The Art of the Magic Striptease

UNIVERSITY PRESS OF FLORIDA

Florida A&M University, Tallahassee
Florida Atlantic University, Boca Raton
Florida Gulf Coast University, Ft. Myers
Florida International University, Miami
Florida State University, Tallahassee
New College of Florida, Sarasota
University of Central Florida, Orlando
University of Florida, Gainesville
University of North Florida, Jacksonville
University of South Florida, Tampa
University of West Florida, Pensacola

The Art of th

University Press of Florida
Gainesville
Tallahassee
Tampa
Boca Raton
Pensacola
Orlando
Miami
Jacksonville
Ft. Myers
Sarasota

Magic Striptease

The Literary Layers of George Garrett

Casey Clabough

Library of Congress Cataloging-in-Publication Data
Clabough, Casey Howard, 1974–
The art of the magic striptease : the literary layers of George Garrett /
Casey Clabough.
p. cm.
Includes bibliographical references and index.
ISBN 978-0-8130-3176-7 (acid-free paper)
1. Garrett, George P., 1929—Criticism and interpretation. I. Title.
PS3557.A72Z63 2007
818.'5409—dc22
2007027534

The University Press of Florida is the scholarly publishing agency for the State
University System of Florida, comprising Florida A&M University, Florida
Atlantic University, Florida Gulf Coast University, Florida International
University, Florida State University, New College of Florida, University of
Central Florida, University of Florida, University of North Florida, University
of South Florida, and University of West Florida.

University Press of Florida
15 Northwest 15th Street
Gainesville, FL 32611–2079
www.upf.com

For Ariel Myers, who has discovered and
secured sources for nearly all my books.

I send you a bouquet which with my own hands
I've just now gathered from these full-blown flowers;
If they had not been picked this evening
They would have fallen to the ground tomorrow.

—Pierre de Ronsard

Who will come here afterwards to blow the dust away
and disturb the peace and oblivion we have earned?

Contents

Acknowledgments

Variations of some of this book's content have appeared in *CEA Critic, Chattahoochee Review, EnterText, Journal of Florida Literature, Texas Review,* and *Virginia Quarterly Review.* I am indebted to the editors of these journals for allowing me to reintroduce those single pieces in a much larger context here. Several individuals contributed to the researching, writing, and overall development of this book. Joyce Pair promptly read the manuscript at each stage of its development: I am thankful for her ongoing attention to my work. I am indebted once more to Ariel Myers, who skillfully and patiently tracked down innumerable elusive documents by and about Garrett. Over the course of my research at Duke University the fine staff in the Special Collections Department (especially Stacey Tompkins, Eleanor Mills, and Alice Poffinberger) provided access to the papers and media from Garrett's immense collection while making my work there enjoyable with their expertise and friendliness. Both my faculty colleagues and the administrative leadership at Lynchburg College contributed to the book as well by encouraging and supporting my research. Marni Fogelson-Teel, a graduate student in English, developed the index. Of special note, my participation in the University of Tennessee Southern Literature Festival: A Celebration of the Life and Work of George Garrett (October 2–4, 2003), allowed me to meet and benefit from the knowledge of a number of the extraordinary writers and scholars (many of them quoted in this book) who have written about Garrett's work over the past half century. My agent, Sorche Fairbank, and University Press of Florida acquisitions editor Amy Gorelick deftly helped orchestrate the project's transition from manuscript to book. And the study owes a special debt to Mr. Garrett himself, who tirelessly responded to innumerable questions and letters, and generously provided access to many of his books and unpublished papers.

Some of the work for this project took place during my time as a 2005 research fellow at the Virginia Foundation for the Humanities. I am grateful for the financial and intellectual support afforded by that outstanding organization during my time in Charlottesville, Virginia.

Abbreviations

BMB   *Bad Man Blues*
BP   *In the Briar Patch*
CG   *Cold Ground Was My Bed Last Night*
CP   *The Collected Poems of George Garrett*
DLR   *Do, Lord, Remember Me*
DOF *Death of the Fox*
DOL *Days of Our Lives Lie in Fragments*
EFS   *Entered from the Sun*
EP   *An Evening Performance*
FM   *The Finished Man*
GSE   *Going to See the Elephant*
Int   Interview of George Garrett by the author, July 9, 2003, at Garrett's home in Charlottesville, Virginia
KM   *King of the Mountain*
KB   *The King of Babylon Shall Not Come against You*
MS   *The Magic Striptease*
MSP   *My Silk Purse and Yours*
OAG *The Old Army Game*
PP   *Poison Pen*
SE   *Southern Excursions*
SFC   *The Sorrows of Fat City*
SUC   *The Succession*
UGG *Understanding George Garrett*
WD   *Whistling in the Dark*
WG   *A Wreath for Garibaldi*
WOE *Which Ones Are the Enemy?*

Introduction

"Art of the Magic Striptease"

Each layer reveals yet another enigma.
—John Towne in Garrett, "Life with Kim Novak Is Hell"

Celebrating the variety and range of the novels of James Gould Cozzens, George Garrett bluntly asserts, "A writer who writes only one kind of book is either obsessive and can't help himself or a hypocrite and the hustler of a single brand name" (*SFC* 83). For more than half a century Garrett has been surprising readers with a dazzling array of fictional topics and forms, spanning everything from the most traditional *Bildungsroman* to historical fiction, satire, and the latest mind-bending metanarrative. Therein also rests the foremost reason for the lack of sustained critical attention his work has received. As Garrett explains, "Artists, I think, by definition are more explorers than exploiters. The one thing that artists who are still alive and growing are most anxious to do is this: not to recall a series of habitual gestures" (Easton 33). How often writers like Garrett and Cozzens, authors who constantly make new gestures, relegate themselves and their overall work to a kind of disparate literary anonymity, the appearance and themes stubbornly refusing to accommodate or fit readily into our most accepted theories and polemics of the day. Betraying an awareness of the cult of literary celebrity rather than a familiarity with Garrett's work, one of Garrett's colleagues at the University of Virginia once labeled him "completely irrelevant" (*GSE* 158). Yet, this is just the sort of critique Garrett invites and, in fact, thrives under. He repeatedly emphasizes the importance of the decision "to go with the flow of the contemporary artistic attitude toward [something], or go in the other direction" (Garrett, Interview), nearly always choosing the latter in his work—a resolution made all the more courageous since it invites censure from the commissars of culture in the form of reactions that employ words such as *irrelevant, radical,* and *irresponsible.*

Garrett repeatedly challenges the assumptions of contemporary literature by calling attention to the unspoken and unwritten rules employed in the United States with regard to publication and cultural interpretation. On a number of occasions he has quoted Alexander Solzhenitsyn's 1978 Harvard University commencement address, applying it to the academy and the ways in which we read and think under a number of conscious and unconscious cultural frameworks. Solzhenitsyn observed:

> Without any censorship in the West, fashionable trends of thought are carefully separated from those that are not fashionable. Nothing is forbidden, but what is not fashionable will hardly ever find its way into periodicals or books or be heard in colleges. Legally, your researchers are free, but they are conditioned by the fashion of the day. There is no open violence such as in the East; however, a selection dictated by fashion and the need to match mass standards frequently prevents independent-minded people from giving their contribution to public life. There is a dangerous tendency to form a herd, shutting off successful development. (quoted in *SFC* 203)

One thing for which readers can be thankful is Garrett's principled, stubborn refusal to follow seasonal literary fashion or dutifully march along with a given finite throng or school. Instead, he stands as a kind of exemplar for the very intellectual freedom Solzhenitsyn found wanting in American culture. Devoid of polemical restrictions, Garrett writes with a kind of reckless impunity. As Annie Dillard has said of his philosophy, "The idea is to let rip. The idea is to give and travel and talk and spend and spend and spend it all" (105). In fact, Garrett's peripatetic, swashbuckling sensibility is evident over the course of his life as well as in his work: from his twenty-page adventure narrative, "Our River Trips," written at the age of eleven, to the diverse notebooks among his papers in the university libraries at Duke and Virginia, composed on spiral tablets from numerous campus bookstores around the country. Garrett's nomadic teaching posts also have resulted in his training of a highly diverse group of successful writers, including novelists and poets such as Madison Smartt Bell and Henry Taylor, each of whom demonstrates a highly distinctive and independent style. In his teaching as well as his writing, Garrett remains true to a perceived authenticity of the narrative at hand, cultivating the most appropriate style and sensibility, even when they go against his own artistic gifts and assumptions.

In his writing, Garrett follows the same principles he employs in encouraging his students. Subordinating the concerns of literary politics and publishing trends, Garrett maintains, "My end purpose has never been to make a living or to be a rich, famous author. It's not very sane; any success is accidental, anyway. What really happens is motives change. Writing was a thing to do, and what I wanted to do all along" (Cross 4). Although writing remains immovably front and center for Garrett, the fact that his "motives change" has often confused and frustrated readers and reviewers. Commenting on the fictional output of Wright Morris, Garrett remarks, "The big trouble with Wright Morris is that he keeps writing and changing. You can't get a line on him. He won't stand there and let them put a name tag on his lapel" (*SFC* 167). Like Morris, Garrett has suffered for his unrepentant desire to accomplish something dramatically new in an original way with each successive project and book. In an unpublished public introduction of Garrett, James Dickey once praised his "receptivity to invention,"[1] and though this aesthetic predisposition has resulted in an enviable array of texts and forms, it also likely has hindered the development of a coherent literary reputation. The scholar James Meriwether recognized Garrett's rich and various gifts as early as 1963 and celebrated them: "The great importance of the diversity of the fields in which he has worked so capably can hardly be over emphasized. For, though he has worked in so many media, he gives no impression of uncertainty, of diffusion of interests" (32). Subsequent readers and reviewers have noticed a similar array of multiple strengths. As Bernice Grohskopf remarks, "George Garrett's writing can't be characterized. The range of subjects, styles and interests in his novels, stories, essays, criticisms, reviews, and poems is unlike that of any other writer" (362). Richard Bausch is even more blunt and laudatory in his assessment: "There is no writer on the American scene with a more versatile, more eclectic, or more restless talent than George Garrett" (*BMB* ix). In celebrating Garrett's gifts, these considerations also underscore their fundamental problematic nature: since he is talented in so many different forms, Garrett's work as a whole seems to suffer from a kind of diffusion of appreciation, its wide-ranging, disparate elements refusing to fit the articulations of readers much beyond a general recognition of their existence.

The dissimilarity of Garrett's interests and output is magnified by the fact that diverse works have sometimes appeared simultaneously. As R. H. W. Dillard recalls, "In 1961 three different publishing houses each published a book by George Garrett on the same day: *Abraham's Knife*, his third collection of poems (University of North Carolina Press); *In the Briar Patch*, his second collection of short stories; and *Which Ones Are the Enemy?*, his second novel (Little, Brown)" (*Dictionary of Literary Biography* 130:170). In fact, an editor actually accused Garrett of not having written *Which Ones Are the Enemy?*, its coarse vernacular style appearing so radically different from anything else he had composed up until that point. If Garrett's books are diverse to the point of negating for many readers any kind of orderly aesthetic or authorial identity, how then may one even begin to assess his work? Rather than attempting to impose a single, meaning-generating, procrustean theoretical framework on Garrett's texts, the answer seems to rest in considering both their distinctive overall differences and those few natural commonalities that appear across them. Garrett himself provides a hint for this kind of reading in his articulation of the term *magic striptease*, Originally introduced by Garrett's most consistently recurring character, John Towne, in an unpublished novel manuscript called "Life with Kim Novak Is Hell." The "magic striptease" refers to an individual capable of assuming any form, which of course carries with it heavy symbolic connotations for aesthetics. As Garrett explains, "He can wear these shapes & forms as one would wear costumes, but of course he remains himself, retains his original identity which is as much or more mysterious than it was before. Whatever he finds, whatever he does with his marvelous gift beings him closer to the truth of the magic mirror where he can see—*himself.*" The practitioner of the "magic striptease" functions as a kind of walking, breathing metaphor for the artist: he meaningfully becomes others while retaining his own identity—a process that successively enriches both his identity and his awareness of it, as well as his art.

Playing many parts and employing numerous forms and approaches in his work, Garrett has practiced a kind of prolonged "magic striptease" over the course of his career, which has confused and dazzled readers even as it has developed and empowered him as an artist. And as his striptease theory demonstrates, Garrett is always aware of his relationship to readers and critics. Even very early in his career he identified the intrinsically minimal, though outwardly influential, role of reviewers and other literary assessors in establishing and breaking the reputations of authors. Writing in 1960 Garrett declared, "The ethics of the scholars are the literary law of the prophets, and there are few of us who will 'scape whipping" ("Review of *William Faulkner*" 215). Though he is cognizant of their potent role in publishing, Garrett frequently teases, plays with, and breaks the laws of the prognosticators by feeding them a steady stream of work that does not cohere to their often pedantic and worn assumptions. As he points out, "A lot of what comes along as scholarship is disguised rerun, a casual and boring wasteland of not-so-instant replay" ("Ending" 17). Refusing to abdicate his work to the mundane arena of trendy literary expectations, Garrett either ignores or plays upon them. As writer Allen Wier observes, "For nearly half a century, George Garrett has responded to what the world has to give and to take away by teaching his readers, among many other things, how to laugh in the midst of despair" (*BMB* xxv). Though he may not approve of the contemporary publishing scene or popular American culture, Garrett does not give into despair, but rather laughs in the face of it, though his mirth sometimes may take the form of a decidedly bleak sound. As he remarks, "Comedy, be it ever so dark or grotesque, is always a shadow dancer in my work" (*GSE* 114). Though he is critical of both the publishing industry and contemporary American media, Garrett remains meaningfully engaged with them, even if his response appears—as it often does—in the guise of inversion, irony, satire, or the macabre leer of a human skull.

Since Garrett always has expressed disdain for the ephemeral and ever-changing fashions of the literary establishment—the "bright young critic, chip on shoulder and one ear cocked for the latest report of the literary stock market" ("Review of *In*" 32)—he is able to perceive his own work both inside and outside the games of publishing and literary identity, which in turn affords him enormous artistic and professional freedom. He once characterized the writer Mary Lee Settle in the following terms: "Never trendy or fashionable, she writes as if she had no interest whatsoever in the intricate games of postmodern metafiction" (*Understanding* 16). Garrett might well be describing himself here, except for the fact that he *does* pay attention to "the intricate games," though, having established their probable outcomes, he almost always chooses simply to break their rules. Like Faulkner before him, Garrett is willing to risk accusations of political irresponsibility and being "out of touch," both in his work and actions, by constantly disagreeing with popular intellectual opinions and going his own way. Recalling his time as an editor for the *Transatlantic Review*, Garrett recounts that the journal's "editorial policy was determinedly and deliberately eclectic. Poetry of all kinds and poets of all schools and cliques were welcomed" ("B. S. Johnson" 280). Implicit here is the preference for good writing over political sensibility or personal favoritism. Literary social connections and polemical solidarity were rejected outright in an effort to attract the best poems from all quarters and movements to the journal's pages.

Garrett believes that theoretical frameworks, which almost always are aligned with political and/or aesthetic schools, eventually defer, over the course of a work, to a writer's talent or the lack thereof. At length he asserts:

> A good writer has the ability to make whatever technique he may choose or wish to employ seem to be not only eminently appropriate, but also somehow inevitable. It is not then, as so many critics suppose, a question of the writer's searching for and sometimes finding the one and only appropriate and inevitable way to tell a given story. That would make of the artist no more than a gifted and lucky treasure-hunter, a kind of pregnant sow sniffing for truffles. Such a notion might of course explain, to the satisfaction of the critic, the difference between an artist and a critic. That it all adds up to pure luck. But the truth of the art is that, for whatever reasons or out of purely intuitive whim and impulse, the artist freely chooses a way to present the story and then summons up all craft and art in order that the work may seem to have found its one and only possible shape and form. ("Technics" 420)

According to Garrett, no matter how a writer (or critic) frames the work, most of the existing patterns in a text are created incidentally rather than methodically, their naturalness or contrived quality occurring in degrees directly proportional to the writer's gifts. Because Garrett successfully employs many different techniques across a host of works, he preemptively complicates any attempt on the scholar's part to relegate his work to a single set of principles. The striptease continues: layer after layer falls away, each discarded form constituting yet another garment from a deep wardrobe of artistic talent.

The "magic striptease," as an overarching theory for delineating Garrett's work, conceptualizes the various facets of his writing as a series of garments, outfits, and costumes: bright, colorful, and sometimes clashing. Forms and genres are donned and shed, the styles and textures of which contain distinctive wrinkles and creases created by the singular manner in which Garrett wears his work. Part I, "Undergarments: The Autobiographical and Regional Writer," discusses the personal and formative regional narratives that lie, sometimes out of sight, beneath much of Garrett's writing. More abstract in its focus on Garrett's work in established genres, Part II, "Styles of Dress: Variations on Fictional Modes," investigates the various fictional areas, the narrative outfits, in which Garrett appears with regularity. Though autobiographical and regional concerns, the undergarments and underpinnings of his art, remain, the visual outward appearance often changes to the point of suggesting a different writer—or, at least, the appearance of a different writer—entirely. This exploration of Garrett's constantly evolving wardrobe continues in Part III, "Costume Change: The Striptease in Poetry and Criticism," before attempting to peel away the garments altogether in Part IV, "The Writer Laid Bare: An Interview and Unpublished Fictional Excerpt"— an offering of new primary material from Garrett consisting of an interview and unpublished piece of fiction.

As the novelist and critic Walter Sullivan warns, "The study of literature is fraught with uncertainty" (*Requiem* xiii), and readers of this book may appreciate a more detailed account of the study's organization. Following Garrett's "striptease" approach to writing, this book considers, chapter by chapter, many of the forms Garrett has worn, discarded, darned, and donned again over the course of his long literary career. Part I specifically highlights his initiation fiction and those narratives that take place in his native Florida and the greater South. At the end of his essay "Three Initiations," Edward Hirsch summarizes his earliest aesthetic reading experience: "I was wounded by its truth. And I was also healed by it" (54). So too young writers often are baptized—challenged and strengthened (or destroyed)—through their encounters with and portrayals of initiation experience, which often serve as metaphors for their artistic coming of age—an understanding of who they are, where they come from, and what they are trying to achieve. This archetypal trend articulates itself under the banner of postmodern poetics in what Brian McHale perceives as a shift "from problems of *knowing* to problems of *modes of being*—from an epistemological dominant to an *ontological* one" (McHale's emphasis, 10). Rendering a collage of Garrett's personal roots and regional concerns, the first three chapters seek to establish a base of aesthetics and identity upon which the essays in Part II may begin to investigate Garrett's separate fictional renderings of specific literary styles, genres, and themes.

Chapters 4 and 5 focus on Garrett's interactions with American culture through the vehicles of the grotesque and satire. Linda Hutcheon believes that a major component of the postmodern endeavor involves "postmodernism's renegotiation of the different possible relations (of complicity and critique) between high and popular forms of culture" (7). Although Garrett's manifestations of popular culture often appear under highly critical circumstances, he maintains a connection with collective mainstream phenomena that betrays a firm belief in their affiliation with personal identity. As Walter Shear says of the literary period following World War II and preceding the 1960s (the period in which Garrett began publishing), "For the immediate postwar years the major task was to create an identity out of a stance toward society using whatever spiritual resources the individual could summon from a personal history" (244). Whereas he often employs satire and irony in representing American culture, Garrett remains seriously engaged with it, its underpinnings maintaining a close, albeit fluid, connection with his artistic identity.

Although Garrett remains interested in contemporary cultural issues, much of his work concerns itself with archetypal forces: those historical variables that manifest themselves continually across time and culture. Addressing Garrett's military and historical fiction, Chapters 6 and 7 deal with the ways in which his writing attempts to portray universal aspects of existence, those that seek to transcend time, place, and self in articulating central aspects of humanity. As John Carr has noted, "Garrett is concerned, perhaps overbearingly, with eschatology, with Final Things: death, the end of History, the afterlife, *la vita nuova*" (21). Garrett's interest in exploring the connections between universal history and the self on a fictional tapestry has come full circle—back toward the concerns of his early self-reflexive, initiation narratives—in his most recent work. In *The Extension of Life: Fiction and History in the American Novel*, R. A. York celebrates writing that demonstrates "on the one hand a passionate loyalty to the facts of history . . . on the other there is an intense inventiveness" (25). And in his 2004 novel, *Double Vision*, Garrett plays with the interactions between fiction and nonfiction, generating a highly autobiographical and historical type of narrative not possible in traditional nonfiction. Although it is not required to tell the truth, it is concerned with truth—the wedding of fact and fiction across time, place, and identity.

As R. H. W. Dillard pointed out in his 1988 critical study of Garrett, "It is difficult to describe the wide range of George Garrett's writing beyond the novels" (*UGG* 193). Yet, this is what is attempted in the book's third section, "Costume Change: The Striptease in Poetry and Criticism." Chapter 8 articulates the shifting themes and appearances of Garrett's later poems—literary legacies, personal mortality, and contemporary meaninglessness, among others. Garrett's is a direct yet complex poetry that employs far-reaching subject matter to attain epiphanies and authenticity in the most unlikely of places and contexts. Garrett's critical output, the subject of Chapter 9, and his verse are wedded through their playfulness and sheer range, the criticism donning and pursuing scholarly threads as various as literature, history, biography, the academy, and the publishing industry in general. Yet, across them all Garrett employs the same sense of celebratory discovery and uncompromising integrity that informs his best poems—the disguises, mischievous posturing, and double talk ultimately giving way to a consciousness wholly devoted to the life of letters. Part IV demonstrates that veiled consciousness directly at work through an interview with Garrett and a previously unpublished work of fiction. In a brief concluding chapter entitled "Redress," I consider again Garrett's various outfits while attempting to gauge the appearance and value of his work and legacy in the context of contemporary American (and particularly southern) literature.

At the end of "Our River Trips," his unpublished book written at the age of eleven, Garrett concludes, "Now we had seen how from a small brook the river had grown very large and had emptied into the sea." Since Garrett has produced such an exceptionally large, rich, and diverse body of work, a deep river of words, it is perhaps impossible to identify each channel and sound every depth. Indeed, just as Heraclitus famously noted that one cannot step into the same river twice, so Garrett's work continues to flow onward while frequently altering its course and appearance. In its attempt to take Garrett's writing on its own terms—as opposed to cladding or wrapping it in ill-fitting threads or clashing colors—this book endeavors to identify a number of promising places to ford the waters and sound the depths. From its protean subject matter there emerge, necessarily, a number of protean concerns.

part I

Undergarments

The Autobiographical and Regional Writer

chapter 1

"The Primary Story"

Initiation Narratives

*The most significant action in a Garrett story or poem is,
then, most likely to occur at a moment of self-discovery.*
—R. H. W. Dillard, *Understanding George Garrett*

Despite its masterful renderings by Goethe, Brontë, Chekhov, Joyce, Mann, and countless others, the initiation story remains a staple of contemporary fiction, seemingly destined to appear, again and again, in various political and stylistic guises with unquenchable regularity. More than fifty years ago, Ray West suggested that the root of initiation is the protagonist's existential dilemma, a problem that must be understood, but is destined to "only a limited solution" (97). While other genres and movements have flowered, evolved, and crumbled, the initiation endures with little having occurred over the past half century to render West's observation dated or moot.

Initiation narratives originally were celebrated in the extended form of the *Bildungsroman*, a category of fiction most often traced to Goethe's *Wilhelm Meister*. The form would become popular among the German Romantics and early Victorians before establishing itself permanently in mainstream literary consciousness. Susan Howe's seasoned definition of the term remains wholly accurate: "[A] novel of all around development" containing "a more or less conscious attempt on the part of the hero to integrate his powers, to cultivate himself by his experience" (6). Less familiar are the more theme-specific categories of *Erziehungsroman* and *Künstlerroman*, the former placing emphasis on a youth's training and formal education, and the latter addressing the orientation of a developing artist. Pervading these specialized categories as well as the general initiation narrative is an overwhelming focus on young people. Hermann Hesse's Knecht journeys to Castilia just as Robert Penn Warren's Jed Tewksbury travels to the University of Chicago. Young Goodman Brown and Andrew Lytle's Lucius Cree negotiate allegorical epiphanies in forest settings, while Cormac McCarthy's John Cole rides away to Mexico. Whether they are aspiring artists, academics, husbands, farmers, or cowboys, all of these young people embark on paths that, however much they loop or shift direction, ultimately have as their common destination the painful, hard-earned, and burdensome reward of human knowledge.

Not surprisingly, a special correlation emerges between young writers and their young protagonists in the initiation form. George Garrett has expressed that "the initial drama of early published fiction is the drama of finding your voice. There are many different ways of doing it; the stories are quite different. That's probably the main theme, at least overtly, that young writers have: who am I and what is my voice? So the initiation story becomes the primary story" (Int).

Just as the young writer's callow protagonist often encounters painful knowledge, so the author himself discovers his own agonizing aesthetic limitations while rendering the youthful characters and milieus that stem from his experience. Garrett might well be relating the dilemma of the young writer in the first section of his poem "Three Short Ones":

> What we spend first of all is innocence
> which after all, we never owned,
> but like a borrowed book returned
> unread, or like a secret was not kept
> but published though the whole world wept.
>   (*DOL* 162)

Over the course of his early narratives the young writer presses against the inherent boundaries of his voice and technique, losing in the process (though he never really had owned them), much of the innocent and idealistic ambitions he had coveted for his art. Yet, from this painful realization, the brutal knowledge of one's own deficiencies and gifts, emerges the vital and necessary capacity for artistic growth.

Though less frequently dramatized or discussed, the possibility for life-changing knowledge and transformation among mature writers and characters is significant as well. William Hoffman's novel *A Death of Dreams* and Katherine Anne Porter's story "The Death of Granny Weatherall," for example, constitute unique and memorable initiation narratives, even though they both center around the dilemmas of mature protagonists. Hoffman's novel was his seventh and arguably his finest, and Porter was nearly forty when she wrote the distinguished story that would appear in her first published collection, *Flowering Judas and Other Stories*. Jerome Buckley makes a crucial semantic distinction between initiation narratives and the variable ages of their authors using the terms *autobiographer* and *autobiographical novelist*. Buckley explains, "The autobiographer is typically the older man" who practices a kind of

> fond retrospect, often more than a little sentimental in his view of his youth, recalling what it pleases him to remember. The autobiographical novelist is usually a younger man, nearer in time to his initiation, self-protectively more ironic, still mindful of the growing pains of adolescence, reproducing as accurately as possible the turbulence of the space between childhood and early manhood. (25)

Inherent in Buckley's distinction is the writer's evolving perspective on youthful discovery, which reflects his own philosophical and aesthetic development across the chasm of time. Skilled veteran writers who repeatedly explore the initiation theme often do so in a manner that promotes their own growth, constructing new patterns and dynamics that, in turn, reflect their shifting philosophical and artistic concerns.

In the autumn of 1958 a young graduate student at the University of Virginia named Richard Dillard asked writer-in-residence Katherine Anne Porter to recommend someone he should read among the many talented young writers of the day. As Dillard recalls, "She didn't even hesitate before giving her answer. 'Read George Garrett,' she said" ("George Garrett: An Appreciation" 461). Like Porter, Garrett is an accomplished and innovative practitioner of the initiation narrative, rendering the form with memorably disparate variables and intentions over the course of his career. From the initial tale in his first collection of short stories ("The Rivals" in *King of the Mountain* [1957]) to the narrative "My Adventures in Fantasy Land (A Story Full of Sex and Violins)" (2003), Garrett approaches the initiation mode as a malleable vehicle for experimentation and knowledge, for himself as well as his protagonists. In an interview with John Graham, Garrett proclaims that he does not like "to blame present actions on past events and circumstances" (Graham 25), a predilection that places the complexities of knowledge and discovery firmly in the time frame of the narrative at hand. After perceptively cataloguing a number of Garrett's central aesthetic concerns in his book *Understanding George Garrett*, R. H. W. Dillard concludes, "The most significant action in a Garrett story or poem is, then, most likely to occur at a moment of self-discovery" (15). Perhaps the most important aspect of Dillard's accurate observation is the focus on a "moment" of initiation, which places the event in the intimately immediate and revealing now-time of the narrative, the reader, and the artist. Since Garrett does not believe in "blaming present actions on past events," his initiation narratives constitute a body of progressively new and developing fiction, reflecting his artistic concerns in the present-tense of composition, even as they successively give way to new interests and narratives.

The dynamic underpinnings of Garrett's ever-shifting relationship with the initiation form—a long, gradual transition, which roughly articulates Buckley's temporal distinction of "autobiographer" and "autobiographical novelist"—is discernible across the body of his fiction. In the early story "The Rivals" an adolescent boy hopes to measure himself against his father by insisting that the two of them run an awkward boat out into a rough Florida surf. The idea of literal and symbolic "measuring" informs much of the narrative's language. In the story's first paragraph the boy attempts "to time his own motion exactly with his father's" (*KM* 7) while paddling across the bay. Later, we learn that the father is possessed of a large, powerful frame while the boy is "slightly built, small for his age" (*KM* 9). Functioning here is an unmistakable element of physical and psychological envy, as the boy seeks to discover his potential against the established power and knowledge of his father. He consistently gauges himself against the older man, wondering if he possesses the potential to grow into an adult of commensurate proportion. In an attempt to feel better about himself the boy initially tries to underscore his father's flaws. When the father brings up his first battle experience at Normandy—his own central and defining initiation experience—the boy remarks, "I bet you were scared, weren't you?" (*KM* 8). After the father attempts to articulate the profound feeling of going into live action for the first time, the boy merely responds, "It sounds like you were pretty scared to me" (*KM* 8). Unwilling to acknowledge the complexity or value of his father's life-changing experience, the boy attributes the older man's trepidation to cowardice while focusing on another weakness: "He's been drinking, the boy thought. . . . When he's drunk he starts to tell about the war. . . . He don't care that it's the last day before we go home and maybe we'll never have another chance to try the boat in the waves. On top of that he's scared" (*KM* 8). Selfishly terrified at the prospect of his own shortcomings, the boy highlights what he conceives to be his father's faults in an attempt to establish his own potential for transcending the mature man's achievements.

The boy's feelings of inferiority and resentment markedly diminish in the wake of the father-son exhilaration that follows their initial successful journey through the heavy surf. Sitting in the boat beyond the breakers, "he felt a curious admiration for his father. They had done this together" (*KM* 14). However, the reality of the older man's skill and his own inadequacy return, albeit without bitterness, when his father insists that the boy paddle them through the breakers on his own. The narrator describes the boy's thoughts on the matter: "It was an awful thing, he thought, to be about to do something that he knew he couldn't. It was different when you didn't know, but he wasn't innocent anymore" (*KM* 15). Equally dangerous is the father's insistence that the boy take them out through the waves, even though he knows his son probably is not strong or agile enough to do it. The result of this mutually ill-considered, though courageous, second attempt is a broken leg for the father, which shatters forever the son's illusion of his father's invincibility: "The boy looked quickly, furtively at his father's legs stretched limp in the water. They had never seemed so long and thin, so easy to be broken. It was a strange thing to think of his father's flesh. He had never really imagined his father as possessing flesh that could be injured, bones that could break" (*KM* 16). As the story concludes, the boy finds himself struck with a greater and more desperate challenge than he had bargained for. Taking the boat to go for help while his father lies injured on the beach, the boy experiences "a strange and precious feeling, as small as the first moment of a catching flame, but hard too, and brimming with an inner glow like a jewel. He kept dragging the boat, pacing himself, measuring his strength because he had a long way to go" (*KM* 18). Burdened by the father's sudden and unprecedented need of him, the boy feels proud and important, even as he is tempered and humbled by his newfound knowledge of life's pain, fragility, and failures.

In "The Rivals" Garrett functions as Buckley's "autobiographical writer," rendering the coming-of-age narrative with utter seriousness from a youthful authorial perspective (Garrett was twenty-nine when the story was published). In fact, given the tale's Florida milieu it is tempting to view the story autobiographically, as a possible event from Garrett's youth. Yet, as the narrative's nameless characters demonstrate, the story's dominant aim and effect is archetypal, exploring the complexities of the father-son relationship with time and setting functioning only as necessary and collapsible props. Whatever personal attachment Garrett may have felt for the characters and events ultimately gives way to a timeless meditation on the dynamics of male initiation.

ı "The Lion Hunter" (1957) Garrett builds upon the father-son dynamics ne establishes in "The Rivals" while using intertextuality and masculine societal expectations as defining themes for knowledge and self-discovery. The story begins and ends with its college-aged protagonist looking back on the time his salesman father took him to see *Death of a Salesman* in New York. Between the structural bookends of this defining event, the narrator struggles to understand his father's personal and professional emphasis on appearance and identity. For example, although the father is moved by the play, he is less interested in the complexity of Willy Loman's personality than in what other characters think of him. As he explains to his son, "In this life you end up being what other people think of you. . . . You just *are* what they decide you are" (*KM* 125, Garrett's emphasis). The story's title serves as the telling symbolic manifestation of this perspective. While at the movies, the boy and his father view a travelogue on Africa in which young men receive lion's mane helmets if they succeed in going out on their own and killing a lion with a spear. As the father maintains, "It's what it *stands* for that matters. That helmet says *this is a brave man*. You either are one or you aren't. And if you are, you just are, you don't have to go proving it and trying to prove it. You do it once and you are brave" (*KM* 123, Garrett's emphasis). Troubling to the son is his father's apparent preference for the approving communal label of bravery over the authenticity of its essence.

Whereas "The Rivals" centers upon the insecurities of a son, "The Lion Hunter" eventually reveals itself as a narrative primarily concerned with a father's desperate fear of failure, both for himself and his son. Having neglected to finish college or succeed as a baseball player, the father never earned his symbolic lion's mane helmet. As a result, he is a manic worker and demanding parent, constantly pushing himself and his son in a prolonged and fruitless attempt to redeem his own past shortcomings. Although, as in "The Rivals," the father and son remain nameless and largely archetypal, the story's guiding symbolic image is unmistakably autobiographical. In his essay "There Are Lions Everywhere" (1971) Garrett recalls an event from his boyhood in which he and his father were looking at a magazine that described the same African ritual of lion hunting. The elder Garrett remarked to his son, "You never run out of lions. There are lions everywhere. You've got to be a lion hunter whether you like it or not" (219). The divergent interpretations of the ritual by Garrett's father and the fictional father in "The Lion Hunter" help underscore Garrett's intentions for the story. Whereas Garrett's father accurately interprets the initiation event as part of an ongoing process—one must constantly prove oneself against life's lions—the fictional father sees the successful negotiation of the single, defining challenge as a trophy or laurel with which to rest—something to be brandished or hoisted for all to see. At the conclusion of "The Lion Hunter" the son remains unconvinced by his father's worldview, even though he is beginning to understand that it is the sad philosophy of many adults. He concludes, "If you have to spend all your time being what other people want or think you are, you'll never find time to find out who you really are" (*KM* 126). In response, the father merely laughs and tells his son that he is "almost a man" (*KM* 126)—a hollow confirmation of his own despairing perspective and lack of self-knowledge.

In his review of a collection of short stories by Reynolds Price, Garrett remarked, "Mr. Price writes his best work about all kinds of love . . . all treated with respect and without vulgarity or cynicism" ("Here" 8). In his early initiation stories involving father-son relationships Garrett demonstrates a similar agenda, attempting to portray the earnest struggles young men undergo in attempting, sometimes unsuccessfully, to love and accept their fathers in the contexts of painfully complex adult worlds. Perhaps the most memorable of these narratives is "The King of the Mountain" (1957), the title piece from Garrett's original collection of short stories and the germ for his first novel, *The Finished Man* (1959). At first glance, "The King of the Mountain" stands out in Garrett's earliest collection because of its compelling, larger-than-life father-figure: a Depression-era Florida lawyer who is beaten severely by local members of the Ku Klux Klan, only to emerge from his grievous wounds and publicly denounce them, eventually becoming a senator and then the state's governor. However, lurking beneath the formidable physical courage and thunderous oratory of the father are the more quiet and crucial impressions of his young son, who is transformed both by his father's beating and ensuing return to public service. What emerges in the ambivalent boy is a tension between pride and resentment for his father's self-righteous moral authority at the risk of his family's safety and his own. At the end of the story the now-mature son comments in retrospect to the story's narrator: "It's a pity . . . that it took a narrow-minded, petty demagogue with a wild desire to be a martyr to stand up for law and order at that time" (*KM* 74). Acknowledging the value of his father's ideals and actions while questioning his personal motives, the son maintains a troubled and irresolute image of the man. In the story's last sentence he remarks, "I really don't know for sure whether I hate him or not" (*KM* 75), a declaration that threatens to dispatch love from the equation. Though he has learned outward courage and idealism from his father, the son, even in adulthood, remains doubtful of the man himself.

The search for one's youthful identity in the shadow of a powerful father and in the midst of adverse political events also serves as the defining endeavor of Mike Royale in Garrett's first novel, *The Finished Man*. Like the formidable patriarch/politician in "The King of the Mountain," Mike Royale's father, Judge Joseph Royale, is epitomized by "Power, but no sign of charity" (*FM* 23). A product of a severe, poverty-stricken, rural upbringing, Joseph Royale has fought for everything he has and remains hungry, despite his poor health and advanced age, for additional political accolades. Having returned to his parents' home in Florida to enter state politics after failing as a husband and lawyer in New York, Mike gropes for his present identity in the shadow of his father's unquenchable ambitions and expectations, even as he meditates on the childhood that has led him to this unmarked crossroads in life. As a result, much of the novel's action is reflective, bending back and connecting past occurrences to events in the present. As a portion of the book's epigraph from Yeats reads,

> What matter if I live it all once more;
> Endure that toil of growing up;
> The ignominy of boyhood; the distress
> Of boyhood changing into man."
>   (*FM* 11)

Seeking to negotiate the turmoil of the present and resign himself to the agonies of the past, Mike undergoes a crisis of identity, which at times threatens to destroy him.

Of fundamental importance in Mike's dilemma is the basic fact that he realizes it is taking place. When he first returns home he discovers his room just as he had left it, but feels "a stranger among the familiar things of his past. For *he* had changed, or thought he had, from the boy who made model airplanes out of balsa wood on rainy afternoons" (*FM* 75, Garrett's emphasis). Despite finding the material accouterments of his youth just where he had left them, Mike still experiences an overpowering sense of unfamiliarity, which stems from his strange presence among them. This feeling of alienation also extends into his professional life; when asked if he is through practicing law, Mike responds, "The main thing I guess is that everything has changed. It just isn't what it used to be, or, anyway, it isn't what I thought I wanted" (*FM* 72). Never having successfully defined himself in youth, Mike embarked on a professional path the promising appearance of which has given way to doubt and disillusion. As his drifting identity has evolved so has his perspective on the everyday phenomena that conspire to construct it. Because he has changed, everything has changed, and he is left with the unenviable challenge of attempting to catalogue the reasons.

Although Mike's dilemma is acutely personal and painful, the narrator informs us that it is hardly unusual, especially for southerners:

If you were a Southerner, whether you liked it or not, you had to live in and with your past. You had to try to make sense out of it. The present was ghosted, shadowed. Nothing you did, but you troubled the dust. Mike's solution, his whim, had been to run away again, to flee this time into the cardboard world of politics, to oversee another's worries. And the fact of the matter was, he guessed, that he couldn't care less what happened, who won or lost. He would throw himself into it with all the energy he could arouse, but whatever happened he would be perfectly safe. He was about as likely to bleed as a stone. (*FM* 111)

Seeking to escape history and time, Mike plunges into the artificial world of politics, attempting to displace and forget his own problems by serving as campaign manager for Senator Allen Parker. Yet, this deferral only serves to suspend, rather than eliminate, an unavoidable rendezvous with his genuine identity. As R. H. W. Dillard correctly has observed, "The real story of the novel is the story of Mike Royale's coming of age, his initiation into the duplicitous and difficult realities of life in the world of lies, and his learning to live as truly as possible in it" (*UGG* 40). However, Mike comes to this realization only after abdicating his identity to Parker's corrupt and flailing campaign. Inspired and distracted by the chaos of election day, Mike feels he is "burning himself up with a dedicated, irrational abandon. He was lightheaded, lighthearted, and careless; strangely for the first time he could remember, he felt, at the pitch of his involvement, wholly irresponsible. It gave him a sense of power. He felt like an invisible man" (*FM* 189). Working manically with little at stake for himself, Mike is able to lose himself—to become invisible—in the toadish abstract world of politics, pouring all his fears and frustrations into a largely vicarious and ultimately meaningless struggle.

Although Mike is able to forget himself for a time in the chaos of politics, "there came a day when all his airy gusto fled him and he was left limp and shapeless as a pricked balloon" (*FM* 189). Just as a decompressing balloon slowly drifts back to earth, so Mike eventually returns to the problems of his own identity. And Garrett's emphasis on an image of decline and descent is hardly accidental. Referencing postlapsarian Christian theology, Leslie Fiedler maintains that initiated protagonists undergo a "fall through knowledge" (22). Descending from the inebriated heights of denial and self-delusion, one plummets through the cold, sobering realm of comprehension, hoping to land without anything permanently maimed or broken, but with a meaningful new appreciation of what it takes to rise and walk again as a man. Commenting on Garrett's early fiction in 1965, William Robinson eloquently observed:

> Garrett's favorite story is an account of moral change, a fall from innocence into knowledge, begotten by a violence without evoking a violence within, of involvement in a power struggle from which there is no intellectual or moral escape. To be a man, his fiction implies, is to be finite and 'guilty': it is to be a part of the world and responsible to it; it is to live in isolated individuality and with uncertainty and change as absolutes yet care, as Garrett does so obviously for all his fallen characters. ("The Fiction" 16)

Although Mike Royale previously may have failed to make the correct decisions in life, at the end of *The Finished Man* he is closer than he ever has been to what the novel's Yeats-derived title implies: a man possessing the unpleasant and hard-earned, though necessary, knowledge of his own finite pain and clumsiness. As Garrett asserts in his early poem "Wishful Thinking," "From failing you can learn the grace/of falling well" (*DOL* 54), and this is precisely what Mike has discovered. In falling well he has attained a kind of grace, both real and theological in its implications. Garrett has observed, "The Protestant is always a creature of mixed feelings, or paradox. His faith, essentially heretical, individual, and anarchic, is in constant conflict with the very institutions he has created to preserve and foster it" (*MSP* 109). In the wake of having undergone and survived a chaotic and even iconoclastic fundamental, moral identity conflict that interrogates the abstract human institutions of politics and family, Mike is able to exercise the Christian imperative of acknowledged imperfection and, in so doing, finally become himself.

Written in Rome in 1958, *The Finished Man* saw Garrett, like many young expatriate writers before and after him, imagining youth in his native culture from the helpful vantage point of an alien one. From afar the complexities of American male initiation returned to him with a vividness that was difficult to ignore. In *The Finished Man* Mike Royale's identity crisis subtly is complemented and shaded by the actions of his older brother, Jojo, the confirmed black sheep of the family. A decorated war hero, Jojo returns to Florida to enjoy a largely desultory existence as a DJ at a small radio station that exclusively plays soul music, shunning all established societal and family expectations. Although Jojo's role in the novel is small, Garrett remained fascinated with his eccentric character, including him in a number of early short stories as well as his eighth novel, *The King of Babylon Shall Not Come against You* (1996). In the unpublished story "A Warfare of the Heart," for example, a young Jojo undergoes an initiation of his own, attempting to reconcile the loss of his father with the overbearing personality of his mother, all the while trying to interact normally with other children his age.

Jojo's secondary endeavor in "A Warfare of the Heart"—to fit in with other children on the way to gaining knowledge—is the primary subject of several of Garrett's baptismal stories, which might best be classified as boyhood camaraderie initiations. In "The Only Dragon on the Road" (1959) Jojo appears again in the context of his ambivalent relationship with T.W., a grade-school bully who grows up to be a paroled murderer. At the beginning of the story Jojo receives a request for money from the recently released T.W., which he immediately fulfills. The narrative then shifts back to a boyhood fight between the two in which T.W., a gang leader at the time, cuts Jojo with a knife, after which they follow separate life courses that revolve around boxing: Jojo attends a distinguished college where he joins the boxing team while T.W. remains a local and becomes a successful amateur fighter. Their paths cross again when Jojo graduates from college and returns home. After one of T.W.'s opponents fails to show up for a match, the promoter talks Jojo into agreeing to serve as a substitute combatant. Their ensuing fight serves as the visceral apotheosis of class and personality difference, the implications of which are not immediately clear: T.W. epitomizes the swaggering, insecure underclass of the community while Jojo constitutes the promising, local-boy-makes-good element. As T.W. informs Jojo before the fight, "You never was really one of the gang" (15), a sentiment expressed for different reasons by Jojo's mother, who harshly characterizes T.W. and his friends as "not our class of people. . . . They're trash" (10). After Jojo bests T.W. in the fight, T.W. laments, "I got to stay around here. You can forget it. I'm finished" (16), to which Jojo helplessly responds, "What are you talking about?" (16). Only years later, after Jojo learns of T.W.'s life of crime, does he realize that his fight with T.W. had dire, far-reaching repercussions. When he reads in the paper that T.W. has shot someone, Jojo remarks, "For a minute I felt like I had killed somebody" (17). Hoping to have redeemed his childhood humiliation and alienation at the hands of T.W. through a literal rematch, Jojo instead ends up stripping from T.W. the local pride and notoriety that had afforded him a positive sense of identity. Whereas Jojo's privilege and education provide him with social mobility and a life beyond boxing, T.W. is left with nothing and turns to crime in a fruitless effort to assuage his inner void.

Adult knowledge transmitted and discovered through the medium of boyhood violence—a familiar dynamic that informs such memorable novels as Calder Willingham's *End as a Man* and William Golding's *Lord of the Flies*—also works as a catalyst in "The Last of the Spanish Blood" (1960), in which the boy-protagonist's violent childhood hero, Harry, commits suicide. A distant cousin of the young narrator, Harry comes to stay with his kinfolk after his terminal father is confined to a hospital. He arrives at a time when the narrator feels "[n]ot a child any more and not yet a man" (*BP* 35), a tenuous period of development during which the narrator is both highly impressionable and brimming with self-doubt. Although Harry and the narrator are roughly the same age, Harry possesses an almost swaggering air of worldliness and confidence, stemming from his harsh and disintegrating family environment, which has forced him to develop an almost adult sense of self-sufficiency. After the narrator and his friends are mugged by a knife-wielding bully and his gang, Harry accompanies them in a second confrontation with the territorial delinquents. To the surprise of everyone, Harry pulls a pistol on the gang members before insisting that the narrator and his friends beat the now-defenseless bully and his companions senseless. The narrator's ensuing feelings of guilt over this act serve to reveal the story's central initiation dynamic. As he confesses to Harry, "It's just I didn't know I had it in me to act like that. We all went kind of crazy. I didn't know I could do like that. I didn't know I could enjoy it" (*BP* 45). Moved to act in a way he hadn't imagined possible, the narrator is shocked to discover that perversity and evil exist within himself. Sometime later, when he learns that Harry has committed suicide, he wonders if "maybe he knew too much about himself and other people too early" (*BP* 46). A living symbol of youthful lost innocence, Harry's violent, self-destructive character conveys the sometimes irreconcilable and unbearable consequences that accompany youth's interactions with evil. At the story's conclusion, initiated into a peculiar understanding of violence and evil himself through the bond he has formed with his cousin, the narrator struggles to perceive meaning and hope beyond his sorrowful knowledge.

Whereas Garrett uses Harry as a condemned symbol for the destructive coupling of youth and evil in "The Last of the Spanish Blood," in "The Test" (1961) he employs a material object, a homemade diving helmet, as a visceral projection of the dissipating impractical dreams of childhood. Once again, the dynamics of boyhood camaraderie serve as the impetus for initiation as three friends—Chris, Bobby, and the unnamed narrator—attempt to construct a primitive helmet that will enable them to search for underwater pirate treasure. Perpetuating each others' dreams, the boys previously had failed in attempting to construct a raft in order "to float along the St. John's River all the way from Sanford to Jacksonville. Then the Mississippi. Then—who knows?—the Nile, the Ganges, the Amazon" (*BP* 3–4). Despite the aborted bid to imitate Huckleberry Finn, the narrator remains confident that "the helmet would be a useful device" (*BP* 4). In this assumption he turns out to be tragically correct, albeit in a manner he could not possibly have imagined. After Chris drowns while using the helmet, the narrator is forced to look full upon the adult world of accountability. As the more mature Bobby explains at length:

> You have all these crazy wonderful schemes and ideas. You don't care what the risk is. And that's all right for you. But somebody has got to watch after you all the time. And when you're all finished with whatever you're doing somebody has got to come along and start to clean up the mess you leave behind. You people are like babies in this world. (*BP* 18)

Angered by Bobby's assertion, the narrator nevertheless admits "there was some truth in it" (*BP* 18). When the speaker finally acknowledges the deadly weight of responsibility for his ideas and actions, the helmet, in retrospect, becomes a kind of sentimental artifact of childhood—the final realized dream from a youthful world forever destroyed by the insistent specters of death and culpability.

Accompanying the highly self-reflexive and archetypal father-son and boyhood-camaraderie narratives that inform much of Garrett's initial fiction are a roguish company of early initiation stories that experiment with specific disparate avenues and areas of development, such as education, art, race, gender, and the grotesque. The last of these elements appears unexpectedly in a story that initially disguises itself in the form of a conventional boyhood initiation narrative. In "Lion" (1959) we again encounter the character Jojo, this time as a curious young boy enamored of the circus. When a traveling carnival pauses in Jojo's town to water its animals, the lion tamer's embittered lover purposefully releases the company's less-than-tame feline out of spite. By chance Jojo is present when this liberation occurs and follows the beast to an old abandoned barn. Local authorities, hostile toward the outsiders, refuse to believe that the entertainers have lost their cat and force the troupe to move on. At the conclusion of the story, Jojo pilfers a steak from his mother and returns to the dilapidated barn, where "holding it in front of him, he began to walk slowly toward the burning eyes" (*EP* 158). What in the beginning appears to be a harmless, obligatory child's fantasy of joining the circus, ends with the menacing implication of Jojo's probable maiming and death. Bakhtin maintained that carnival settings traditionally function as symbolic phenomena in which appearances often are bent and disfigured to the point of becoming grotesque (32). With its carnivalesque elements and violent implications, "Lion" sees Garrett exploring an episode of childhood naivete that likely will result in the young protagonist's grisly physical, as well as psychological, disfigurement—an insinuated, knowledge-bearing, traumatic event that very well may transform the child into a grotesque.

While the boy in "Lion" idealizes the circus life against the mundane qualities of his provincial upbringing, the older twenty-something protagonists of "A Hard Row to Hoe" (1957) and "The Seacoast of Bohemia" (1957) both attempt to reconcile their unsophisticated formative backgrounds with the knowledge-bearing, alien environments in which they find themselves. In the former story, Bill and the protagonist, both Princeton seniors from Georgia, have "a tacit understanding that we were both spies in a foreign country" (*KM* 104). Since it takes place in a college setting, "A Hard Row to Hoe" possesses some aspect of a *Erziehungsroman*, the young men sitting around together and marveling at what it feels like "to be a melancholy senior" (*KM* 102). Yet, this theme quickly is subordinated to the significance of regional and socio-economic origins. Popular and polished at school, Bill is humiliated when his father, visiting him for the first time at Princeton, arrives at the dormitory drunk and belligerent. As the inebriated sire proclaims to Bill's friends, "My boy Bill is a nice college boy and his old daddy is a hick, a country boy, a plain Georgia cracker" (*KM* 107). Bill's embarrassment appears most acute to the introverted narrator, himself a native Georgian who feels as if he somehow does not belong or fit in at Princeton. Like Quentin Compson in *Absalom, Absalom!* the two southerners, having left their native region for college, find themselves more immediately engaged with their cultural pasts than they ever would have been at home.

A similar dynamic of reflective, displacement-based initiation informs "The Seacoast of Bohemia," a *Künstlerroman* describing a young southern writer's attempt to forge a literary career and find meaning in Greenwich Village. Arriving from rural Florida, the protagonist looks up a slightly older female acquaintance from the same parochial town. The woman, Diane, is a thoroughly urbanized, struggling painter whose "subjects seemed to suffer in wisdom and by choice" (*KM* 49). Not surprisingly, a knowledge-based dialectic emerges between the protagonist and Diane, who warns him that once his naive ideals are lost, "they aren't like sheep. They never get found" (*KM* 55). Diane also accurately characterizes the narrator as being "full of all kinds of exotic first impressions of this grubby city" (*KM* 53). Inevitably, the protagonist is destined for a painful change in perspective toward the city and himself, both of which he dangerously has idealized. In retrospect, he marvels at himself and the two other young artists with whom he shares an apartment: "The truth is we were happy and the lively arts thrived. I wonder, now, at our innocence and ignorance" (*KM* 50). However, not content to limit the story to the concerns of an individual young artist and southerner, Garrett sought to touch upon the initiation dynamics of an entire epoch. As the narrator explains, "Our generation had come to life after the war and though the world was tragic it was all new to us and for the taking" (*KM* 55). Becoming cognizant of the world's recent evils, the young people of the late 1940s and early 1950s, not unlike southerners of all generations, found it possible to feel new and make their own discoveries even as a dark historical cloud loomed behind them. As the protagonist summarizes, "We grew older very quickly, but I think we carried with us childhood's wisdom that nothing is impossible. Nothing, good or evil, is impossible any more" (*KM* 60). Making use of temporality and cultural difference, "The Seacoast of Bohemia" successfully abstracts the initiation experience into the historical realm.

Historical and regional distinctions give way to conflicting perceptions of racial difference in "In the Briar Patch" (1957), the title narrative from Garrett's 1961 short story collection of the same name, which records a young white boy's ambivalent discovery of racism and duplicity. The tale's central action is generated by the controversy surrounding the juvenile protagonist's new nanny, Velma. When the boy's elderly former babysitter Lizzie "got through cleaning up the house she would go sit at the kitchen table and read out of her Bible. . . . Sometimes she would have to get me to read to her and I was only in the second grade" (*BP* 84). Although Lizzie and Velma are both African-American women, they are otherwise utterly disparate figures. As the protagonist observes, Velma "had lipstick on and smoked cigarettes. She could work twice as fast as Lizzie and if nobody was around she'd go sit in the living room and smoke and drink coffee and read the paper or a magazine. She played the radio and she talked on the telephone. She was pretty and nice to us but she had her own way of doing things and Mother didn't like her" (*BP* 84–85). Reflected in the transition from the elderly, barely literate, kitchen-confined Lizzie to the independent and self-possessed young Velma is an important generational and cultural change. The boy's frigid mother characterizes Velma as "one of the new kind of maids—so uppity" (*BP* 86), a condemnation which fails to blunt the boy's fondness for Velma. In fact, the young narrator willingly conceals from his parents the fact that Velma takes him and his younger siblings on long walks in a nearby park so that she might encounter her deadbeat love interest, Leroy, a charming soldier gone AWOL. After her relationship with Leroy sours, Velma notifies the authorities of his whereabouts, after which he breaks into the protagonist's house one night and attempts to kill her. Walking in on this scene, the boy's horrified father drives Leroy away with a pistol. When the police bring Leroy back to the house for identity verification the protagonist recognizes a difference: "I could see he was scared but he was acting scareder than he really was and he was bent over trying to look small" (*BP* 90). As Leroy pleads for the police not to hand him over to the army the boy is reminded of a Br'er Rabbit story read to him by Lizzie and can't believe that the cops "were so dumb. I couldn't see how they couldn't catch on that he was pretending" (*BP* 92). Whereas the perceptions of the white adult characters remain mitigated by their racism, the boy recognizes Leroy's manipulative signifying tactics through his relative innocence of prejudice and with the aid of a children's tale. Twisting the initiation narrative in an innovative manner, Garrett demonstrates how naivete on occasion may function as a marked advantage in acquiring accurate knowledge. Free from the adult disease of racism, at least for the time being, the boy is able to understand Leroy's actions and intentions better than his parents or the police.

Garrett also explores the intersection of culture and initiation in a number of development narratives that center around young women. As R. H. W. Dillard has observed, "For a male writer of his generation especially, his ability to write successfully and with sensitivity from a woman's point of view is one of his real and distinctive strengths" (*Dictionary of Literary Biography* 130:173). In stories such as "Hawk in the April Wind" (1961) and the unpublished "Beach Party," Garrett stakes himself the arduous task of convincingly evoking female characters' transitions to womanhood. In the former narrative a country girl receives several kisses from a poor hitchhiking urban boy and abdicates her pail of buttermilk to him, before and after which they exchange their foreign worldviews. Like several of Garrett's other initiation stories, "Hawk in the April Wind" goes beyond the protagonist's personal development to reflect cultural conditions as well. Informed of a world beyond her pastoral mountain home, the adolescent girl acquires knowledge of another kind of living even as she begins to embrace the life of a woman.

A similar element of shattered provincialism also informs "Little Tune for a Steel String Guitar" (1976), a play originally composed in the 1960s under the title "Gentleman from Georgia." Like the girl in "Hawk in the April Wind," the bored, small-town female protagonist of "Little Tune for a Steel String Guitar," Betty, is duped by a seemingly cosmopolitan outsider, who eventually turns out to be an escaped criminal named Bill Starkey. Assuring Betty that "[a] lawyer don't never tell a lie" (60), Starkey proceeds to con and titillate her with the illusionary joys of city living until the police arrive to reveal his true identity. However, at the drama's conclusion, undeterred by Starkey's fraud, Betty still yearns for the superficial qualities of urban existence—an idealized world beyond her own still waiting to be unmasked for what it truly is.

Whereas Betty is all too prepared to be seduced by an outsider and escape her one-horse town, the protagonist of "Song of a Drowning Sailor: A Fabliau" is exactly the opposite, never quite willing or able to give herself over to experiences beyond her strict local upbringing. Originally published as "The Long and the Short of It" (1976), the story's narrative drive, at least on the surface, is generated by unrequited love. Adam Peterkin, the handsome darling of a small Florida town, falls hopelessly in love with Lucy Birdsong, an attractive girl "born with the soul and vocation of a nun" (*EP* 376). Frustrated by his failed efforts to win Lucy's attentions, Adam leaves town and becomes a sailor in an attempt to subdue his persistent agitation with distance and adventure. However, rather than forgetting Lucy, he drowns at sea, as obsessed and frustrated as ever. Soon thereafter, Lucy shows up at the seedy residence of Katie Freeman, the local soothsayer, claiming that Adam's spirit is haunting her. From there on, the story's events become ambivalent, careening between the psychological (Lucy is experiencing a manifestation of guilt in the wake of having ignored Adam's love) and the supernatural (perhaps his ghost really has returned to haunt her). Regardless of the literal interpretation, the main thrust of the story remains focused on portraying the adverse implications of turning one's back on life and knowledge. Having ignored Adam rather than confronting his advances head-on, Lucy remains haunted by her inability to act or embrace experience.

Lucy Birdsong's reluctance to participate in life—to be initiated for good or for ill—also functions as a negative symbolic manifestation of Garrett's perspective on art and writing. Unperturbed by the complexities of representing alien experience, the ambitious writer attempts to tackle foreign subject matter in the interests of his own aesthetic growth. Limitations and failures are inevitable but to shirk the responsibility of pressing against those boundaries is to knowingly curtail one's maturation. Thus, the young Garrett did not shy away from challenging characterizations of girls who become women, yearn to leave their small towns, or seek to make monasteries of their lives. Reflecting on his early stories in his notebooks, Garrett remarks, "I was very young when I wrote many of them, young enough to be careless in the daze and spell of inexhaustible energy and inspiration. Careless enough to play all tunes by ear." Cognizant of his inability to read different styles of music—a metaphor for his youthful ignorance of many established fictional forms—Garrett nevertheless intuitively played the pieces to the best of his ability and, as it turns out, with a remarkably attuned ear. To return to Buckley's distinction, the young "autobiographical novelist" attempts to reproduce "as accurately as possible the turbulence of the space between childhood and early manhood" (25). Relating initiation experiences from a perspective not very far removed from those of his young protagonists, Garrett rendered his early compositions with an energy and immediacy that genuinely reflects the pangs and frustrations of young people, even as—beneath this topical layer—he was experiencing his own initiation as a writer: finding his voice, experimenting with and mastering different forms, and learning through experience the hard truths surrounding his gifts and deficiencies.

That these early stories taught Garrett a great deal is evident in his more recent initiation narratives. In stories such as "A Letter That Will Never Be Written" (1998) and "My Adventures in Fantasy Land (A Story Full of Sex and Violins)" (2003), Garrett uses initiated young men as protagonists but with a fullness, abstracted wryness, and wisdom of voice that links the youthful individual agonies of knowledge to lives, times, and truths beyond their own. When asked about his evolving relationship to initiation narratives, Garrett remarked that there are "a couple of elements. One is that you are more apt to see yourself as comic, if you have survived long enough. It was not comic at the time but essentially you are working with a recapitulation of a certain point of view in which it is now possible—and I've done several stories of this kind—for the elder version of the same person to be more tolerant of youth and its foibles. That story has changed a little bit" (Int). Such a perspective, replete with comedy, forbearance, and historical abstraction, takes place in "A Letter That Will Never Be Written," a partially epistolary tale set in the spring of 1626 and narrated by "*a kind of clerk, secretary and companion to Robert Carey*" (*BMB* 29, Garrett's italics). After a memorable night of debauchery in London, the nameless young man lies drunk in his bedchamber composing in his head a repentant letter to his idealized love interest, Priscilla. With a stodgy wistfulness that comes across more comic than poignant, he laments, "Oh, why did he not go and join the Godly people, the Puritans?" (*BMB* 30). Removing his initiation narrative to seventeenth-century England and infusing it with irony, Garrett achieves a universal quality that actually serves to strengthen the tale's immediacy in the present. Strip away the historical trimmings and the protagonist could well be a twenty-first-century young man, thoroughly soused and chastened after one too many nightclubs. In London the bookish youngster has discovered "the limits of my body and the emptiness of my purse" (*BMB* 36), feeling as if he has become "[a]n ape disguised in a scholar's gown" (*BMB* 37). Yet, the self-imposed agonies of his sins and yearnings for Priscilla are tempered unconsciously by his relationship with the elderly Carey. Carey confides in the protagonist that long ago he had married for love, earning Queen Elizabeth's censure. Describing Elizabeth as an exemplar of logic and forethought, Carey maintains that she "always cultivated a most strictly practical kind of wisdom" (*BMB* 31). Although Carey's counsel would clearly benefit the young man, his young companion abjures his experience and wisdom: "Forgive me, my dearest Priscilla, these old stories of old people. Such things are my daily bread now. The Earl talks to me and I must listen" (*BMB* 34). Rather than learning from Carey's life experience, the protagonist tiresomely belittles it as dated and useless, secure in the assumption—shared by most young people—that he knows best, though he may know very little. Instead of confronting the complexities of his current situation the young man yearns to take Priscilla and flee both his predicaments and the anti-quated atmosphere of England: "Let us then make a new beginning. Let us leave and go to the New World" (*BMB* 43). Behind the young man's idle dreams and impatient exclamations, one just barely hears the quiet and in-dulgent laughter of Carey and perhaps Garrett as well; not a mocking sound but forgiving and warm, perhaps even a little nostalgic, at the timeless fool-ishness of youth.

Buckley maintains that the older "autobiographer" often indulges in "fond retrospect, often more than a little sentimental in his view of his youth, re-calling what it pleases him to remember" (25). The tension between the nostalgic reconstruction of youthful experience and objective fact stands near the heart of "My Adventures in Fantasy Land (A Story Full of Sex and Violins)," a tale that weaves back and forth between the separate memories and facts of a fourteen-year-old protagonist named Frank and a much older projection of himself, both rendered by an apparent fictional projection of George Garrett. The story's narrative dilemma is apparent before it even begins. An epigraph from V. S. Naipaul reads, "I would prefer fact," while another from John Updike asserts, "Nothing gums up fiction like facts" (13). From these two conflicting dedications emerges a kind of double vision—in fact, this story originally was part of Garrett's novel *Double Vision*—with regard to a single event experienced and remembered by the young and old Frank, respectively. The primary setting of the story—there are several dis-parately minor ones—is the bathroom of Frank's boyhood home, "where the boy is, now and forever, and so is the Geezer more than half a century later" (33). Locked in the bathroom with a collection of dirty magazines, the two Franks (young and old) remain always and forever on the threshold of being discovered by their father. Focused on a key event rendered from dual perspectives across time and memory, the story becomes a kind of meditation on the act of telling. In fact, the narrator remarks that the tale "hasn't really ended yet since the old man, who was the young boy at the beginning of the story, still remembers it as if it happened only moments ago. Whether it will end when the old man, that's the young boy as well, is dead and gone or when, at last, living or dead, his file of memory is nothing but trash and dust in the wind, remains to be seen" (22). Compressing, expanding, and folding back upon itself, the story establishes and then investigates a series of shaky boundaries between times, narrators, characters, events, and—ultimately—fact and fiction.

At the center of the linguistic rendering of fact is the creative process. Even objective historians indulge in pejorative language when delineating the so-called irrevocable data of an event. For the adolescent Frank, sex becomes the medium through which he develops his artistic imagination. As his confidante Esther summarizes, "You look at these magazines and then make up stories about the women in the pictures" (15). Yet, the complexities of this process are not left entirely for the young Frank to show us. In the midst of the adolescent's erotic narrative involving a Roman orgy, a mature narrative voice humorously butts in to justify the moral course of the story, relating that he has "been married to a wonderful woman for many years (more than fifty years in fact) now. And I plan to stay that way" (19). Later, the mature narrator jumps in again to spoil the story's drama, revealing that the boy will be devastated when he loses his collection of dirty magazines. Yet, he assures us, "In the future the whole story will be a lot funnier than he was capable of guessing in the tumultuous years of his adolescence" (20). Possessing a mastery of both the initiation experience itself and its repercussions down the line, Garrett offers the event in all its youthful angst while simultaneously disrupting time and the narrative with a more mature perspective. Although this technique occasionally blurs both the event and the life at hand, it also has the capacity to focus and enrich an experience's meaning through its interactions with a single protagonist across the jumbled oceans of time.

Phillip Tew once characterized the English writer B. S. Johnson as attempting "to embody truth in a vehicle of fiction that mostly refuses to do so. Johnson looks back to his earlier years for the bulk of experience common to both his fiction and his life" (Tew 198). Historically, Garrett and Johnson were linked by their successive editorships of the *Transatlantic Review* and in Tew's observation they are brought together again: two skilled veteran writers offering up highly self-reflexive experiences in styles that sometimes threaten to bend and distort the experiences themselves in an effort to some-how say more. Not content with telling similar stories in the same ways, Garrett, unlike many seasoned writers, has become progressively knowl-edgeable and ambitious with the passing of the years. Having accurately dis-covered through his sometimes painful early initiation narratives his voice and identity, Garrett, rather than comfortably lulling himself to sleep with the sound of that voice, ever continues to tweak, exercise, and occasionally strain it. At the beginning of "My Adventures in Fantasy Land" the youthful Frank notes that just outside his window, "A mockingbird is right now try-ing on some new voices and making up new songs" (13). So too, the reader suspects, is George Garrett.

"The Wind Shuffled the Palm Fronds Like New Money"

Garrett's Florida

*If you look at Florida it's changing right before your eyes.
Like time-lapse photography of corn growing. In that sense
maybe it's just an exaggerated version of the whole country.*
—Garrett, The King of Babylon Shall Not Come against You

With its emphasis on aggregate international commerce, law and inter-
vention, and a perceived collective evolution toward a world village, the
globalization phenomenon presents itself as a massive and confused, yet
sometimes menacingly single-minded, conglomeration of ideologies and
economics, the cacophonous totality of which habitually threatens to drown
out the complexities of its own more minuscule, though often vital, components. The general theory of globalization maintains that more nations
are depending on worldwide conditions relating to communication, the international financial system, and trade. As a result, the world scenario progressively becomes more integrated through international economic and
cultural transactions.

Accompanying this dominant reading of globalization as a great homogenous, culture-enforcing conglomerate is a smaller collection of observations
that, instead of referring to a single new world order, perceive an emergence
of a variety of new regional systems. In this context, regionalism refers to
a series of areas linked by a geographical relationship, as well as a degree
of mutual cultural and economic interdependence. Regional communities
necessarily are subordinate ones, functioning beneath the more impersonal

national and global human systems. Nevertheless, they help to construct the larger communities and often demonstrate the potential for meaningfully influencing them, culturally and otherwise. In this sense, considerations of regional place, contrary to popular consensus, remain as important as ever.

Over the course of the last several decades, the study of place under various theoretical agendas has lingered as a popular vehicle for scholars attempting to establish and investigate the complexities of a given region and the peoples and cultures it produces. Speaking in the realm of southern literature, Louis Rubin captured the obviousness of its importance: "What makes the oft-remarked Sense of Place in Southern fiction so important is the vividness, the ferocity even, with which it implies social and community attitudes" (33). As memorable as autonomous characters and writing styles can be, it is often the dynamics of the place a writer articulates that haunts the reader beyond a book's final pages. Yoknapatawpha, Mississippi; Asheville, North Carolina; Winesburg, Ohio; John O'Hara's Gibbsville, Pennsylvania; and the respective East Tennessees of Cormac McCarthy, Charles Wright, and Madison Smartt Bell stretch out before us, imaginative landscapes made real through the deftness and detail of their renderings. And both in and beyond these places, to varying degrees, lies a portion of the imaginative landscape of the writer's mind and the experiences that have generated his fiction. As George Garrett maintains, "Where we begin, though, the home place and home plate of all our stories, is not first of all with the history of the tribe or crew we were born into, but with our own personal history and our own stories" (*BMB* 181). From the home place of the painfully acknowledged self, writers stretch out their tentative feelers, collecting and translating through their art the intricacies of their surroundings.

Garrett, himself, over a number of memoirs, stories, and novels across several decades, provides an intriguing example of how a writer's personal imagined relationship to his home place may develop and change, even as his undeniable place of origin, the region from which he hails, undergoes radical transitions in appearance and culture with the passing of time. The prospect of geopolitical change is especially palpable in much of Garrett's work because of his close personal ties to the Orlando, Florida, area of the 1930s and early 1940s, a rural region destined for jarring, unprecedented shifts in its economy, culture, and fundamental identity. At the beginning of a talk delivered to the Florida Historical Society in Orlando in 1991, Garrett remarked, "I hunted and fished and biked all over what is now this city and most of Orange County. I would have sworn I knew every inch of it, but I got lost today trying to find this new hotel." A provincial town in the 1930s, surrounded by large tracts of farmland covered mostly by cattle and citrus groves, Orlando would undergo a sudden dramatic change with the arrival of the United States Army in 1940 and the 1941 establishment of the Orlando Army Airfield, a site made significant in literary history through its detailed rendering in James Gould Cozzens's Pulitzer Prize-winning World War II novel *Guard of Honor*. Stimulated by the influx of more than 10,000 military personnel and the industrial complex that accompanied them, Orlando's population would rise from approximately 27,000 in the early 1930s to nearly 53,000 in 1950. Subsequent lucrative corporate contracts proceeding in part from the arrival of the space industry in the 1960s and the opening of Disney World in 1971 resulted in additional growth, with Orlando's twenty-first-century population well on the way to 200,000 and Orange County's pressing the one million mark. During a trip to the area around the turn of the century, Garrett observed, with a mixture of humor and poignancy, "I could see, at one point, the house where I grew up, but I couldn't figure out how to get there" (Int). Stuck amid the numerous on-off ramps and suffocating traffic of a towering modern interstate designed for fast, convenient travel, the native Floridian found himself unable to reach his home place, completely bemused in an environment bearing no resemblance to the place he knew so well, even though it occupies the same, identical space.

Familiar with the gaudy contemporary complexion of Orange County and expert in its pre-World War II identity, Garrett explores both worlds in his work, occasionally mingling them in such a way as to flirt with larger assumptions about the phenomena of historical change and place. Having written an extraordinary trilogy of historical novels set in Elizabethan England, Garrett is as comfortable portraying convincing fictional worlds from the past as he is assembling representations of contemporary times. In his Florida Historical Society address Garrett remarked that for him the "Orlando of the 1930s and 1940s is more vividly present, more 'real,' then, than this bright and shiny hotel ballroom and the world beyond these windows, where massively towering bank buildings, vaguely Babylonian, brood over this city by day and by night." Raised in and shaped by Depression-era Orange County, Garrett remains imaginatively tied to that place in a way that makes its immediacy more genuine than the bustling landscape of today. Furthermore, Garrett's description of contemporary Orlando as "vaguely Babylonian" helps to articulate his personal perspective on the region's modern development. The Bible relates in the book of Ezra that the wealthy city of Babylon was razed, its people driven out, and its legendary wealth and power forgotten. Later, in Revelation, Babylon is associated with Rome, perceived by early Christians as the doomed heart of empire and idolatry during that epoch. This biblically based symbolic association between contemporary Orlando and Babylon/

Rome bears literary fruit in Garrett's eighth novel, *The King of Babylon Shall Not Come against You* (1996), the fictional Florida setting of which boasts grotesque, idolatrous celebrity references and high-stakes economic hustling while attempting to link characters and historical causality across decades. The novel's narrator, Billy Tone, has the unenviable task of wading through a sea of decadence and cultural detritus in order to discover the meaning of an almost forgotten event. In Christian theology the king of Babylon often is associated with Satan, and in seeking to arrive at accurate historical and personal truths Tone must overcome the fiendish disguises and deceptions of both his shiny, opulent Florida community and himself.

In much of his autobiographical writing, especially *Whistling in the Dark* (1992), Garrett refers to his Florida family (past and present) as a "Tribe." Translated in the Assyrian tablets, the name *Babylon* means "the city of the dispersion of the tribes." A crapulous place of indiscriminate wealth and power, Babylon rushes toward an excess-driven *Götterdämmerung* of its own making, disintegrating the distinctive community and familial ties of its people until they are erased from history. Over the course of his fiction, Garrett plays upon a similar historical transition in the context of the Orange County area, from reflections on the provincial and pastoral aspects of its tightly knit, Depression-era identity to its impersonal modern existence as a prosperous, image-driven, international metro area. In the process of becoming a global city, which champions a place called Disney *World* (a kind of Babylon unto itself), Orlando has relinquished forever much of the distinctiveness and sense of community that once made it unique.

In his autobiographical piece "Under Two Flags" (1992) Garrett offers a brief but detailed snapshot of the Orange County town of Kissimmee, Florida:

> Picture this, if you will. Kissimmee, Florida, in the heart of the Great Depression. A small, shabby little place. Then, blessed with the rich shade of live oaks and so offering a few moments of shadowy respite from the heat and dust and glare all around for miles. Walt Disney is near there now, and the old place looks pretty, pretty much like every place else. But it was a cow town then, a hard, tough place where life was hard and tough and had turned bitter for many decent people. (*WD* 193)

Describing Kissimmee past and present in a few spare sentences, Garrett evokes a broad historical transition from autonomous, local struggle to homogenous prosperity. "Shabby" and "hard," 1930s Kissimmee was a poor place possessing the simple "rich shade of live oaks." By contrast, the modern area is "pretty," but also "pretty much like every place else," its nondescript population, flourishing economy, and real estate values boosted by the endless flow of pilgrimages to Disney. And just as many of its oldest live oaks have been cut down in the interests of widening roads and developing land, so most of its old identity has been stripped and transformed into something new and almost unrecognizable.

Garrett closes his autobiographical description of Kissimmee with a reference to its Depression-era people, for whom the place and life in general had turned "bitter" in the wake of their economic suffering—a travail that would be slow to depart them, if ever. At the beginning of the early short story "The King of the Mountain" (1957), Garrett's anonymous narrator elaborates on the enduring effects of that period:

> There's a whole generation of us now, conceived in that anxious time, and if we're fat now, flash a wide advertisement grin at the cockeyed careless world, we know still, deeply as you know the struggles of blood on its long pilgrimage of flesh, the old feel and smell of fear, the gray dimensions of despair, and, too, some of us, memory of the tug and gnaw of being hungry. (*KM* 61)

However much he might attempt to assuage his past with fat living and commercial amusement, the Depression-era Floridian finds it difficult, if not impossible, to abdicate his reluctant historical ties to fear and hunger. As the narrator in "The King of the Mountain" summarizes, "[W]here you suffered first, acquired your first wounds and scars, is where you've hung your heart once and for all and called it home" (*KM* 62). As much of Garrett's fiction and autobiographical writing attest, the narrator's declaration is true both for Garrett and his work, which increasingly has demonstrated a reflective focus on the dynamics of his own life and those of his extended family. "The King of the Mountain" constitutes a very early manifestation of this theme. Although it skillfully captures the dynamics of 1930s Orange County, it is more concerned with telling the tale of a local lawyer, closely based on Garrett's father, who is beaten severely by the Ku Klux Klan but survives to defeat them in the courts and become a powerful political figure. In "Uncles and Others" (1992) Garrett records how his lawyer father and a partner, braving death and terror, literally "drove the Ku Klux Klan, then a real political power, completely out of Kissimmee, Florida" (*WD* 49), a veritable act of heroism performed in an era of dashed hopes and widespread suffering. An exemplar of courage and idealism, Garrett's father and veiled manifestations of him appear throughout Garrett's writings, early and late, fiction and memoir—from his first novel *The Finished Man* (1959) to more recent autobiographical essays such as "The Right Thing to Do at the Time" and "Heroes" (both collected in *Bad Man Blues* [1998]). In evoking his father and the temporal Florida milieu to which he is linked, Garrett often seems bent on capturing both the worst and the best of that time—the suffering, ignorance, and bitter hate of the hopelessly downtrodden, as well as the enduring honesty and courage of hard-pressed individuals and their tightly knit communities.

While tokens of Garrett's father and the dramas of his life appear across his work, Garrett's own relation to the place of his youth is evoked quite differently and shifts from story to story. Whereas the various projections of Garrett's father are prime participants in local adult incidents of the Great Depression, many of Garrett's own literary silhouettes look on through the rosy lenses of a child narrator or youthful character, only vaguely interested in the adult affairs around them and focused mostly on the pastoral aspects of a largely juvenile world. In the more recent story "Gator Bait," for example, Garrett's young autobiographical character lists a "lightly grassy playground" (*Empty* 165) as his major concern in life. Several of Garrett's early short stories possess similar figures, youthful and nearly always bound for some kind of maturing, life-altering event. Unconcerned, as of yet, with the burdens of adulthood, these young characters are backgrounded by a sylvan Florida, which serves as their playground, itself still unspoiled by destiny and developers. Thus in "The Rivals" (1957) the young male narrator—not a boy but also not yet a man—undertakes a Florida boating expedition with his father across a remote bay to a beautiful, empty beach ("a splatter and a flash of pure whiteness" [*KM* 9]), the violent aftermath of which leads to a harsh initiation into adulthood. Barren of sunbathers, boardwalks, and lifeguards, the tale's now-unfamiliar Florida shore remains a convincingly forsaken place, fraught with danger, loneliness, and beauty.

Like "The Rivals," most of Garrett's recollections and early narratives that evoke the Florida landscape contain memorable narrative-shaping descriptions of beaches and water. In the autobiographical "Under Two Flags" (1992) Garrett describes his grandfather sailing home with his two sons: "Sun going down, wind touched with a chill and the salty sense of the open sea" (*WD* 224). Having recently lost his fortune, Garrett's grandfather nonetheless is able to find comfort in the hint of a limitless ocean, the nearness of his sons, and a boat skillfully brought to dock. Just as the benign coastal weather conditions reflect the inner peace of Garrett's grandfather in "Under Two Flags," so changes in the Florida climate mirror dramatic action in the early story "A

Game of Catch" (1960). Having departed for the Florida shore, a small group of youthful acquaintances—TeeJay and Courtney (who are brothers), and Naomi (TeeJay's girlfriend)—arrive at the beach to discover "a perfect day. The sun was bright, the water was blue and scaled with the white caps of a brisk east wind" (*BP* 132). However, planting a subtle sense of foreshadowing, Garrett notes, "The tide was down, but rising" (*BP* 132). While the wind and water roll in and TeeJay and Courtney begin to quarrel, a storm becomes visible on the horizon. As the squall nears and the brothers foolishly refuse to depart in favor of their softball throwing contest, Courtney crouches in TeeJay's vehicle, worried that they all will be struck by lightning or stranded on the beach by the rising tide. A picturesque watery setting turned sour and deadly also appears in "The Test" (1961), in which a trio of boyhood friends try out their homemade diving helmet in a deep local spring. Like the ocean in "The Rivals" the inland water setting of Wekiva Springs is beautiful but forsaken and potentially dangerous. As the narrator relates:

> The spring is the source of a stream that winds away through a dense green jungle of palms and palmettos and water oaks and cypress, the trees covered with vines and the stream choked with green hyacinth plants. Farther along, up the stream a few miles are some hunting camps, and if you go by boat to one of them, you'll see huge alligators and the biggest water moccasins you ever laid eyes on. Or imagined. You might as well be in Darkest Africa; it's easy to pretend you are. Weikiwa Springs is a lonesome, beautiful, abandoned place. (*BP* 9)

Making the locale scenic and remote to the boys' liking, Garrett then peppers it with menacing peripheral references to snakes and alligators, as if to remind readers that the world remains a dangerous place, though a child may think it a playground. When one of the boys drowns while using the helmet, the tragic lesson is brought home to his companions, revealing also an Edenic allegory, the boys' ill-considered pursuit of knowledge in a pristine setting having destroyed forever their innocence.

Now a seven-thousand-acre state park, the Wekiva Springs area is one of the few Florida milieus from Garrett's early fiction that exists much as it was in his youth (with the exception of convenient canoe rentals and drink machines). Beyond the narratives that seek to capture the precommercial Florida landscape, Garrett also explores the process, by turns subtle and sudden, of the state's transition from pastoral agrarianism to prosperous tourist haven. Driving across the state in the late-1950s setting of *The Finished Man* (1959), the novel's protagonist, Mike Royale, describes the altered essence of his native landscape at great length:

There are old towns in West Florida, plantation towns from the antebellum days, left behind like curious sea creatures tossed up, then relinquished by a retreating tide, quietly with their histories and their scars. There are the old Spanish settlements, now tourist attractions under their glowering forts, like Pensacola and St. Augustine. There are the port cities, Jacksonville and Tampa. There are industrious new towns, little cities like Orlando. And there are the fantastic, unabashedly vulgar, blaring tourist cities ringing the coasts, outposts with all the glare and gilt of carnivals, adolescent day-dreams of *luxuria*. (*FM* 64–65, Garrett's emphasis)

Even with Disney still more than a decade away, Mike Royale's midcentury Florida already is in the process of becoming defined by its "vulgar, blaring tourist cities," its storied historical sites and towns having been either assimilated into commercial tourist packages or cast out and left to suffocate and rot like marooned fish on a beach. Accompanying the historical places, Florida's natural beauty is drawn beneath the banner of commercialism as well. Evoking Florida in the poem "Four American Landscapes," Garrett describes how "the wind shuffled the palm fronds like new money" (*CP* 41). No longer a feature to be admired on its own terms, nature becomes a commercial resource, its physical qualities suggesting dollar signs to opportunistic developers. Of course, the irony of this relationship, repeating itself throughout American history, is that the developer usually ends up destroying much of the unique environment he wishes to market, the majestic dunes sacrificed for ocean-front houses and motels. Mike Royale experiences a kind of dark epiphany surrounding this geopolitical transition in *The Finished Man*:

[M]onstrous, fabulous hotels sprung like exotic plants from the weary imaginations of winter-bound Easterners, opulent daydreams of the tropics, rising out of the sand and scrub of what had been, only a generation or so before, a tidal bog humming with the song of mosquitoes. Nothing real, nothing dangerous could happen against such a background. No matter how serious the complexities which might arise, all things were bound to end with fanfare and a song and dance, a buck and wing. All of the East Coast beginning with the preserved Spanish town of Saint Augustine was like that, each town, each cluster of motels and tourist courts, designed to meet the need, the desire for something that never was and hadn't been there before. (*FM* 117)

Recurring in Royale's description is the alien quality of Florida's development boom—the new hotels are "monstrous" and "exotic," fully realized foreign projections created to satisfy the blind desire of a new shared consciousness: something that "hadn't been there before." In the throes of this transition, nothing seems real anymore to Royale, the concrete certainties of his provincial Florida youth having given way to the superficial dreamworld of a transitory tourist culture.

Whereas Mike Royale delivers a kind of grand declaration on the destiny of Florida, Garrett is much more subtle in his treatment of the state's cultural changes in other narratives. Suggestive of Madison Jones's account of Brady, Tennessee's, somewhat slower transformation in his first novel *The Innocent*, these stories contain hints of societal oscillation and threatened traditions while relinquishing the big picture for the reader to assemble. In "The Confidence Man" (1959) a supposedly prudish and very traditional middle-aged Florida widow, Miss Alma, has an affair with a dashing young con-man who rides into town on a motorcycle and dupes her out of her money. Alma's apparent association with an older, now-extinct Florida is established early in the story through her relationship with the local fishermen: "She was the only person in the world still allowed to market right there where the boats came in instead of uptown at the new Fish Market. Nobody had the heart or the inclination to tell her that long ago all that had changed" (*BP* 60). Characterized by the townspeople as a venerable, long-suffering link to the past, Alma unexpectedly puts her neighbors back on their heels, in the unfamiliar position of enforcing the local morality, when she flaunts her new love interest and then displays no guilt or sorrow after he jilts her. Wholly satisfied with the trade-off, Alma functions in the end as the unlikeliest of liberated, progressive women, championing personal pleasure over small-town mores and linked to the outside world through her relationship to the controversial wanderer.

Garrett again makes use of a prudish elderly woman in order to underscore reactions to cultural change in "Thus the Early Gods" (1959), which records the tensions between an established Florida family, the Grims, and their impoverished new waterfront neighbors, the Quiglys. However, in direct opposition to Miss Alma, Mrs. Grim, as her name powerfully reinforces, is a stalwart champion of tradition and social condescension. For example, she complains to her son's northern-born wife, Jane, that when the family's cottage was built,

> there wasn't another cottage for miles. It was so peaceful. Now houses are popping up everywhere like the heat rash. Like pimples. They're tearing the dunes down, and new people—not the kind of people you'd care to have around if you had any say so about the matter—are com-

ing here by the hordes to live. They're ruining the place. They're like a lot of weeds choking us out. (*BP* 114)

Likening the recent beach-front development to a "heat rash" or "pimples," Mrs. Grim develops her disparaging analogy further by comparing her new neighbors to "hordes" of "weeds," whose pesky, unattractive presence threatens to "choke out" her presumably rightful, indigenous presence at the beach. Conveniently oblivious to the fact that her own family once razed the dunes and carved out a place for themselves on the shore, Mrs. Grim laments and attacks the same desire in others. That the head of the Quigly family, Joe, is both a "cracker" and a bulldozer operator—a literal, threatening harbinger of cultural and environmental change—outrages her all the more. As Mrs. Grim's son Harper explains to Jane:

> It's just that she was born out of her time or, anyway, that she had to live on beyond it. She's a lady living in a time when that word doesn't mean anything. And all she sees around her is change, change, change. Change and decay. The good, happy, comfortable world she grew up in turned inside out, turned into something else after the Depression and the War. She's just a minor, eccentric victim of the great social revolution. A bewildered mastodon, wandering around in the postglacial age. (*BP* 115)

Offering an intriguing alternative to his narratives that criticize the process of Florida's development, Garrett here portrays the dangers of irrationally clinging to an idealized past. Stubbornly choosing to remain in the world that was, Mrs. Grim is unable to establish any constructive role for herself amid her changing surroundings. Unwilling to adapt, she condemns herself to a kind of bitter living death.

Garrett continues to investigate the prospect of change with regard to backward-looking elderly characters in "Goodbye, Goodbye, Be Always Kind and True" (1961). Having been wounded in the First World War and received a wooden leg, Peter Joshman spends his days in a rocking chair on the front porch of his son-in-law's central Florida farmhouse, idly gazing off into the distance. However, Joshman's routine is altered abruptly when the state begins laying a new highway across his son-in-law's land. As the narrator relates, "[T]he big machines, the rollers and levellers and graders, hurried through the early spring, smoothing the wound that had been made in his field of vision" (*BP* 151). Troubled, like Mrs. Grim, by the alterations to the landscape, Joshman allows, "I don't know as I can get used to what they done" (*BP* 152). Shortly thereafter the narrator elaborates on Joshman's uncomfortable ambivalence: "Pretty soon the tourists would be coming down it, making a short-cut to the East Coast with its splendid beaches, the sun and waves and sand as white and fine as sugar there. Peter sat in his rocker, gripping his heavy cane with knuckles whitened from impotent anger" (*BP* 152). As in "Thus the Early Gods," development-related change informs the heart of the story, Joshman appearing unnerved, yet powerless to resist, the alterations rendered upon his accustomed way of life. However, unlike Mrs. Grim, Joshman eventually learns to accept the prospect of transformation. Whereas the embittered elderly woman holds her new neighbors in contempt and repeatedly dehumanizes them, Joshman eventually is moved to love the new highway through the glimpsed humanity of its travelers. As the narrator explains, "That was entirely different, a road with *people*" (*BP* 152, Garrett's emphasis). Largely alienated from his family and the world at large, Joshman determines "that he ought to *participate*, share in some way that hurtling moment of gleaming speed. He wanted to offer his benediction" (*BP* 154, Garrett's emphasis). Initially waving at travelers from the curb and then constructing a collection of roadside dummies to accomplish the same purpose, Joshman achieves an eccentric variety of peace and union with the new road.

In the wake of his initial novel *The Finished Man* and his first two short story collections—*King of the Mountain* (1957) and *In the Briar Patch* (1961)—Garrett's work would revisit Florida milieus and themes with diminishing frequency, and those few writings from the 1960s and '70s that returned to the state did so in a manner that contextualized Florida within a larger nation and world. For example, in the novella "Cold Ground Was My Bed Last Night" (1964) a self-satisfied local sheriff named Jack Riddle is forced to look beyond the scope of his uneventful rural county when his cocksure deputy, Larry Berlin, shoots a gun-wielding interloper. A nondescript village along a Florida highway, Riddle's charge, Fairview, "is small and old" (*CG* 153), a blur in the window of tourists rushing to vacation spots like Daytona Beach. As the narrator relates, "The town endures now in the affluent middle of the century without thriving and without really changing much, a preserved relic, it seems, of what at least from this anxious point in human history was an easier, gentler, more relaxed time to be alive" (*CG* 154). Its culture frozen in time, Fairview, as its name suggests, functions as a quaint visual depiction of an earlier, more leisurely era. Into this insular world speeds Tony De Angelo, a Brooklyn native who has recently shot a store clerk—fatally, it turns out—during a robbery in Daytona Beach. Shortly after picking up a hitchhiker named Ike Toombs, De Angelo is pulled over for speeding by Riddle's deputy, Larry Berlin, who guns down De Angelo when he gets out of his car while attempting to draw a pistol from his coat. With De Angelo dead, Riddle is stuck with trying to establish Toombs's relationship to him, from which stems the story's central drama. Although Riddle, true to his name, never satisfactorily establishes Toombs's guilt or innocence, he is affected powerfully by the outsider's perspective on Fairview. A wandering musician and ex-con, Toombs is highly adept at characterizing places. For example, he notices that the calendar in the sheriff's office is a month behind, thinking to himself, "A month or two don't make no difference in a place like this" (*CG* 173). Refusing to plead or employ diplomacy with Riddle, he instead lectures him on the insignificance of his town and, by association, himself: "It's a great big world, Sheriff. There's thousands and thousands of miles of it and all of it is outside of this crummy county" (*CG* 174). Although Toombs arouses the malice of the good-natured sheriff, Riddle, in the end, grudgingly accepts his worldview. He concedes, "The world came into town in the morning paper and on the TV. Lying with a smile and killing with a kiss. The world had an Italian name and lived in a cheap hotel in Brooklyn, New York" (*CG* 198). Never having carried a gun before, Riddle understands that he would be dead if it had been him in Berlin's shoes. As Berlin, immature but cruelly realistic, bluntly muses, "You can sit on your ass around a place like Fairview and forget about a lot of things" (*CG* 203). No longer able to conduct his office according to the passive, genteel rules of the Mayberry-like Fairview, Riddle dons a revolver, a symbolic gesture which reflects his painful recognition and acceptance of the dangerous forces beyond Fairview and himself.

Visions, both disturbing and promising, of life beyond a small Florida town also inform the stories "Little Tune for a Steel String Guitar" and "Song of a Drowning Sailor: A Fabliau," both published in 1976 but composed in the 1960s. In the former narrative, a naive small-town waitress named Betty is charmed with tales of the good life in faraway Atlanta by a suave visitor, Bill Starkey, who turns out to be an escaped convict. Momentarily drunk on Starkey's tales of the exciting world beyond the town of Paradise Springs, Betty is swept away, only to come crashing back to reality when the police arrive to apprehend her seducer. As dull as her small world may sometimes appear, it nonetheless is an honest one. Let down by Starkey, Betty comes to realize that the indistinct and idealized outside world is as full of as many lies and disappointments as dreams. Falsehoods and dreams also may inform "Song of a Drowning Sailor: A Fabliau," which records the psychological or supernatural hallucinations of Lucy Birdsong, who is haunted by her former admirer Adam Peterkin, a local boy who had loved her desperately but eventually despaired and departed. After Peterkin drowns in a storm at sea, Lucy complains to the local psychic, Katie Freeman, that his ghost is haunting her. In this manner, the story shakes loose the restrictive yoke of Paradise Springs and strays into the realms of the psychological and supernatural. Underscoring the dangers of the world beyond one's home, Peterkin believes it was his decision to leave his small Florida town that initiated all his troubles. As his ghost confesses to Katie Freeman, "I never should have left Paradise Springs in the first place. It's just as easy to die there" (*EP* 384). In the end, charged with a bewildering number of interpretive possibilities reminiscent of Henry James's *The Turn of the Screw*, the reader is left unsure whether Lucy is purposefully lying, psychologically plagued by guilt, or perhaps genuinely haunted. Fortunately, the story's subtitle provides some direction on how it all should be taken. A short, comic tale usually conveyed in verse, the fabliau plays with and teases the reader while often delivering cynical commentary on places and institutions. Seen in this light, the story becomes a mischievous evocation of naive provincial love, the boy having forsaken his parochial community with a broken heart and the girl remaining guilty and unable to imagine his life and afterlife in worlds beyond her experience.

Although the aim of "Song of a Drowning Sailor: A Fabliau" partially is comic, the story opens with the narrator's haunting declaration that "we have our share of ghosts in old Paradise Springs" (*EP* 373). When Garrett's writing finally returned to Florida settings in the 1990s with the largely autobiographical *Whistling in the Dark* (1992) and the novel *The King of Babylon Shall Not Come against You* (1996), shades of the past—family members as well as unrelated figures—haunted the pages. Whereas *Whistling in the Dark* generally is backward-looking, much of the writing dealing with Garrett's youth in Orange County, *King of Babylon*, while exploring historical themes, takes place in contemporary Paradise Springs, an updated 1990s version of the setting of much of Garrett's earlier short fiction.

In spite of its late-twentieth-century setting, *King of Babylon* contains references both to Florida's past and Garrett's earlier Florida fiction. Near the beginning of the novel, Billy Tone reveals that he is related to the Singletrees and Royales (*KB* 3), influential local families that figure prominently in *The Finished Man* and several of Garrett's early stories. This important connection, casually related by Tone in passing, creates both a meaningful link to the preceding Florida generation and an intertextual relationship with Garrett's earlier fiction. From the beginning then, *King of Babylon* is not only about itself. Rather, it embodies a historical continuity of place as well as an extension and revision of fictional themes across nearly four decades.

Paradise Springs in the 1990s is conceptualized by most of its citizens as a progressive, forward-thinking area, liberated from the violence of its past—a perspective that does not always hold up to close scrutiny. In "Bad Man Blues," a section of *King of Babylon* that was cut from the novel's final version and published separately, the prosperous African-American lawyer Willie Gary recounts to his white colleagues the area's last lynching, to which one of his listeners responds, "None of us is eager to listen to Willie tell us about the last lynching in the county or, for that matter, about any lynching at all, early or late, first or last. All that ancient history has nothing to do with any of us. Not really. Think of us as being like young yuppie lawyers anywhere in America. Might just as well be in Connecticut or Iowa" (*BMB* 73). Although they would prefer to think they have moved beyond the brutality of earlier local generations and become culturally indistinguishable from their colleagues in other regions of the country, the uneasiness of Gary's white associates indicates that the event lies uncomfortably closer to their own lives than they would like to acknowledge. When the speaker asserts that the event does "not really" have anything to do with them, he only succeeds in inviting ambiguity and uncertainty—he would like to think he is removed from the experience but cannot be entirely sure.

Although genuine changes in the belief systems and people of Paradise Springs are left open to debate, alterations in the place itself are undeniable. Dudley Hagood, editor of the local newspaper in *King of Babylon*, says of Paradise Springs:

> What people once would have called a "typical small town" is now a type only of the dead and wilting stalks left on the vast cornfield which was once America. The said field is scheduled to vanish forever, proba- bly to be covered up with asphalt, and the asphalt covered with painted arrows and parking slots, all aiming to become the biggest continuous shopping center in the history of the world." (*KB* 4)

Abstracting the fate of Paradise Springs to that of the rest of the country, Ha- good simplifies the area's transition into a shift from pastoralism to sprawl- ing commercial development. At the heart of this change are people such as the developer Penrose Weatherby, who acknowledges his complicity in the area's growth but clings stubbornly to the worn, time-honored gospel of capitalist opportunity and wealth at all costs. As he explains to Tone, "We are running out of water in this state. People keep coming and building, and living here and pretty soon Florida will be nothing but one big toxic sand pile. Sure we have got problems, but you can't blame them all on the developers" (*KB* 11). Rather than recognizing the prominent role of his profession in the difficulties that accompany Paradise Springs' rise to economic relevance, Weatherby redirects blame toward outsiders: "Yes, dope problem has reached even here, little old Paradise Springs. . . . Mostly it's the outsiders, dope dealers and that ilk, people from large urban ghettos who cause all the trouble" (*KB* 13). Of course, what Weatherby misses or willfully ignores is the fact that an area's economic and population growth irrevocably connect it, through trade and migration, to other areas. In this manner, economic development usually lies at the heart of cultural change. Accompanying new money and fresh people are new markets, not all of them beneficial or legal, which carve out their own niches in localities that never have known them before.

In "The Pornographers," another section from *King of Babylon* published separately, the specter of outside influence and altered culture is brought home through the story of a twelve-year-old girl who supports her extended family by starring in porno movies. As Paradise Springs' uncommonly astute sheriff Dale Lewis explains, "There is no escaping the moral climate of the modern world. It comes here, too, of all places, in all of its twisted fury and madness. . . . And all of the plagues and diseases of the times have been visited upon us" (*BMB* 21). Opened up and linked to the rest of the country through commercialization and development, Paradise Springs no longer enjoys the peace of a severed cultural backwater and must stomach, for better or for worse (mostly, it seems, for the worse), the complexities of the outside world. Economically rewarded by the transition but largely unaware of the new culture they are inviting and the old one they are destroying, developers like Weatherby function as unwitting harbingers of a bland, uniform future. In fact, Jojo Royale defines Weatherby and his ilk as

> The man of the hour. Sometimes I find myself thinking that he is the man of the future, too. It's true (isn't it?) that we are rapidly turning into a nation and a people without any real and serious principles. A people without any core. Led, at the moment, by a President [Bill Clinton] who suits us (we *deserve* him) perfectly. A man without a core or even a shadow. (*KB* 200, Garrett's emphasis)

Just as Dudley Hagood relates Paradise Springs' developmental shift to that of the rest of the country, so Jojo compares the local "man of the hour" to the national one, each possessing the lack of principle and identity necessary to make everything the same—a kind of empty homogeneity, constantly feed-

ing itself and growing, without any real purpose other than its own prom-
ulgation.

Seen in this unfortunate light, the process of change, instead of containing the prospect of widespread social and economic liberation, becomes
a local capitulation to prosaic national and global forces. Regional subjec-
tivities become consumed, assimilated into a larger agenda that disguises
a move toward uniform sameness beneath a blinding veneer of promising
visual alteration. Aware of this process, the perceptive Dale Lewis sees

> Everything changing all the time. New people, new faces, even new
> flora and fauna down in south Florida around Miami. New plants and
> animals (and probably viruses) from South America, Africa, India.
> If you look at Florida it's changing right before your eyes. Like time-
> lapse photography of corn growing. In that sense maybe it's just an
> exaggerated version of the whole country. The United States busily
> (and without regrets) reinventing itself every decade at the least. (*KB*
> 234)

Singling out Florida as the most obvious manifestation of a great national
shift, Lewis ominously portrays the transition as a blind and repetitive end
within itself—all of its promising variables of diversity incongruously functioning in a formula that works toward national homogeneity. In this observation Lewis also inadvertently connects *King of Babylon* to a particular
late-twentieth-century literary tradition. Like Gloria Naylor's *Mama Day*
(1988), Thomas Pynchon's *Vineland* (1990), Percival Everett's *Zulus* (1990),
and several other books from the 1980s and 1990s, *King of Babylon* is an
American novel with strong millennial connotations, uncertain about the
future of humanity. In these types of books the folly of mankind takes center
stage and, usually assisted by powerful technological and economic forces,
foreshadows a collective human fate that looms closer and more dangerously than we might have imagined.

Linking Florida's flashy new contemporary denizens to its earliest inhab-
itants, Lewis notes, "Florida is a pretty place, a postcard place, filling up, day
after day, with strangers. But then, that was always so. Even the Seminoles,
the oldest people among us, were strangers" (*KB* 236). Invoking history,
Lewis reminds us that no human group, neither the Americans, Spanish, nor
the Seminoles, has ever really owned Florida. Subordinating human beings
to the context of place, Lewis's foreboding comment paints contemporary
Americans, like the Seminoles, as just passing through the area for now.
Like the biblical Babylon, the American concept of Florida and even the
United States itself is not beyond dispersion and oblivion. Garrett originally

had intended *King of Babylon* to be the first part of a three-novel project, which he referred to as his "American Sequence," and the book's ability to encapsulate a regional identity, as well as a national and human one, across history demonstrates that its agenda stretches far beyond its local narrative action and milieu. The same might be said of Garrett's collective body of Florida narratives. Journeying back and forth among decades with regard to a single place, Garrett tells the story of a little corner of twentieth-century North America. Yet, in performing this task perceptively and thoroughly he contributes to the universal story of change unfolding before our eyes, everywhere, all the time. We have long known that the best regional works are those that transcend their geographical and temporal boundaries in speaking to human experience everywhere—a communion of the local and global made possible by the gifted artist. Ultimately abstracting experience beyond their provincial settings, Garrett's Florida narratives ambitiously attempt to participate in this tradition—striving to somehow tell us something more through their collective evocations of a single place.

Garrett's South

A Literary Image

Ever since the Civil War, the southern writers who had any kind of national ambitions or aspirations, or the writers who worked in special forms—the drama, for example—whose principle centers of commerce and appreciation are elsewhere, have been forced to live up to an alien image of what the southern writer is supposed to be and to say; and, behind that, the subject itself, the truth presented in approved and certified southern literature, must conform to an outsider's image.

—Garrett, *Southern Excursions*

Well-worn and much-maligned, the interdisciplinary concept known as globalization generally espouses the vision of a borderless world dominated by multinationals and markets, vanguards of a homogenized culture shaped by western values and a grand narrative of reason. However, beneath this imagined oneness reside a number of lingering, though perhaps doomed, systems and paradoxical elements. For example, the concept of nationalism continues to present itself as a complex socio-political phenomenon, constantly in formation, deformation, and reformation in response to various other catalysts of change. The dominant state form over the last five centuries or so, the nation-state emerged on a broad historical canvas out of dramatic processes of social change that incorporated empires, city-states, tribes, and feudal lords. Often taking the defensive in light of its tenuous mutability, the nation-state usually is portrayed by globalization proponents in terms of its narrowness, selfishness, and exclusiveness. Delving deeper, beyond nationalism, we spy the stubborn, familiar phenomenon of regionalism, nearer to each of us though sometimes more difficult to perceive. Often depicted by globalization thinkers as a smaller, meaner, more nostalgic form of nationalism, regionalism perpetuates a collective set of visions and values aimed at the establishment of a local system, formal or informal, within a specific geographical area. Yet, for all its backward provincialism, the regional context finds itself attracting increasing recognition from observers of international relations, international political economies, and development, as well as governments and other stakeholders in civil society and the private sector. Increasingly, economic and cultural leaders find themselves searching for regional solutions to the problems and challenges presented by national and global forces. Much energy, therefore, now is being devoted to studying how regional processes relate to globalization: how regional trade arrangements may be stumbling blocks or stepping-stones to ever-increasing free trade, and whether regional integration, economic as well as cultural, can be understood as a way of negotiating nationalism and globalization or creating a social buffer against their potentially disturbing effects.[1]

As strange as it might seem, these issues and revelations are not particularly new or unrecognized in the literature of the American South, a regional genre of writing long conversant with the pressures and complexities of national and, increasingly, international discourses and economies. After all, with the notable exceptions of university presses, small admirable publishing houses, and marvels such as Algonquin Books, it is to the large (inter)national presses and the still-dominant literary region of the Northeast that southern writers continue to turn, and often move into, in the hopes of garnering publication and reputation. This long-standing diasporic intellectual trend—lamented by writers as far apart in chronology and sensibility as William Gilmore Simms and Lee Smith—also manifests itself on the international level, as witnessed by Faulkner conferences in China and the odd phenomenon of Christine Chaufour-Verheyen's work of criticism *William Styron: Le 7e Jour* appearing in France as a mass-market paperback and outselling hosts of novels.

Although many writers have commented knowledgeably on the shifting place of southern literature in national and international literary contexts, the single figure who has invested the most time and ink examining the tension between southern writers and the national publishing scene over the past half-century is George Garrett—one of the region's few remaining distinguished men of letters. Editor, translator, dramatist/script writer, Virginia poet laureate, award-winning fiction writer, teacher and mentor, and wide-ranging reviewer and essayist, Garrett—by turns donning the armor of poetry, prose, or spoken rhetoric (his father was an admirably hard-nosed and uncompromising lawyer)—consistently wades headlong into the issues at hand, be they aesthetic, historical, social, economic, political, or otherwise. Over the years, the South and the publishing dilemma for southern writers have remained particular and constant points of interest—from his first two published essays in 1957, dealing respectively with the work of Faulkner and Garrett's Georgia relative Harry Stillwell Edwards, to his 2003 collection of essays and reviews pertaining to the South, *Southern Excursions*. In fact, Garrett's critical facility as a scholarly essayist and reviewer was noticed nearly as quickly as his gifts in fiction and poetry. Writing in 1963 the Faulkner scholar James Meriwether asserted, "No examination of Garrett's literary accomplishment is complete without mention of his critical writing, which has produced two of the best articles ever written on Faulkner" (29). The ensuing years have born out Meriwether's declaration, and there might have been more scholarly work. A notebook entry dated January 29, 1965, finds Garrett expressing an intention to write a critical study entitled "The Southern Past: A Literary Image"; two years later he told an interviewer that he hoped to "write a short critical book on certain aspects of recent southern fiction" ("Writer" 1). Yet, for all this scholarly enthusiasm, during this period Garrett's most celebrated literary achievement, the historical opus *Death of the Fox*, also beckoned, and one would be foolish to argue that his time would have been spent better on literary criticism. In fact, Garrett's fiction and criticism are not so far apart as one might suspect. Just as his historical Elizabethan novels interact with vast stores of scholarly knowledge in making unique philosophical statements about the nature of human history, so his fictional southern narratives subtly complement his critical essays on the southern literary genre—together delineating an idea, as well as a practice, of the regional form.

In order to articulate Garrett's conception of southern literature and its relation to the rest of the country and the world, one must first attempt to understand him both as a southerner and a writer. In a 2003 interview Garrett recounted the following anecdote:

> In the 1930s I used to visit my grandfather who lived in a place called Naples, North Carolina, which doesn't exist anymore I'm told. It was between Asheville and Hendersonville. All around there were developments that never got off the ground: street lamps and sidewalks without houses or buildings. That was the norm growing up: that you would see things that came to nothing. Very surreal. I didn't even know what a development was. I would get on my bike and go out

in the woods and suddenly come upon an area with driveways, sidewalks, beautiful street lamps, and sometimes an old abandoned hotel.
I thought, naturally as a child does, that's the way the world is: it's full
of abandoned places and buildings. Then everything changed radically
and I began to feel, as many others do, the need to preserve some
memory of that earlier version of place. (Int)

Struck by the haunting image of a world full of empty, abandoned places, the
young Garrett initially glimpsed writing as a means of immutable historical
preservation, an endeavor he would later identify as definitively southern.
More than thirty years before our conversation, he had written, "Change and
decay have always been primary subjects in southern literature. Because it
is characteristic of the southern writer (especially in prose fiction) that he
feels compelled to capture in words and describe things as they are before
they crumble and vanish forever" ("The South" 33). At the heart of this sensibility is both a critique and an embrace of the inevitability of change, the
future ever-abandoning an unrealized present. Though less polemical and
more detached, the approach vaguely echoes the earlier perspectives of the
Agrarians, and, in fact, Garrett specifically evoked the pastoral South in the
early 1960s, remarking, "You can hardly find a Southern writer who does not
love the land he writes of. . . . [It] sings lyrically in their work . . . even the
cities and suburbia and the new industry cannot efface the almost instinc-
tive affection for the land—for there is too much of it and it is too strong. It
triumphs over our best intentions" (Meriwether 31). Such an outlook, voiced
early in Garrett's career, attempts, perhaps a little stubbornly, to recognize
and confer with a prior southern tradition of land-based literature, even as
the inevitable, encroaching dark cloud of industrialization threatens to alter
it forever.

At their worst, such aesthetic philosophies of preservation flirt with a
kind of implacable, sentimental romanticism, denying the inevitable changes
at hand while wistfully memorializing a way of life and *Umwelt* now gone
with the wind. Yet, Garrett defends the objectivity of his approach: "I think
there's not so much a sense of nostalgia as there is something akin to the
urge to fill a photograph album before everything has changed" (Int). Although this attitude is noble, its practicality presents formidable difficulties
to the artist. Pictures—as professional photographers can attest—do not always accurately capture objects. The image-shaping eye of the photographer
and the person who views the picture conspire—not unlike the author and
the reader—to create an object and its meaning in a new way. Likewise,
exploring and portraying history—what Eliot called its "cunning passages"

and "contrived corridors"—is not so easy as it might seem, the historian and the reader bringing their respective interpretive agendas to so-called factual events. However, a masterful renderer of historical fiction like Garrett recognizes and welcomes this danger. Writing about the Civil War in his essay "Under Two Flags" (1992) he concludes, "In spite of growing and towering mountains, huge slag piles of factual history and many kinds and forms of poetry and fiction, and even the wonders of television, it is still very difficult to imagine the Civil War accurately and honestly" (*WD* 198). In fact, one might argue that the numerous layers of conflicting interpretation and representation only serve to cloud the immediacy of the event, with the latest scholarly contributions resembling—to extend Garrett's metaphor—a gratuitous sprinkling of pebbles on an already enormous mountain of rock.

Confronted with the equally perilous dangers of nostalgia and numerous, disparate historical theories, serious writers of historical fiction often are left to draw on their own histories and experiences as means of interpreting and portraying the human element of antiquated events—a technique traditionally suited to southern writers. In a 1958 review of Robert Penn Warren's *Promises* Garrett notes, "The South, his as well as ours, is haunted by its ghosts, benign or malevolent, but omnipresent. History, personal or public, is always here and now. . . . For the Southerner, rooted in his living history, time is an intricate network, an ever-spinning web" ("Review of *Promises*" 106–7). Living in their own times, yet irrevocably anchored to earlier ones, Garrett's and Warren's southerners roam, whether they wish to or not, "out of history into history and the awful responsibility of time" (*All the King's Men* 464). Whether dealing with the recent dynamics of racial and sexual conflicts or the more distant legacy of the war of 1861–1865, most southern writers still employ some measure of generational inheritance in their narratives. In Garrett's own early military vignette "How the Last War Ended," the final section of the story "Comic Strip" (1957), the protagonist Captain G. tells his unidentified captor, "I know what it's like to be defeated. . . . I am a Southerner" (*KM* 99), thereby invoking the bequeathed shadow of a lost cause described by C. Vann Woodward and many others. Yet, for all its complexity and psychological baggage, the lingering specter of the past is not without its artistic advantages. Perhaps most notably, it infects objects and places with useful characteristics and narratives. As Garrett explains, "Precisely because I *am* a southerner, I believe that places are enchanted. Rich with spirits. All houses, sooner or later, are haunted" (*SE* 105, Garrett's emphasis), the aesthetic implications of which were summarized best by William Robinson: "Garrett is a Southern writer and *the* subject of the Southern imagination is history" ("Imagining" 35, Robinson's emphasis).

Accompanying history, particularly southern history, is the common and sometimes unavoidable phenomenon of guilt, which in the South most often is associated with race and the legacy of slavery. In his notebooks for the novel *The King of Babylon Shall Not Come against You* (1996), Garrett admits, "[S]ince it deals with the South and some Southerners during the late 1960s and now, it likewise has to deal with various kinds of racism among other things." Demonstrating a much earlier interest in racial conflict, Garrett's notebooks from the 1950s include an untitled fictional account of a lynching in a small southern town. More than forty years later, a similar episode would appear in the title story of the collection *Bad Man Blues* (1998), reworked into a fable narrated by the African-American lawyer Willie Gary, a character from *King of Babylon*. However, just as Gary's lynching anecdote serves as a single episode in a much larger narrative, so Garrett's historical view of the South includes racial conflicts while weaving them into an enormous tapestry containing numerous other historical catalysts. Including race under the general moniker of southern history, reviewer Adam Mazmanian suggested that the protagonist of *King of Babylon*, Billy Tone, is concerned "not with the crimes he studies but with the South itself and with the accumulated psychic debt of history" (176). Mazmanian's linking of personal crimes to the great currents of history is all the more significant since it concurs with an earlier observation from Fred Chappell: "Garrett's vision of civilization as the relentless sacrifice of individual personality for the sake of order and continuance is deeply tragic" ("Fictional" 74). Built upon the tension between isolated historical phenomena like guilt and racism, and the impersonal, interweaving historical forces beyond any individual's control, Garrett's historical view of the South documents the local joys and agonies of citizens even as it simultaneously, and often a little reluctantly, abstracts them into the vacuous realm of human history—small footnotes in an enormous, multivolume, ongoing drama.

In admirably attempting to propel southern history and literature beyond reductive polemical and regional contexts and into a tragic human universality, southern writers like Garrett inevitably encounter a new set of difficulties. As William Robinson has summarized, "One of the problems about trying to write about southern politics or anything set in the South is that there are so many clichés and conventions that people expect or look for to identify, besides the fact that it takes place in a certain place and has a certain dialect and quality of language" ("George" 84). In addition to combating one's own temptations to memorialize or critique a given southern tradition, southern writers also must account for the sometimes debilitating expectations of their readers. With a hint of irony, Garrett observes,

"The southern novel has gradually become a genre, every bit as formulaic as science fiction, the thriller, the historical romance, or the old-fashioned western. . . . The southern novel advances through a minefield of habitual gestures and conventions, edging closer and closer to the pure and simple status of irrepressible cliché" ("It's True South," *SE* 167). Established to the point that both writers and readers entertain a common expectation of specific tropes and rules, most contemporary southern literature, to Garrett's thinking, runs the risk of forsaking immediacy and relevance for the mastery of a long-established, though now less culturally applicable, form.

If much contemporary southern literature conspires to constitute a collective cliché, how then may its more useful and unique narratives be identified? One solution is to read for language as much, if not more, than content. Garrett has noted that "The prose fiction of the South has an enormous range as compared to the prose fiction of other regions of the country. Even at his most literary, the Southern fiction writer doesn't go too long on a high tone. Even Miss Eudora loves to drop into the colloquial. They love variety of speech, from public rhetoric to the rhetoric of movies and the pop culture" (Israel 44). The scope of convincing voices, whether rendered by Faulkner and Erskine Caldwell or Alice Walker and Dorothy Allison, has long been a strength of southern literature, and this dynamic informs narrative relationships between southerners and nonsoutherners as much as it does purely regional ones. For example, in Garrett's short story "A Hard Row to Hoe" (1957) the narrator describes his friend Bill, a Princeton undergraduate from Georgia, as "a Southerner with a rich amusing accent and idiom that gave whatever he happened to be saying a strangeness which made people listen" (*KM* 103). Possessing an usual, compelling voice in a foreign setting, Bill captivates his Princeton acquaintances with the peculiar sound and method of his storytelling as much as for the stories themselves. And among southerners a writer's use or rejection of certain types of southern voices sometimes may lead to assumptions about his or her own personality or societal views. As Garrett humorously notes, "Some southern writers would rather die slowly and badly than admit to a touch of trash. They will go to great lengths to deny there's any such (of a) thing as a Cracker in their gene pool or a Redneck in the woodpile" ("Don't Try" xi). Of course, the voices in Garrett's own southern narratives are both inclusive and unpredictable with the working-class southerner often appearing as a prominent figure. In his unpublished 1950s poem "The South," a kind of experimental montage of southern voice and identity, Garrett writes, "The South is a pinch-faced, deep eyed sharecropper / Face to face with poverty and death for life." Later, Garrett articulated several different voices and points of view, nearly all of them lower- or working-class, in the novel *Do, Lord, Remember Me* (1965), the depth and richness of which have been summarized by R. H. W. Dillard:

> The South of *Do, Lord, Remember Me* is, like Chaucer's England, a confused landscape in which religion and sex, honesty and petty evil, the haunting dream of purity and the fallen world of lies are so subtly interwoven that no one can judge another or even himself or herself, and in which the most serious of religious pilgrimages is at once an occasion for true religious feeling and unrestrained bawdiness. (*UGG* 87–88)

Just as Chaucer jumped from disparate personality to personality amid the dramatic action of a religious journey, so Garrett leaps among his odd assortment of characters, deeply embracing each individual while using them collectively to perambulate toward central philosophical aspects of existence.

Though language and narrative technique function as the potentially liberating and self-defining implements of many southern writers, there remains much that makes them uneasy about their aesthetic decisions and the genre in which they are attempting to participate. Beyond specific literary conventions, many—perhaps too many—of southern literature's achievements and current expectations still are traced to the work of Faulkner. As Garrett notes, this is a fact to which writers readily must resign themselves: "It is impossible for any Southern writer aware of his place and people and aware of his own literary tradition *not* to be influenced by the towering energy and example of Faulkner. Those who pretend otherwise (and there are a number) are either trying to fool themselves or us or both at once" ("Foote's" 86, Garrett's emphasis). For Garrett, the southern writer who refuses to confront Faulkner is practicing an ill-advised conceit and playing a dangerous game. Yet, unlike many writers, Garrett does not view Faulkner as a potentially abusive literary father or menacing intellectual shadow. Instead, Faulkner's work stands as a kind of rich resource, a vein to be mined with great reward. He explains at length:

> Faulkner's work offers consolation and direction to the contemporary Southern writer. It offers a challenge as well: the writer is dared to divorce himself from easy habits of thought which are prevalent in the overall culture. Dared, by that towering example, to cultivate his art without regard to present systems of praise or blame and, indeed, without embarrassed or inhibiting reverence for the immediate

past, the past, which includes the achievement of William Faulkner, of Thomas Wolfe, of all of the Fugitives and other masters. By example, he demonstrates that the Southern past is not dead or disposable and cannot be ignored. It remains a resource to be wisely *used*. (*SFC* 213, Garrett's emphasis)

Secure in the ideas behind his own work and convinced of the value of southern literature's cumulative achievement, Garrett heartily recommends Faulkner as an exemplar of aesthetic integrity and for his unique ability to make relevant and alive his particular southern past.

Faulkner's mark on Garrett's work is glimpsed most readily in his numerous narratives involving the Florida Singletrees, who, appearing over the course of several stories and novels, call to mind Faulkner's recurring Mississippi families. Mike Royale, the protagonist of *The Finished Man* (1959), originally was a Singletree before Garrett decided to give the name to his mother's side of the family. Later, Garrett intended to use a character named Angus Singletree as the protagonist for the novel *Which Ones Are the Enemy?* (1961). Other Singletrees include Raymond ("Bread from Stones"), Courtney and TeeJay ("A Game of Catch"), and—despite his last name— Fergus McCree ("Man Without a Fig Leaf"). Revisiting the Singletrees and their fictional Florida community of Paradise Springs enabled Garrett to build a small imaginative world that grew with each new narrative while also establishing an interesting intertextual historical continuity across his writings. Garrett also embraced and used Faulkner, rather than ignoring him, by giving at least two of his southern protagonists some knowledge of Faulkner's work. For example, in *The Finished Man* Garrett has Mike Royale imitate Faulkner's narrative style in one section of the book for the purpose of demonstrating his familiarity with him. Yet, this playful reference only served to confuse and anger reviewers. As Garrett accurately summarizes, *The Finished Man* "was praised, for the wrong reasons, by one crowd of Southerners and damned and savaged by the Fugitive point men, also for the wrong reasons" ("George Garrett," *The Fugitives* 24). Baffled by Garrett's unusual references to Faulkner, some reviewers attacked him for unimaginative imitation, while others, equally wrong, lauded what they perceived to be straightforward thematic applications of southern literature's most popular and relevant writer. However, Garrett's use of Faulkner hardly is essential to his achievement and almost always appears more whimsical than vital. For example, in "A Hard Row to Hoe" Bill humorously critiques Faulkner in passing: "Why, that man's characters are much too civilized. Where I come from Erskine Caldwell characters are fine ladies and gentlemen" (*KM* 104).

Later, when the story turns serious, Bill tells an aristocratic southern friend, "You can't be yourselves and you won't allow anybody else to be either" (*KM* 108). Over the years, critics have attacked other writers, southern and non-southern, for perceived imitations of Faulkner—Cormac McCarthy, Ernest Gaines, Reynolds Price, to name but a few—to the point that one might apply Bill's advice to reviewers of southern fiction. Ingrained with Faulkner's legacy, which inevitably intersects with the experiences of other southern writers, and a formulaic set of expectations for southern literature, critics rarely afford writers the opportunity to wrestle or play with the master, choosing instead to guard assiduously his hallowed ground.

Citing his versatility and openness, Madison Smartt Bell has argued that Garrett actually "has influenced more writers than Faulkner" (Novel Panel), an assertion that is difficult to dismiss given Garrett's long years of teaching and his scores of successful students, including Bell, who now are published writers. To be sure, Garrett plunges into literary scenarios involving southerners that likely never entered Faulkner's mind. For example, in an untitled play from his notebooks, Garrett planned to have all his characters, including a Singletree, appear as ghosts in a graveyard. Slightly more grounded though still unconventional, Garrett's short story "Bread from Stones" (1964) follows Raymond Singletree, a well-bred, habitually impoverished southerner who infrequently strikes it rich by serving as a companion for mature wealthy women. Although a story concerning a male escort from the South certainly is not traditional, near the beginning it contains a line that might have come from one of Faulkner's characters: "[I]t is all right to be southern and poor if your ancestors were southern and rich" (*CG* 81). Drawing on the vagaries of southern wealth, class, and identity, the story's opening passages call to mind Faulkner characters such as Quentin Compson. Like Quentin, Raymond, the "black sheep" of his family, desperately and futilely attempts to escape his southern history. However, the disparate and equally unpromising avenues of liberation he follows separate the story from Faulkner's work. For example, at one point he invites self-parody, hosting a mock square dance for his love interest's wealthy, northeast Jewish acquaintances. Part of Raymond's problem is that he is drunk on appearances, a remnant of his aristocratic upbringing. Lacking wealth, he nonetheless desires the appearance of it and seems to believe that by denigrating his southern heritage he may somehow escape his past and embrace a new image. Yet, as his wealthy female benefactor confides to Raymond's visiting brother, what he really desires is some little sign of approval from that crummy Tobacco Road family of his" (*CG* 96). For all his posturing, Raymond cannot desert the importance of his southern values even though they are mocked and disowned both by his friends and himself.

The wealthy northeasterners in "Bread from Stones," half-serious observers of Raymond's mocked southern background, continue to appear in the literary world today as national readers and publishers who expect to encounter a specific constructed image of the South that is consistent with their preconceived cultural notions of a region they know little about. As Garrett explains, not without some bitterness:

> the history, nature, and character of the South (thus of all southern traditions, including the literary) have been so distorted and clouded by an accumulation of misinformation as to require major rehabilitation before we can think or talk sensibly about the subject. For more than a century since the South was defeated in our most savage and destructive war and subsequently treated (that is, mistreated) worse than any enemy the United States has ever battled, for more than a century the victors have written the history of the South, and the revisionists have also continuously modified that history. (*SE* 46)

Entertaining sometimes drastically different images of the region, (inter)national observers and southerners periodically still find it difficult to locate common points of cultural and historical agreement by which to communicate and move forward. For nation-state Americans the South usually is critiqued in a way that most contemporary southerners find offensive and/or outdated. Too often southerners still find themselves attempting to explain or apologize for cultural and historical issues that reach back to the Civil War and beyond—a phenomenon that has been noted and criticized by Garrett: "I, too, must bear my burden of contemporary guilt like a student's obligatory backpack. But I flatly refuse to add to it one ounce, one feather's weight, of *historical* guilt for anything. I am not guilty of or for the actions of anyone but myself" (*WD* 38, Garrett's emphasis). Some of Garrett's characters are less certain; in *The Finished Man* the theme is played out between Mike Royale and his wife: "she was from New England and different enough to find his ways and assumptions a little strange. And in the mirror of her eyes he had felt compelled to justify not only himself, but also his whole region, its past, its faults and follies as well as its virtues. . . . Like many a Southerner he loved and hated his history just as he loved and hated himself" (*FM* 178). Confronted with his wife's New England background, Mike, a lawyer by profession, feels as if his own culture constantly is on trial. Yet, the ambivalent nature of his region makes it impossible to defend in rational terms; he is both proud and ashamed to be a southerner and the duality is never successfully resolved—it is hardly surprising that their relationship ends in divorce.

Significant in Mike's dialogue with his wife is the fact that his culture, never his wife's, is the one on trial. A northeasterner by birth, Mike's wife functions as an agent of the dominant, culture-enforcing region of the nation-state. Spilling over into the literary world, an almost identical relationship exists between most southern writers and the people who publish their books. As Garrett recounts:

> Ever since the Civil War, the southern writers who had any kind of national ambitions or aspirations, or the writers who worked in special forms—the drama, for example—whose principle centers of commerce and appreciation are elsewhere, have been forced to live up to an alien image of what the southern writer is supposed to be and to say; and, behind that, the subject itself, the truth presented in approved and certified southern literature, must conform to an outsider's image. (*SE* 4)

Once again, Garrett's critical observation also finds expression in his fiction. In "Man Without a Fig Leaf" (1964) Fergus McCree, originally bearing the name Angus Singletree, is described by his Jewish New York friend, Sam, as a "crazy southerner with a taste for elegance and no money to support it" (*CG* 52), and, in an earlier unpublished dramatic version, as "a malcontent, gifted, ambiguously mad." Throughout the story, Fergus repeatedly takes it upon himself to speak for his region while lamenting the debilitating ways in which it has kept him from succeeding as a writer in the culture of New York. Well-meaning and sympathetic, Sam, in the unpublished version, playfully tells Fergus that he looks like "the walking, decaying corpse of the Deep South. You're all covered with ringworm and hookworm. You're pellagra-ridden, illiterate and thoroughly corncobbed. If I looked like you I'd join the Ku Klux Klan just to have a chance to hide my face behind a sheet." Although Sam is joking with his friend, there is more truth in his jest than he suspects, and Fergus does not laugh. Though he would have Sam think otherwise, Fergus genuinely is troubled and hindered by the negative aspects of his region and their unavoidable connection to his tenuous identity and dysfunctional life.

Whereas Sam means well and wishes to help Fergus, his aid repeatedly takes the form of condescension, a relationship that symbolically translates into the literary world. As Garrett notes, "They (the Other, Yankees and such, as they say) do still take us Southerners, the men and the women alike, to be at best a kind of literary junior varsity" ("Literary Ladies" 163). Concerned with the vast (inter)national literary stage, the American literary establishment allows southern writers their own provincial bush league. Of course, the irony in this relationship is that southern writers consistently transcend the limitations of regional categorization by writing memorable novels that take place in national, international, and historical milieus. In an address to the Richmond, Virginia, Women's Club Garrett noted two contemporary regional novels of New York City and Washington, D.C., written by southerners: Tom Wolfe's *The Bonfire of the Vanities* (1987) and Garrett Epps's *The Floating Island* (1985). Ignoring authors' southern roots when it is convenient, the national establishment never hesitates to claim and assimilate those talented writers whose work does not espouse a strong regional interest. Thus, Tom Wolfe, who lives in New York and whose work is national in flavor, generally is not referred to as a southern writer, but Cormac McCarthy, with his collection of undeniably southern and southwestern material, is. Categorized and shaped by the ambivalent rules of a national literary establishment that is itself anchored to a very small region and cast of players, southern writers—even the best-selling, award-winning ones—discover, sometimes painfully, that their reputations and identities ultimately are out of their hands.

Not content to weather silently the ongoing colonization of southern literature, Garrett continually has referenced the problem in essays and readings, while also stubbornly refusing to conform his creative work to the rules and expectations of the national publishing scene. In this practice he is not alone. Citing writers such as R. H. W. Dillard, Lewis Nordan, Barry Hannah, and Jim Grimsley, Garrett notes, "All these people have worked away from and played with the expectations of audiences and publishers of what a good Southern novel is supposed to be" (Int). Infusing the genre of southern writing with nontraditional subject matter and parody—from violent, sex-crazed Confederate officers to unprecedented, courageous homosexuals—such writers strive to reinvent the form for various new aesthetic and philosophical purposes. One of the single most ingenuous examples of playing upon traditional southern tropes appears in R. H. W. Dillard's title piece from a short story collection coedited by Garrett, *That's What I Like (About the South)*, in which each section is preceded by a phrase—"family bonds," "local tradition," etc.—from the collection's introductory essay on what constitutes southern fiction. Consciously building a fictional narrative around the traditional formulaic variables of southern literature, Dillard skillfully appraises the genre while toying with the expectations of readers and conventional publishers.

In view of Dillard's short story, it is significant to note that *That's What I Like (About the South)* is the publication of a southern university press rather than a northeast/(inter)national/commercial one. Although its contents convey something new and innovative with regard to the established regional genre, the book's publisher, residing and predominantly marketing within the same region, ensured that its revelations probably would not reach the national readers who likely would benefit from them the most. As things stand then, the most groundbreaking southern writing is likely to remain well below the radar of the (inter)national literary establishment—a significant regional subjectivity generally unrecognized by the cultural commissars of the greater nation-state. However, as Garrett's criticism and fiction keep telling and showing us, this is nothing new and, for all its inauspiciousness, not something that should cause aspiring southern writers to despair. In the summer of 2003 Garrett observed, "Right now the commercial world is not real interested in southern points of view but that's not very meaningful. We have such a strong tradition, I suspect it'll just go on" (Int). Continuing to evolve and articulate itself in spite of national forces that threaten to misinterpret or, worse, ignore it, southern writing carries on much as it has, fueled by the small, dedicated regional presses and periodicals that provide its largely regional readership. Having done more than his share over the past half-century to document and critique the South's ambivalent literary image in this national context, Garrett makes his own forecast of southern literary endurance all the more possible and likely.

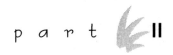

Styles of Dress

Variations on Fictional Modes

"Maggots in the Basement"

Garrett's Grotesque House of Fiction

George Garrett's house of fiction has as many dark rooms as sunny ones,
and there are maggots in the basement.

—William Peden, "The Short Fiction of George Garrett"

In an unpublished lecture fragment from the 1960s George Garrett remarked that the grotesque "holds up a mirror to nature, but it is a mirror taken from the Glass House or the Crazy House." Implicit in Garrett's comment is the idea that the grotesque possesses the capacity for expressing meaningful and unconventional aesthetic truths through the art of reflective distortion. Yet, it also may leave one asking the questions: What nature? Which mirror? It goes without saying that natural systems, those both with and without humans, are highly diverse, as are various fun house mirrors: Is the mirror of choice the one that makes objects enormously tall, short, wide, thin, or otherwise? Garrett's writings promptly answer the question of nature; for the most part, his grotesque narratives take place in the environment and culture of the American South. However, the makeup of his aesthetic mirror is less readily apparent and much more complex. Sharing commonalities with the grotesque looking-glasses of other southern writers such as Flannery O'Connor and Truman Capote, Garrett's particular mirror nevertheless remains uniquely and notably his own.

Cultural observers have often unsympathetically contextualized the South as the crazy house of American society. At the conclusion of *The Phenomenon of the Grotesque in Modern Southern Fiction* (1983) Maria Haar meditates at great length on the underlying reasons that inform the region's strong associations with aberrance:

> As to the question of why the mode of the grotesque is so common in Southern fiction, the answer seems to lie in the distinctiveness of the South. This distinctiveness has, in brief, been brought about by historical factors (e.g., the defeat of the Confederacy in the Civil War); geographical considerations (e.g., the climate that made the plantation system possible which, in turn, gave rise to the racial problem between blacks and whites); sociological factors (e.g., the homogeneity of the white citizens, which has aggravated the racial conflict and increased violence in general); and economic circumstances (e.g. the comparative poverty and isolation of the rural South, which has led to a low level of education, inbreeding and abnormality). . . . The South, then, has become a good breeding ground for the grotesque; the Southerner's love of a good tale and his innate ability to tell one have presumably achieved the rest. (204–5)

Inclusively cataloguing the southern grotesque in terms of its many peculiar cultural factors, Haar remains focused on the sources for the genre's narrative content while limiting her discussion of its formal qualities to a very general comment on the southern love of storytelling. Although Haar's study is by far the most exhaustive published account of the southern grotesque, it shares interpretive space with a number of like-minded, culture-based considerations. Throughout the 1960s and 1970s commentators on the southern grotesque portrayed and analyzed the genre mostly in terms of its odd, violent personalities and milieus. For example, observers such as Alan Spiegel eschewed its formal implications in favor of its memorably bizarre characterizations. Others, like William Van O'Connor, interpreted it as a brand of shock-value social commentary. In the late twentieth- and early twenty-first centuries, scholars such as Patricia Yaeger and Sarah Gleeson-White began applying the interpretive models of Mikhail Bakhtin in emphasizing the potentially liberating implications of the grotesque for southern female writers and their characters.[1]

Since Garrett's use of the grotesque has been only sparingly noted and discussed by scholars, it is difficult to place his work specifically in the context of contemporary scholarship on the genre. Yet, even very early in his career, his use of the form was apparent to editors and various fellow writers. In fact, in the late 1950s Garrett had trouble publishing several of his stories because editors kept accusing him of sounding too much like Flannery O'Connor. Unaware of O'Connor's work at the time, Garrett humorously recalls, "I just thought it was some guy from Ireland. It bugged me because I hardly could have been influenced by somebody I never heard of and thought was an Irishman" ("Interview," *GSE* 134). However, making for a memorable literary anecdote, O'Connor would endure the association on her end as well when Katherine Anne Porter, an early admirer of Garrett's work, informed her that she wrote "a lot like George Garrett" ("Interview," *GSE* 134). O'Connor and Garrett also are brought together in terms of the ambivalence and occasional hostility with which some of their fiction was greeted by more established members of the southern literary community. For instance, Garrett recounts that with his 1958 *Sewanee Review* Fellowship in Poetry "came a message from Andrew Lytle that the award was *not* by any means to be misconstrued by me as offering any approval whatsoever for my prose fiction which was, in those days, sassy and irreverent and indifferent to (though not at all ignorant of) certain standard rules and regulations of acceptable Fugitive fiction" ("George Garrett," *The Fugitives* 23–24, Garrett's emphasis). Though generally admired for his poetry, Garrett had greater trouble gaining acceptance and encouragement, at least among the southern literary establishment, for his fiction. Employing unprecedented tropes and techniques, many of which appeared "sassy" and "irreverent" to more traditional southern sensibilities, Garrett's early fiction alienated him to a significant degree from many older writers, as well as his more tame contemporaries. Like other postmodernist southern writers who have employed the grotesque with great profit—for example, Calder Willingham and, later, Harry Crews—Garrett was made to endure an indeterminate period of neglect for his unique and generally unpopular aesthetic choices.

Although much of Garrett's early fiction was construed as different or radical, his specific conception of the grotesque does not deviate significantly from familiar constructions of the term. For example, during an interview in 1963, Garrett evoked the well-traveled correlation between the importance of southern family and the grotesque: "If we live in families extending through threads of cousins and uncles and aunts, then we must come to terms with *characters* and eccentricity. A big family has a place for this, just as, curiously, our small towns do, a place for the winners and the losers, the proud and the misbegotten" (quoted in Meriwether 31, emphasis in original). Suggesting the close bonds between grotesque figures and their families and small local communities, Garrett's point calls to mind such disturbingly significant familial relationships as those that exist between Benjy Compson and his dysfunctional siblings, or the wise blood Enoch Emery inherits from his daddy. Yet, significantly, even as we wonder at Enoch's relationship to his father and what "wise blood" really means, we cannot help but snicker a little at the absurdity of the situation—just as O'Connor sometimes laughed aloud while reading from her manuscripts at the Iowa Writers' Workshop. In his review of Robert Penn Warren's *Promises*, Garrett admiringly observes how Warren draws "from his region something of the native wit and humor, both dominant characteristics of significant Southern literature" ("Review of *Promises*" 106). Although Garrett is not discussing Warren's poetry in terms of the grotesque, his observation is notable for its focus on the pervasive importance of jest in southern writing. Elsewhere, Garrett is more specific, noting that southern humor often is "the humor of the grotesque" (Meriwether 31), its gentle rhythms and ribald storytelling giving way to the leer of a grinning skull. In this manner, grotesque humor, a dark form of laughter to be sure, becomes the *modus operandi* for reconciling narratives to events and characters otherwise too terrible to confront or handle.

Often accompanying the element of humor in the grotesque is a pronounced degree of perversity. In Poe's "The Imp of the Perverse" the narrator contends that scientists fail to account for the fact that human beings often do things for no better reason than to hurt themselves and/or others. Driven by destructive, irrational forces, human actions frequently and inexplicably shirk the yoke of reason—a dynamic that reveals itself repeatedly in Garrett's fiction. As Fred Chappell notes, "Most of George Garrett's short stories, even the funniest ones, deal with uncomfortable or downright perilous situations which occur most often because the characters have willed—or sometimes merely allowed, which more or less amounts to the same thing—these situations to come about" ("The Lion Tamer" 42). Often built on a foreshadowing narrative of individual perversity, the "perilous" aspects of Garrett's stories usually appear in terms of visceral implications or actions—hard-hitting, literal events that develop slowly and convincingly out of perverse subtleties and extensive psychological wavering. As Chappell observes in the same notable essay, "The Lion Tamer: George Garrett's Short Stories," "There is one kind of achievement which I think ought to be pointed out as belonging preeminently to George Garrett. The treatment of physical action" ("The Lion Tamer" 45). Rather than flirting with subtle, diaphanous portrayals of activity, Garrett's, and in fact most, grotesque narratives utilize the carnal functions and excesses of the body, sometimes in comic terms. In this way, the grotesque impacts and disrupts the themes of normality and constraint, sending bodies and narratives spiraling out of control, fraught with extremes and uncertainty.

In his review of Warren's *Brother to Dragons*, Garrett asserts, "The Pasiphae myth as a part of the ecstatic Cretan religion serves as a symbolic background for Lilburn's specific crime, and it is the disregard of this fact, the terrible potential of mankind for irrational ecstacy, good or evil, which Warren sees as the fatal defect in Jefferson's vision" (313). Summoning the Greek fable as a means of contextualizing Warren's poetic play in terms of "irrational ecstacy," Garrett couples the archetypal tale of the woman who gave birth to the monstrous Minotaur with the human propensity to mindlessly act upon groundless compulsions. The result of this unlikely combination is a vision at once horrible, fabulous, absurd, and compelling. Correspondingly, Garrett has described Federico Fellini as his favorite director while characterizing his work as "preposterous" and "corny" (Robinson, "George" 183). Capturing images that are memorable for their unconventional weirdness, as well as their ability to disturb and captivate, Fellini combined an unorthodox technical approach to filmmaking with content that was inherently capricious. As William Robinson has noted, a similar interaction between technique and subject matter occurs in many of Garrett's narratives:

> Garrett's fiction clearly is not an elegy for a dying society or for time-weary man but a vigorous voice of the New South in the making. Energy sweeps through its intense or grotesque characters who are or become involved in the rough give and take demanded by assertive living and its direct, lucid, masculine style, especially effective in the Southern vernacular dialect, a vehicle for the raw power of life. The energy is present also in the rush of action and fury of emotion, impelled by passion and culminating in violence, which characterize his narrative technique, and in experiments with point of view, tense, character types, and plots—resulting from Garrett's persistent quest to tell the true story about change. (15–16)

Unknowingly countering Andrew Lytle's notion of the nontraditional and "irreverent" unsuitability of Garrett's fiction, Robinson emphasizes the visceral, dynamic nature of Garrett's form and content, which conspire to abandon a "dying" southern society while attempting to articulate the cultural and formal nature of the present and future.

Beyond its accurate portrayal of the general active immediacy in Garrett's writing, Robinson's observation is important for its description of the appropriate similarity between Garrett's vigorous, destabilizing narrative content and equally energetic and disruptive formal techniques. Outside of his own work, this is something Garrett admires in other successful writers. In a taped 1988 lecture he remarked that post-World War II writers such as Joseph Heller, Kurt Vonnegut, John Hawkes, and Thomas Pynchon deal "mainly with the grotesque, with the distortion of the real into forms of fable and fantasy" (*American Literature of World War II*). Manipulating content, "the real," in addition to the various formal techniques by which it is expressed, such writers demonstrate the practice of the grotesque as a technical, as well as cultural, endeavor. At the conclusion of his memorable study of southern fiction, *Death by Melancholy*, Walter Sullivan warns that disorder "is everywhere, and we must encompass this fact in our work without either disordering the work itself or suffering an accompanying disorder of our own spirits" (129–30). Flirting with technical and cultural bedlam—walking a kind of tightrope between innovation and chaos—Garrett's practice of the grotesque heeds Sullivan's warning only just barely. Pressing the boundaries of order, Garrett repeatedly strives, occasionally to the point of unraveling the narrative, to say something original in an unprecedented way.

Garrett's grotesque narratives generally fall along two distinct lines: those that explore individual perversity, usually by way of irony, and those that use elements of the grotesque in order to critique various aspects of society. Clearly, the greater ambition rests with the latter type of story, and it is significant to note that Garrett appeared to move exclusively into that specific form after dabbling and experimenting for a time in the former, individual-based approach. All of the stories that have as their primary focus a perverse individual appeared between the late 1950s and mid-1960s, whereas the society-based narratives began around the same time but kept Garrett's attention much longer, stretching from the late fifties to the end of the twentieth century. Experimenting with both approaches at the beginning of his career, Garrett discovered over a span of a few years the richer possibilities of his civilization critiques, not least of which was an opportunity to evaluate the marked cultural changes of the 1960s and the mushrooming power of the American media.

Although they are wanting in societal commentary, Garrett's grotesque narratives that center around individual and interpersonal dynamics are important for their convincing and sometimes memorable representations of unusual characters and events, as well as for their eccentric and subtly humorous use of irony. For example, in "The Victim" (1959) an escaped North Carolina convict takes a man hostage only to be killed by his captive after becoming careless. In the first section of the story, the reader sympathizes with the nameless hostage, whose gun has been taken and who is forced to flee through the woods with his anonymous captor. However, once the "innocent" hostage steals his gun back, we discover, in a heavily ironic sequence, that he actually is far more evil and dangerous than his kidnapper. Espousing the philosophy that "[i]f you hate yourself, you got the right to hate everybody else in the world" (*BP* 57), the liberated hostage tells his former captor he may go free, only to shoot him in the back as he walks away. Imagine the proselytizing grandmother in O'Connor's "A Good Man Is Hard to Find" wresting away the Misfit's gun and shooting him with it. Struck by the grotesque reversal in the story's circumstances and expectations, one looks on in horror as the violent action unfolds, yet suppresses a chuckle at the tale's conclusion, Garrett's ironic treatment of victimization having set the story's title and readers' assumptions on their heads.

A similar measure of violent, perverse humor informs "A Game of Catch" (1960), in which two brothers, Courtney and TeeJay, and a female friend, Naomi, drive to a nearby beach for what they hope will be an afternoon of relaxation and fun. However, the oddness of the brothers and the tale's perverse capacities are revealed just three pages in when the two young men get into an argument over the particulars surrounding a man who had gathered his family together for a photograph only to execute them with a shotgun. As if that were not enough, Garrett further foreshadows the story's aberrant agenda when he reveals that Courtney is "just out of the State Asylum" (*BP* 128), his commitment having been a result of his wife's shameless elopement with a glamorous fishing tackle salesman named Billy Towne. With the two male characters possessing such idiosyncratic backgrounds and interests, one is not completely surprised later when the men stubbornly continue playing their game of catch on the beach as an ugly storm begins blowing in off the Atlantic. Understandably desperate to depart, Naomi is told that she must strip and dance before they will think about leaving. As the story nears its conclusion, we are treated to the bizarre image of two men furiously hurling a softball back and forth without gloves while a frightened, naked woman dances and a terrible storm draws near the shore. Once again, as in "The Victim," the narrative action suggests violence and perverse brutality even as its visual ridiculousness verges on absurd comedy.

In at least two of Garrett's stories perversity and humor manifest themselves in the form of singularly greedy, manipulative protagonists. In "Time of Bitter Children" (1961) a strange, disfigured, hitchhiking con-man with the made-up name of Bill Thibault exploits well-meaning drivers out of their money and cigarettes. Described as "almost a kind of dwarf, old and dirty" (*BP* 73), and possessing a "sharp rodent's face" (*BP* 69), Thibault projects a grotesque appearance, which is matched in his behavior by a creepy, persistent ability to provoke handouts from the people who give him rides. Like the hostage in "The Victim," Thibault initially cuts a wronged and abused figure, only to discard his shroud of victimization and eventually hustle his highway benefactors. The last line of the story records "the expression of simple childish pleasure and victory on the old man's face" (*BP* 80), and his drivers not being especially sympathetic or inconvenienced, one nearly is tempted to smile with him. It is also difficult not to smile at the actions of Raymond Singletree for similar reasons at the conclusion of "Bread from Stones" (1964). Functioning in a more up-scale social environment than Thibault, Singletree nonetheless is a con-man, acting the part of foppish companion to lonely women of means. Possessing expensive tastes but lacking the resolve to attain them through conventional labor, Singletree uses wealthy women in order to experience fleeting brushes with the good life: "He had even been slightly rich once or twice" (*CG* 84). Viewing people purely as financial means, Thibault and Singletree function as symbols of an avaricious, perverse humanity—a theme that would reach its apotheosis in Garrett's unpublished screenplay "The Binge," which critiques the dehumanizing nature of American materialism via credit cards.

Just as women appear as coveted, idealized means to wealth in "Bread from Stones," so a similar dynamic of desire exists, minus the materialistic element, in "And So Love Came to Alfred Zeer" (1962)—the strange story of a man's obsession with the shadow of a woman that appears nightly in the window of an apartment across from his own. Succumbing to "powerful and inscrutable forces" (*WG* 101), Zeer watches the shadow regularly and begins making assumptions about the woman's habits and personality, which ultimately generate grotesque implications for himself. Setting fire to his apartment and standing on a windowsill in a sad, extreme bid to attract the shadow woman's attention, Zeer loses his balance and plummets to his death. The identity or reality of the shadow remaining veiled to the reader, one is left uncertain whether or not the image was actually the ghostly form of a woman or some manifestation of Jung's feminine shadow visited upon a lonely, middle-aged bachelor. Just as Zeer is preoccupied by a compellingly unusual image, so the reader is left wondering at the story's absurdly tragic and comic implications, haunted by the bizarre vision of Zeer's final attempt to make contact with his idealized ghost.

Garrett's female characters make more definitively visceral appearances in several grotesque narratives that investigate the dynamics of marital dilemmas. For example, the two stories that fall under the heading "The Insects Are Winning (Two Versions of the Same Tale)" in *An Evening Performance* focus on a pair of couples who seek to escape the worn, mundane qualities of their marriages and their persistent, perverse yearnings for empty ephemera such as money and sex. Possessing the same conclusion, the stories use similar themes veiled in different events as means of arriving there. The first story, "The Moth," begins with Harry and Grace appearing late at a matador movie, the dynamic action and visual appeal of which contrast with their bland, obese features and uneventful lives. Also functioning as a counterweight to Harry and Grace's drab marriage is the figure of Grace's friend, Flora, who is "tough, cynical, good looking, rootless, and ageless" (*EP* 407). In an early unpublished dramatic version of the tale, Grace, impressed by Flora's lifestyle and depressed by Harry's behavior, laments, "What happened to all the *men* in the world?" A similar degree of spousal frustration appears in the alternative version of the same story, "At Least They'll Have Candlelight," in which Lucille muses upon the silly bedtime image of her husband, Sam: "In silk pajamas, his uniform of love, he looks like some kind of clown" (*EP* 414). Instead of functioning as masculine beings with initiative and passion, Harry and Sam both are cast as borderline grotesques. Their vigor and virility diminished by stagnant jobs and unrewarding lives, the husbands appear physically soft, tame, and world-weary. However, at the conclusions of both stories, when the men kill moths that have frightened their wives, they regain a measure of primitive masculine aptitude in the eyes of their women. Of course, the culminating actions are also highly ironic in the sense that they constitute small, temporary victories by limited, largely uninteresting people. Although the reader vaguely hopes their relationships may improve, it is difficult not to chuckle at the overall pathos and triviality of their concerns.

Whereas the people and literal events in these marital stories may appear to be of little consequence, the overall intentions behind them are not. David Slavitt observed that because of the two versions of "The Insects Are Winning," "the focus of our attention is redirected away from the actual tales to some other plane of engagement" (59). In essence, the exercise in reading becomes one of both comparison and thinking beyond the actions at hand, meshing similar and dissonant themes across the linked stories as a means of weighing the tales' deeper philosophical implications. Considered together, Garrett's marital narratives do in fact reveal something akin to Slavitt's "other plane of engagement," serving as the site of Garrett's transition from the insular perverse concerns of memorably unique characters to a larger societal agenda. Writing in his notebooks in the 1960s, Garrett remarked, "I sometimes think the image for our times is divorce," the prospect of which subtly informs all of his stories about married couples. For example, in "At Least They'll Have Candlelight" Lucille muses, "When a marriage breaks up, they always blame the woman anyway" (*EP* 415). Similar thoughts and anxieties inform a host of unpublished marriage stories in which Garrett attempted to trace and evoke the problems, cultural and personal, of married life: "Don't You Remember That Time in Florida" takes as its subjects a perverse, cheating wife and her naive, alienated husband; "Entered from the

Sun" contemplates a divorcé's severed relationship with his son; and "The Many Marriages of William Rich" humorously delivers on the promise of its title. Focusing on various aspects of nuptial friction, Garrett repeatedly attempted to interrogate the innumerable causes and dynamics of divorce as an avenue of engaging society through his art.

Beyond using marriage narratives to address divorce as a defining phenomenon of contemporary culture, Garrett also employed them for the purpose of demonstrating the grotesque bigotry of small communities. In "My Pretty Birdie, Pretty Birdie in My Cage" (1964) Henry Monk and his beautiful wife Ilse become the brunt of their provincial community's perversity and self-hate. Garrett's long, wonderfully vivid description of Henry associates him with

> a grotesque dwarf, thick-torsoed, powerful-shouldered as big men twice his size with long loose arms dangling down ending in huge, hopelessly awkward hands. . . . He had a dented cannonball of a head with short curly hair clinging to it like some kind of fungus, squint eyes, red-rimmed and muddy, forever blinking. . . . His lips were pouting, nearly colourless and formed in bold exaggerated curves like the trick ones made out of wax that people put on for a joke, and his nose was peaked and warped and broken. Legs? They were incredibly short and thin and frail. (*WG* 76)

Henry's abnormal physical qualities are countered or balanced by the limited intellect of Ilse, whose beauty conceals "the mind of a small child" (*WG* 82), "as inwardly deformed as he is outwardly" (*WG* 83). Condemning this varied modern retelling of the beauty-beast fable are the outraged townspeople, who hate the fact that Ilse is beautiful and believe that Henry instead should have married an appropriately disfigured counterpart who would produce for him "a whole family of clowns" (*WG* 78). The "clownish" quality of Henry's prospective family is preceded by the narrator's remark, "When you looked at Henry Monk you had to laugh" (*WG* 76). Though physically repulsive, Henry inspires neither fear nor disgust in the townspeople, but comedy, which further aligns him with the spirit of the grotesque. Yet, for all their difference, Henry and Ilse are not inherently perverse, but rather are constructed as such by their neighbors, whom together constitute a kind of collective grotesque. At one point a townsman sneaks over to listen at Henry and Ilse's window and then shares what he hears with everyone else. Furthermore, the narrator remarks that if Henry were gone, there "would be plenty of others to take his place—the strange, the weak, the drunk, the over- and under-sexed, the feebleminded, the diseased, dwarfed, deformed, and dispossessed—to be offered up in propitiation, in true and perfect sacrifice, that the safe, the sane, the whole might preserve at least some fragile notion of their self-esteem and human dignity" (*WG* 77). Convenient and replaceable victims in an ongoing archetypal ritual of demonization, Henry and Ilse allow their fellow citizens to feel good about their own bland normality and the homogenous rules by which they live, which channel all of the community's evil and perversity onto the Monks.

Similar elements of communal outrage and perversity appear across several of Garrett's other stories. In the unpublished tale "Strangers to the Town" a young man becomes a boarder at the home of a widow, only to discover "the terror of village talk." In another unpublished story, "Susanna of the Suburbs," the citizens of a wealthy neighborhood verbally condemn a young nocturnal female skinny-dipper, even though most of the men repeatedly show up to watch her swim. As the narrator recounts, the community consists of "elders of the town. This was a highclass, respectable neighborhood . . . all dominated by the vexing boredom of old age." The perverse voyeuristic yearning of these stodgy venerable men takes on slightly different forms in "The Rare Unicorn" (1957) and "An Evening Performance" (1959), the former story capturing the temporary madness of a blood-thirsty crowd at a boxing match, and the latter tale describing a small town's perverse reaction to a dangerous carnival routine.

The circus-like setting of "An Evening Performance" is also significant in that it embodies Mikhail Bakhtin's assertion that carnivals traditionally function as distinctive phenomena in which appearances and social norms often are bent and disfigured to the point of becoming grotesque (32). Even before the act arrives in town, "grumbling adults" rip down the strange, suggestive advertisement posters, which the narrator describes as "lurid and unsettling as a blast of trumpets" (*BP* 164). Portraying a scantily clad woman diving from a high platform into a flaming tub, the posters shock and titillate the townspeople, forcing them to confront a strange, fantastic event utterly divorced from their own drowsy existence. Yet, as the act's manager explains, the feat is not predicated on difference or deception, but rather on the human ability to achieve amazing things:

When Stella climbs that tower and dives into the flames she's doing something anyone could do who has the heart and the skill and the nerve for it. That's what's different and special about our show. When Stella sails through the air and falls in the fire and comes up safe and

smiling, she is the living and breathing proof of the boundless possibility of all mankind. It should make you happy. It should make you glad
to be alive. (*BP* 171)

Consistent with the violent herd-mentalities of communities from Garrett's
other stories, the townspeople ignore the manager's remarks, eager to witness the dive or, more likely, the prospect of someone's death. However, after
Stella successfully performs the act, the event plants itself firmly in the town's
consciousness with preachers denouncing it as sinful, local barflies adding
exciting details, and children clamoring for an encore. As in "My Pretty
Birdie, Pretty Birdie in My Cage," the community chorus is both outraged
and fascinated by those who practice or present an image of something different. Conceptualizing their local "others" as grotesques, the townspeople
succeed only in limiting and dehumanizing themselves.

The coupling of otherness and the grotesque reveals itself in at least two
other Garrett narratives through unlikely applications of fantasy and trickster figures. In the children's play *Sir Slob and the Princess* (1964) Garrett
filters the Cinderella fable through a poor, doltish peasant boy who wins the
hand of a princess with his good heart. Along the way, Sir Slob, as he comes
to be called, is demonized and denigrated by his community for his humble
origins and negligible wit. Yet, in the end, he unknowingly functions as both
a critique and redeemer of the other people in the play, teaching them the
importance of love and sincerity through the example of his honest simplic-
ity. Whereas Slob helps to stabilize his society, returning it to morality-based
order, the figure of the Goatman in "Cold Ground Was My Bed Last Night"
(1964) works in a completely opposite direction. Described as a "fool without cap and bells," he "is somehow needed to question the value of disguise
and appearances" (*CG* 165). Like Slob, the Goatman "lives outside the neat
boundaries" (*CG* 163), his otherness and alienation functioning as a silent
rebuttal to the tired customs of his community. Whereas Slob helps to stabilize his surroundings through ethical conduct, the Goatman is an alcoholic
lawbreaker, a regular, though harmless, foil to the peace-keeping endeavors
of Sheriff Jack Riddle. Both making their appearances in 1964, Slob and the
Goatman constitute two sides of an unusual coin. Possessing similar degrees
of remote otherness, their nonconformist roles in their respective communities demonstrate similar techniques in achieving opposite ends.

In Garrett's poem "Four Local Characters," the narrator muses,

the ways of God are crazy, daze
a skeptic mind like summer lightning.
Others false and foolish as you (and I)

have been chosen, and so chosen
babbled more wisely than they knew.
You bow your handsome goathead and
God springs from your lips like a snowy dove
    (*CP* 18)

Addressing not the Goatman, but a praying man with a "goathead," the speaker describes the phenomenon of regular people possessing the ability to "babble more wisely than they know," transcending their own knowledge and experiences with a rich, unexpected awareness of indeterminate origin. Characters who go beyond their severe limitations in revealing wisdom that would seem beyond them make up the cast of Garrett's third novel *Do, Lord, Remember Me* (1965), which in early manuscript form included a Chaucerian epigraph for each of its fictional personalities. Like the figures in *The Canterbury Tales*, Garrett's characters represent a wide variety of human faults and aspirations, all conveyed in a visceral, sometimes comic mode that frequently strays into the grotesque. As reviewer G. H. Pouder said of the book's individuals, "These people live in an inferno and their frightening ruminations as they look into the past and present seem to symbolize the human comedy and the futility and tawdriness of the life struggle" (D5). Surrounded by debilitating adversity, the figures in the novel struggle to find meaning even as their efforts paradoxically evoke humor and despair. Yet, as Monroe K. Spears noted, "The mixture of the earthy and religious in these 'low' characters is presented with nothing but sympathy" (49). Creating an eccentric group of working-class people, Garrett staked himself the challenge of making them genuinely compelling, even as he periodically dehumanized them with elements of the grotesque.

Not unlike some of the struggling characters in his book, Garrett faced a degree of adversity in trying to get his manuscript accepted for publication. Running, at one point, to more than 1,500 pages, *Do, Lord, Remember Me* was rejected by several publishers before a much-abbreviated version finally found a home—a concession that likely damaged the book's reception. As R. H. W. Dillard maintains, "The editors who cut the larger novel before publishing it and the critics who failed to identify the novel's true coherence and identity did Garrett's readers a great disservice" (*UGG* 109). In fact, when the novel finally was published, it actually appeared as two different versions, its British and American editions containing several notable incongruities. Garrett has admitted, "For various reasons, I favor the British version" (*GSE* 24), which stems from the fact that the British edition is more true to his grotesque vision of the book. He cites as an example an episode of flatulence that was removed from the American version at the insistence of the publisher (Int). Originally written as a play, Garrett never satisfactorily completed *Do, Lord, Remember Me* to his liking, its characters and events translated, recontextualized, and augmented to varying degrees in the narratives "To Whom Shall I Call Now in My Hour of Need?" (included both in an issue of *Red Clay Reader* and in the "anti-anthology" *The Girl in the Black Raincoat* [1965]), "Moon Girl" (1971), "The Satyr Shall Cry (a Movie Sound Track in Various Tongues and Voices)" (the final novella in *The Magic Striptease* [1973]), and *The King of Babylon Shall Not Come against You* (1996). Each version contains character modifications, alternate aesthetic forms, and new grotesque episodes usually interpreted from the perspectives of various townspeople who, not unlike the local citizens in many of Garrett's stories, collectively function as a kind of framing chorus.

The number of perspectives and voices in *Do, Lord, Remember Me* also conspires to create a peripatetic book—one that distorts itself grotesquely at times only to arrive at moments of startling clarity on an ensuing page. Furthermore, the novel resembles Robert Penn Warren's *The Cave* and much of the work of Wright Morris in the way it moves across and compresses time, employing this technique to unite important events and motivations across temporal gulfs and to disturb both narrative continuity and the reader's comfort. Garrett's decision to distort through multiple voices and temporal shifts appears to have been based partially on a desire to complement the tension and ambiguity of the novel's narrative action. In terms of plot, he recounts that the book "was about a mildly insane revivalist preacher who actually could heal people . . . it had to do with being possessed by powers that you don't understand. The other people around him, his immediate group, were like a cult" (Sussman 210). Tapping into madness, faith healing, and a messianic following, Garrett required a form that would convey to readers the nuances and complexity of belief and insanity as irrational, nonlinear constructs. In an interview, Garrett compared the narrative's string of unrelated events to Boethius's attitude toward predestination, "where he tries to describe how God can have foreknowledge but we can have free choice" (Garrett, Interview). As an author, Garrett possesses a godlike omniscient and linear foreknowledge of his narrative; however, the reader ultimately must make a faith-based decision with regard to interpreting the novel—reconciling the disparate parts and voices in an effort to achieve meaning. As the speaker declares in Garrett's poem "Revival," "Chaos has pitched a tent" (*CP* 15), and whatever relevance emerges from the anarchy of *Do, Lord, Remember Me* is mostly contingent upon the reader's trust or skepticism with regard to Garrett's authorial intentions. For believers like John Carr, the book's evangelical protagonist, Red, is a legitimate Christ figure who functions as a kind of redeemer of the grotesque (22), cleansing through sacrifice the ugly pettiness and perversity of the plagued people who surround him. More skeptical readers might point to the greater symbolic importance of the psychologically complex girl in the black raincoat,[2] whom poet Daniel Hoffman once described as "incarnat[ing] memory and desire" (195). Finally, for those who do not accept Garrett's intentions and techniques at all, the book itself becomes a chaotic grotesque—bent, disfigured, and ultimately defeated by an overly fervent and misguided aesthetic agenda.

Not fully satisfied with the themes of *Do, Lord, Remember Me*, Garrett established an almost identically elaborate formal and philosophical flirtation with the grotesque several years later in "The Magic Striptease" (1973), the opening novella in the book of the same name. Both intrigued and perplexed, reviewer David Tillinghast characterized it as "so outlandish and mischievous that the reader really questions its intention" (23), a comment that just as easily might describe *Do, Lord, Remember Me*. However, *The Magic Striptease* is much more overt than the earlier work in revealing its cultural agenda, Garrett explaining that "two thirds of it was written in reaction to the sixties, and those two thirds are grotesque comedy. It's really hard to sustain any seriousness when you're writing about the sixties, I guess" (quoted in Israel 48). Earlier, writing in 1965, Garrett's perception of the decade had been quite different: "It isn't news to anyone that we live in a bad time. A world getting worse, and with typical modern pride we revel in it" ("Against" 221). Contextualizing the 1960s as a debilitated era of misplaced pride and comedy, Garrett hints at a perverse cultural relationship between adversity, humor, and vanity. Elsewhere, in an unpublished speech, Garrett remarked that the grotesque "may be sometimes only the truth of the age exaggerated," which both reconciles his earlier comments and embodies the societal agenda of "The Magic Striptease."

Garrett foregrounds the cultural nuances of his novella by infusing it initially with traditional manifestations of the grotesque. Invoking Bakhtin's observation of the relationship between carnivals and the grotesque, Garrett has his protagonist, Jacob Quirk, compare his unusual gift of shape-shifting to the talents of circus "freaks": "*Rope climbers! Fire eaters! Sword swallowers! Mystics standing on one leg, like a crane or something, for hours at a time*" (*MS* 4, Garrett's italics). The grotesque nature of Quirk's talent is further augmented by its subtle ties to violent, abusive elements of his childhood. For example, in a scene of domestic brutality and squalor reminiscent of Stephen Crane's *Maggie: A Girl of the Streets*, Quirk's hulking mother kills his father with a devastating, two-handed blow from a gin bottle (*MS* 9).

From these hard-hitting, traditional elements of the grotesque emerge the philosophical agenda of the novella. Revealing the aesthetic implications of his gift, Quirk remarks, *"No poet or novelist can ever imagine to blend himself, to wed himself so completely, into the flux and flow of an imaginary creature's being"* (MS 18, Garrett's italics). Reveling in his ability to take on the physical appearances of others, Quirk contextualizes it as a superior art form—one that goes far beyond any other medium of imagining identity. In allowing him to become other people, Quirk's gift also makes him, like the narrator of Sherwood Anderson's *Winesburg, Ohio*, privy to the lives and disparate grotesque qualities of the people in his community. For example, the prostitute, Mrs. Carnassi, functions as a grotesque in terms of her singular, self-destructive fixation on fine clothing:

> *The apartment of the widow Carnassi is bare and empty. No furniture of any kind at all except for one old ripped and stained mattress in the middle of the floor. No objects of any kind. No chairs, no rugs, no curtains, nothing! Except that all the closets are open, bulging and overflowing with clothing. The closets glittering and glowing like open jewel boxes, overbrimming with an abundance of extravagant, beautiful clothes.* (MS 21, Garrett's italics)

Fixating on clothes to the exclusion of all principles and other materialistic concerns, Carnassi, along with several others, enlightens Quirk to the perverse and self-destructive greed and blindness of human beings.

Aligning his shape-shifting ability with the human propensity for ownership and desire, Quirk eventually "decide[s] that people see what they want to see and believe what they care to believe. And this in itself, he ascertained, was at once the strength and the secret of his art" (MS 22). Revealing that his ability to change identity is based more on how people apprehend objects—their misguided, distorted gazes—than his own inherent aptitude for reorganizing matter, Quirk points to the empty, illusory nature of twentieth-century values and culture. This nihilistic realization leads him, as his gift progresses, to become "Nobody" (MS 43) and then nothing. Yet, this mostly despairing (d)evolution is not without an element of grotesque irony and humor. Shortly after using his gift to drive a girl into madness (MS 54), Quirk is institutionalized himself. And once Quirk seemingly disappears for good, out of the ashes of his nihilism and madness arises a bizarre brand of New Age spirituality. As people learn the strange story of Quirk's life two religions emerge: "The Temple of the Primitive Proteus on Sunset Boulevard" (MS 104) and "the more conservative and respectable Temple of Protean Mysteries, located in Beverly Hills" (MS 105). Having dedicated his life to a search for the evasive truths that lie behind appearances, Quirk ironically becomes merely a compellingly inscrutable image in the end. Furthermore, the ironic and grotesque appropriation of Quirk's identity and legacy by others also concludes Garrett's point about late-twentieth-century culture: that beneath nearly all popular ideas and media images resides a collection of misguided individuals whose own yawning emptiness of self compels them to create a facade of principles—bright and shiny, yet vacuous.

Writing in 1963 Garrett remarked, "The beginning of high fashion may, indeed, be a striptease, but it is not my purpose to create a new generation of Sally Rands" ("One" 166). A groundbreaking erotic dancer, Rand was arrested four times for indecent exposure on the first day of the 1933 World's Fair in Chicago because she appeared to be dancing nude behind feather fans. Actually, it was an illusion: she wore a flesh-colored body suit that only made her look nude. The arrest and publicity afforded her lasting fame as a "fan dancer." Critiquing popular culture in heavily ironic and grotesque terms, Garrett was careful to avoid inadvertently celebrating it or offering up something equally monstrous in its place. However, over the course of his career, he has not stopped writing about the phenomenon or working it into his narratives. In *The King of Babylon Shall Not Come against You* (1996)—in some respects, a sequel to *Do, Lord, Remember Me*—Garrett employs numerous cultural developments while meditating on the grotesque lifestyle of late-twentieth-century Florida and the United States as a whole. As one anonymous reviewer observed, "Clearly, Garrett's intent is to draw a picture of the moral breakdown of American society, using 1968 as the defining year that the culture changed for the worse" ("Review of *The King*" 58). As in *Do, Lord, Remember Me*, the disparate personalities participating in the narrative serve to frame and interpret the novel's big philosophical questions in different ways. Like the characters in Lee K. Abbott's *Living after Midnight*, whom Garrett characterized in a review as "crammed with the excess and detritus of our popular culture" (*MSP* 147), the figures in *King of Babylon* view, struggle against, and interact with vulgar media forces beyond their control.

The fact that media phenomena ultimately are beyond anyone's control makes its most grotesque articulation in "The Pornographers," an omitted chapter of *King of Babylon* that would appear later in the collection *Bad Man Blues*. Taking as its subject a twelve-year-old girl who is pimped out by her family on the way to becoming a porn star, the piece recounts the apathy of society and ineffectiveness of the law with regard to the girl's unfortunate situation. In her stardom, albeit in a deviant genre, generating money and a following, the media image of her identity swallows up or renders irrelevant the essence of who she really is. Correspondingly, in his essay "When Lorena Bobbitt Comes Bob-Bob-Bobbing Along" Garrett recounts the powerful evolution of the celebrity figure in American history and its implications for nonentertainment sectors of society: "Some had talent and some didn't. Talent became, finally, irrelevant to stardom. So, soon enough, did other factors like character and integrity. . . . [T]he star system has spread first to all other shapes and forms of show business and entertainment, but also into all other aspects of our lives including politics and the professions, all the arts and crafts" (*GSE* 172–73). Titillated by and addicted to the images of mass media, society finds itself increasingly accommodating the value(less) structure of the "star system," incorporating it into other walks of life instead of interrogating its underpinnings. It is precisely this sad degeneration of essence into image which informs much of *King of Babylon*'s narrative action—the inefficient and farcical roles of society (especially law enforcement and the press) suggesting nonfiction books such as Vincent Bugliosi and Curt Gentry's *Helter Skelter*, which unintentionally captured the ridiculousness of the trial following the Tate-LaBianca murders and attracted Garrett's attention in the form of a book review. Coupling the grotesque absurdity of media and celebrity forces with the tragic, ignored sorrow of real lives, Garrett established for himself the difficult task of infusing a comedy of hyperbolic popular images with the essence of authentic human loss and knowledge. In his review of David Madden's novel *Brothers in Confidence*, Garrett characterized the book as "serious enough, but the tone and substance are comic, thus charitable and compassionate from first to last" ("Con" 9). One reaches nearly the same conclusion at the end of *King of Babylon*, as we leave the protagonist, Billy Tone, groping among superficial scoundrels and media-distorted information for a difficult truth that must necessarily come forth from within himself.

When informed, during the course of an interview, of William Peden's comment that his "house of fiction has as many dark rooms as sunny ones, and there are maggots in the basement," Garrett laughingly responded:

> Well I'm rather fond of maggots. You know they used to use them for wounds since they only eat dead flesh. Now what they would be doing in the basement, I'm not so sure. They like sun. We're doing a lot of laughing here but with the flip of a coin the grotesque can turn serious. I think that's part of the fun: not knowing when that coin is going to be flipped. (Int)

Deeper than the assessment of any of his critics, Garrett's response thoroughly contextualizes his admiration for and practice of the grotesque.

Despite their disgusting popular connotations, maggots attract Garrett's fondness for the necessary beneficial functions they perform. Furthermore, they do not thrive shut away in a basement, but rather out in the bright, warm sunlight. Much like the workings of maggots, Garrett's practice of the grotesque functions in the open, drawing obscene, terrible, and comic manifestations of aberrant difference into the brightly lit arena of his constructed fictional worlds. There, they are used most often as a kind of cleansing mechanism for both society and the reader: in confronting the ugly and the obscene we as readers embrace the prospect of healing and change. Continually flipping the coin of the grotesque across his stories, Garrett consistently delights, disturbs, and instructs—forcing the reader to confront and sift through life's macabre ugliness in search of the human hope that allows one to laugh, heal, and grow.

Life in the Academy Is Hell

Academic Narratives

In some important sense, the world of academe is more like the child's
game of Monopoly, played with funny money.
—Garrett, *The Sorrows of Fat City*

Looking back over his literary career in his autobiographical essay "Under Two Flags" (1992), Garrett confesses, "I am astonished to have to admit that much as I love the lively arts, including the art of letters, to which so much of my life has been dedicated, I cannot accept that a life based mainly upon aesthetic principles can be anything but harmlessly silly at best and, in view of all this world's desperate needs and hungers, shameful at worst" (*WD* 211). Not comfortable raising the abstractions of aesthetics above the real and immediate woes of everyday life, Garrett espouses a philosophy that contextualizes the writing life as "a way of life" as opposed to "a life"—an all-consuming, tunnel-visioned undertaking that absorbs all of the intellect, emotion, and miscellaneous energy of an individual. Though he remains wholly dedicated to his art, Garrett's ability to see life and himself outside of it allows him to perceive his vocation with a penetrating irony and occasional levity that eludes all but a few of his literary peers. Having once stated in an interview that writing "won't make a better person out of you—but it will keep you so busy, you can't get into trouble" (Cross 5), Garrett humorously emphasizes the impact of the profession on the writer's existence beyond the craft.

Although his statements on the literary life often come across as ironic or amusing, Garrett is less genuinely comic when examining the writer's relationship to the academy. A cofounder of the Association of Writers and Writing Programs (AWP), Garrett has witnessed the thriving or monstrous (the adjective here depends on one's point of view) growth of graduate writing programs in the United States over the past thirty years, which has produced unprecedented benefits for writers as well as new challenges. Never contented with the writer's expected and sometimes restrictive allegiance to a given departmental or institutional agenda, Garrett has warned, "One good reason for writers to disassociate themselves from academe is to avoid the bad company there, including the bad company of each other" (*GSE* 39). In addition to suggesting the inevitable friction between writers and their more traditional academic colleagues, Garrett's statement suggests the ways in which academic appointments, salaries, awards, and other less palpable factors can produce jealousy and division among writers who would be better served thinking about their next projects. Although he does not specifically indict traditional departmental teachers and scholars as catalysts for misunderstanding in terms of a writer's employment, Garrett does point to the prevalence of trendy literary theory as a distracting force in the writer's departmental role, which has led him to the confession, "By hook or by crook, by pure luck and whimsical fortune, I have managed to arrive at an age where almost all literary theory bores me to tears" ("George Garrett," *Sudden Fiction* 257–58). Though Garrett himself thrived in the academy as a teacher and colleague, he does not hesitate to critique and reject the fashions and aspects of it that he deems unsavory or useless. While he remains seriously engaged with the difficult challenges writers face in academic settings, he makes it clear that his art is infinitely more valuable to him than any finite institutional academic concerns: "In some important sense, the world of academe is more like the child's game of Monopoly, played with funny money" (*SFC* 14). Trivializing the petty politics and power relationships of the academic world, Garrett frequently delves into their underpinnings even as he ultimately satirizes and dismisses them.

Over the course of his career Garrett repeatedly has employed academic figures and milieus, fictional and nonfictional, as means of revealing and interrogating the more ridiculous phenomena of the academic world. Surprisingly, some of the more bizarre and unbelievable accounts revolve around incidents of nonfiction. For example, at Rice in the 1960s Garrett discovered that "all the football players came from the . . . Commerce Department, a mysterious brick building off by itself and close to the shadow of the huge stadium. . . . The chairman of Commerce was Jess Neely, who did double duty as the football coach" (*BMB* 95). Bribing his fellow department heads with lucrative football profits, Neely practiced an amiable form of corruption that kept his boys on the football field and Rice's high academic standards dutifully intact. Although Neely is a singularly memorable figure, most of Garrett's protagonists fall under the more conventional academic roles of scholars and writers. However, while the professional situations remain quite typical, the personalities of the academics involved usually are not. For example, in "How to Do the Literary" (1992) Garrett describes the "Mystery Professor," an elderly gentleman who dutifully and obliviously showed up nearly every day for forty years at the American Academy in Rome to conduct indeterminate research. As the account's narrator remarks, "Oh, he must have wondered once in a while as governments and armies came and went. But he had his work to do (whatever it may be). And the rest of the world, in peace or at war, was without much meaning" (*WD* 149). A kind of walking symbol of the ivory tower, the Mystery Professor embodies the sometimes remote alienation from the real that comes with highly specialized, esoteric academic research. Blindly living through World War II and a host of other significant national and international events, the Mystery Professor remains wholly absorbed in a subject that for him renders the world's events irrelevant.

Many of Garrett's early academic fictional characters resemble the Mystery Professor in their general alienation and pathos, haplessly caught up in stale, insular academic existences. In the earliest of these, "The Accursed Huntsman"—the third vignette in "Comic Strip" (1957)—Professor B., whom Madison Smartt Bell has characterized as a "wearisome pedant" (315), performs extensive genealogical research, living almost exclusively in a world of dead people and long-forgotten events. However, when he discovers that one of his ancestors was a mass-murdering slave trader, he is jarred into a more immediate understanding of existence and experiences "a new confinement" (*KM* 95). As Bell has summarized, Professor B. is "a radically changed individual: inwardly he is disillusioned and cynical, but he also seems to have won the outward appearance of a wise man (in the eyes of everyone except his long-suffering wife, of course)" (324). Stripped of any romantic notions regarding history and his ancestors, B. acquires an air of bitterness, which makes him a less happy individual but also a more genuine person. In short, the event humanizes him for his colleagues and students who now perceive a human being touched by experience rather than a monastic intellectual isolated and obscured by abstractions.

Garrett uses a similar academic figure to work in an opposite direction in "My Picture Left in Scotland" (1959). Like Professor B. and the speaker in Garrett's poem "Salome," Professor Dudley is a "dancer of the abstract fancy" (*Collected* 6), juggling his rich, albeit doleful, life of the imagination with his hectic and less-than-ideal family situation. However, whereas Professor B. moves toward an uneasy acceptance of life's painful realities, Dudley increasingly desires to withdraw from them. Like B., Dudley is a man who has become generally dissatisfied with his academic existence. As Garrett says of Dudley's meeting with a hopeful young writer, "Dudley toys with him, cat and mouse, needles him in several ways, leaves him crushed. The reason? Mixed. Partly it's because he's bitter about his own wasted talents." Later, when Dudley meets with a pretty female undergraduate, Garrett explains that he flirts with her "out of loneliness and folly." Garrett proceeds to balance Dudley's fanciful, abstract student interactions with a stressful, action-filled family life. When he arrives home to a scene of domestic chaos Dudley retreats again into the haven of the imagination, delivering a make-believe lecture to his students in which he implores them to "never marry an intellectual woman . . . and . . . keep your grubby, cotton-picking, unwashed fingers out of the lively arts, lest, bitten by the bug or burned by a gemlike flame, as the metaphor may go, so to speak, lest you become infected with ambition and desire and then struggle yourself gray-headed and black in the face trying to be what you most patently are not" (*CG* 116). Embittered by middle age, an unsatisfactory marriage, and his inability to succeed as a writer, Dudley indulges in a dreamworld where he is lord—damning undergraduate papers, seducing female students, and self-righteously pushing students away from the arts as a result of his own shortcomings and failures.

After visiting a hatchet-job upon an aspiring novelist's manuscript, Professor Dudley dismisses him with the disingenuous remark, "I'd like to think I'll see the day when I'll open a package in the mail and find an autographed copy of your first novel" (*CG* 106–7). Garrett's story "Last of the Old Buffalo Hunters" (1963) follows up on this idea, recording a pompous scholar's reaction to a former student who mocks him in a novel. "[A] real old-fashioned snob" (*EP* 427), Professor Harvey Peters swells with pride when he learns that an ex-student has published a novel, only to discover that a thinly disguised character based on himself is extensively satirized and caricatured in the book. Although Peters experiences considerable embarrassment and humiliation, the reader's sympathy for him is tempered by the fact that the novel's assessment of Peters seems to be fairly accurate. For example, it turns out that Peters is indeed clownishly bureaucratic, having formed the ridiculous and redundant "Lightening Committee, a group of earnest professors making a close study of how much time was being lost by their colleagues through committee work" (*EP* 429). Like Professor B.'s genealogical research, Peters's perusal of his student's novel forces him to discard his unearned pride and confront and accept a number of hard, ugly truths regarding his personality and life.

Although Garrett employs humor at his professors' expense in most of these academic tales, the underlying identity implications generally remain serious and immediate. This is less true in Garrett's stories involving provincial schoolteachers, which lean more toward traditional comedy and nonsymbolic manifestations of the absurd. "The Gun and the Hat" (1961), for example, presents the comic confrontation between an effete fourth-grade teacher named John Pengry and an outraged parent. Believing that Pengry has insulted his obese son, the angry farmer drives to Pengry's home with the intention of shooting him. However, having been "alone now since his mother had died and his sister Louise had left" (*BP* 24), Pengry has acquired personal habits and a grasp of reality that are both pitiably eccentric. When he answers the door wearing only his mother's bathrobe and his grandfather's gaudy Confederate hat, he presents such a ridiculous and pathetic appearance that the farmer is incapable of shooting him. Equally goofy and hapless is the geeky high school science teacher, Elmer Adelot, in "The Farmer in the Dell" (1959). Like Pengry, Adelot lives alone in a house he has inherited from his mother, alienated and apparently sexless in his seemingly inevitable bachelorhood. Yet, when Adelot gets "behind the desk in the Science Room, he is a little tin god and everything has got to be just so" (*CG* 119). Highly particular and retentive, Adelot is despot of his classroom but pitiably alienated in nearly all other aspects of his life. However, subtly manipulating this characterization, Garrett implies at the end of the story that Adelot probably is having an affair with the wife of his friend, Johnny Spratling, adding a teasing measure of misdirection and irony to Adelot's otherwise limited attributes and life.

When Garrett throws us a narrative curveball with an insinuation of Adelot's affair, he breaks his mold of hapless, morose, dreamy, scholarly figures, providing Adelot with a functional, though deeply buried and concealed, initiative and engagement with the real world. As opposed to Garrett's teacher/scholar figures, nearly all of his writer characters possess this quality. In fact, though most of them are struggling and/or unstable, Garrett's scribblers remain wholly involved with their surroundings. Unlike the more stolid scholars and teachers, their powerful gifts of perception enable them to recognize, often painfully, the extent of their misfortunes and artistic shortcomings. In

"What's the Matter with Mary Jane?" (1963) a pregnant woman named Mildred chides her husband Bill, a failed poet, for flirting with an actress at an artsy party. Deeply aware of and depressed by his wasted promise and unrewarding life in academia, Bill dallies with the actress as a temporary means of escaping the burdensome limits of his job and marriage. Attempting to exact revenge, Mildred asks him, "You wanted to be a poet. . . . Whatever happened to you?" (*EP* 443), a harsh question, which causes him to weep. Unlike Garrett's scholars and teachers, Bill, though he is a failed writer, essentially possesses a poet's heart, discerning his identity, his wife's cruelty, and life in general with a degree of honesty, detail, and feeling that forces him to cry. Unlike the stodgy scholar protagonists, Bill does not retreat into the realm of intellectual abstraction; rather, he drinks the bitter dregs of existence, unwilling to shrug the responsibility of naked experience.

The engagement of Garrett's writer figures is equally apparent in other stories and ultimately would serve as a bridge to lengthier projects. In "Man Without a Fig Leaf" (1960) the frustrated and possibly insane writer Fergus McCree places his wreath of woes at the feet of his best friend, only to reason that brotherly goodwill and a nice job will not ease the burden of the things he so intensely perceives and feels. Similarly, in "More Geese Than Swans" (1962) the writer-protagonist Sam Browne possesses an ungovernable compulsion to weave a long narrative of English Department scandal for an exhausted and hardly interested married couple who have just returned from a long sabbatical in Europe. The resident writer and bachelor of the English Department, Browne weaves his bawdy tale with descriptive relish, obviously enjoying the act of telling as much as or more than the actual content. As the academic narrator concedes, "Sam can be a fine story-teller, given a certain kind of material" (*CG* 19), namely sleazy material. Delighting in the visceral human follies of his colleagues beyond their abstract functions in the academy, Browne humanizes his stiff, intellectual cast of characters through his vivid account of their human shortcomings.

Writing in his notebooks in 1962, the same year that "More Geese Than Swans" was published, Garrett called Mark Harris's *Wake Up, Stupid* (1959), "Very good, funny, clever, imaginative and quite possibly the best 'academic' novel I've read in years." Written in an epistolary format, Harris's novel thoroughly satirizes its academic milieu through the actions of its protagonist, a lapsed Mormon named Lee Youngdahl, who, in a letter to the Harvard University English Department chairman, asserts, "I am a scoundrel and a blockhead, and I trust you are the same" (81). Like Sam Browne, Youngdahl delights in critiquing his academic surroundings by focusing on the seedier aspects of his colleagues' lives, and the success of his biting, epistolary approach was not lost on Garrett, who began experimenting with the form himself in a number of half-serious unpublished stories involving sleazy protagonists such as "The Decline and Fall of Dave O'Hara," which portrays a swindling, down-and-out Hollywood promoter, and "Feeling Good, Feeling Fine," the protagonist of which asserts, "When it comes to morals, I can take it or leave it." These fictional exercises were accompanied by the mid-1960s phenomena of Garrett's literary friends reading strange, comic letters attributed to Garrett at various parties. In 1967 Garrett would publish the first set of these dispatches in *Rapier* under the title "Exemplary Letters from *The Realms of Gold* (An Excerpt from an Upcoming Novel)." Ascribing the composition of the letters to a person named R. C. Alger, who was a character created by John Towne, himself a fictional invention, Garrett introduced the epistles as examples of "the genre of the poison pen letter, for they are intended to bug, distract, irritate and insult the people he is writing to" (6). Calling down religious leaders, politicians, and celebrities with vitriolic, satirical glee, "Exemplary Letters" marked a radically new wrinkle in Garrett's fictional oeuvre.

His praise for *Wake Up, Stupid* notwithstanding, Garrett remarked in 1970 that among the bad things arising from the writer's association with higher education is "that ungainly weed, 'the academic novel'" ("Teaching" 62). However, as his "poison pen" letters accumulated over the course of the late 1960s, Garrett began cultivating a distinctive novelistic weed of his own called "Life with Kim Novak Is Hell." A symbol for the gaudy, weird dynamics of celebrity existence, the vixen in the book's title also appears in Garrett's poem "Celebrity Verses: Figures from the 60's": "[I]t's Kim Novak's secret and she never tells / why she's blonder and blander than anyone else" (*CP* 97). As the novel's title and the poem's lines imply, Garrett was working toward a satirical indictment of both the celebrity cult and American popular culture at large. In fact, satire had been on Garrett's mind throughout the 1960s, as evinced in his 1965 introduction to an edition of *Gulliver's Travels*:

All satire, whether it is grotesque and seemingly cruel or mild and benevolent, is intended to point out faults and abuses and, by doing so, to encourage correction. Which means that satire can never be really negative. It calls for change, implying therefore that change is possible. Satire is, then, never tragic. For the satirist, it is never too late. Otherwise, in all honesty, he could not write a satire. Satire is like comedy and is founded on the proposition that a happy ending is at least possible and that laughter is better medicine than tears. ("Introduction" xiii)

Having confronted and embraced the celebrity landscape of the 1960s as a means of critiquing the questionable culture and society that created it, Garrett employed satire, attempting to arouse awareness and laughter with regard to the increasingly pervasive and influential presence of media forces.

Of course, Garrett's use of satire does not stop with his celebrity subjects but spills over into other areas, including the academy and the characterization of the dominant protagonist-writer figure of "Kim Novak" and the poison pen letters: John Towne. Towne himself does not admit to satire, boasting, "Let it be others who scoff and scorn, criticize and satirize. Jack Towne has no (pardon the expression) truck with Nay-sayers. I laugh at winter and say yes to life. In short, undefeated and undaunted, I am out to get mine and to get it here and now while I can still enjoy it" (*PP* 34). Although he rejects satire, Towne is satirized himself through the ridiculously elevated and clumsily hyperbolic, life-affirming tone Garrett ascribes to him. Furthermore, Towne functions as the necessary centerpiece around which nearly all of Garrett's satirical workings move. An academic writer figure, Towne provides Garrett with an additional narrative level of expression, a kind of trashy echo, which often makes it difficult to perceive whether it is Towne's or Garrett's voice that is speaking at any given time—a fundamental interpretive problem that has hindered the work of scholars like Lee Holmes. Towne also is confusing simply in and of himself. Although he appears in the Garrett manuscript called "Life with Kim Novak Is Hell," he claims he is working on a novel with an identical title. Yet, he hardly ever discusses it, favoring instead another manuscript called "The Insects Are Winning." Clouding the waters further, Garrett asserted in his notebooks that he was "trying to make a real novel" out of "Insects" and hoped to submit it to publishers under a pen-name, presumably John Towne. However, he also was exploring the idea of writing "a thoroughly *pornographic* book" (Garrett's emphasis), apparently different from "Kim Novak" and "Insects," using Towne as the author.

Summing up the collective plan for these projects while providing no real clarity, Garrett has Towne conclude, "Now, of course, *Life with Kim* isn't really a *novel*, as I have no doubt stated. And *Insects* will be even less of one in its own inimitable way" (Garrett's emphasis). Although Garrett/Towne leads us through elaborate meditations on what will be written and achieved, we end up with absolutely no understanding of what Garrett/Towne ultimately is really trying to accomplish, which may in fact be purposeful. Even when we know we are firmly in Towne's grubby narrative hands, things still are apt to become confusing, a partial byproduct of his strong dependence on prescription drugs as means of firing his composition process. For example, in a chapter from "Kim Novak" called "Pornography," Towne asks, "[C]an you tell that I'm calmer than usual? Because this time I'm on *Dexamil*" (Garrett's emphasis). Later on in the novel, in a letter to his agent, Towne laments, "The effects of coffee and goof balls are wearing off fast." Corresponding to Towne's variable drug use, the styles of the different "Kim Novak" sections are highly erratic, reflecting Towne's various levels of inebriation and diverse consumption of uppers and downers, prescription drugs he pilfers from various friends and neighbors. This dynamic also lends an appropriately tacky 1960s-era, *Valley of the Dolls* atmosphere to Towne's exploits and narratives, which often appear gratuitous, meandering, and without purpose.[1] In fact, one of the interesting things about "Kim Novak" is that nearly all of it takes place in a kind of foggy textual limbo, never truly taking shape. Towne repeatedly indulges in the art of the literary "cop-out," bragging about and describing his novel at great length to his dead, cuckolded friend, Ray Wadley, but never actually writing it. As one of Towne's hapless editors explains, "'KIM NOVAK' is a sort of cop-out, as it were. For [Towne] is always hiding behind the device of addressing someone in particular." Enamored with his grandiose ideas for the book and the sound of his own self-important voice, Towne talks a great deal but accomplishes nothing of real worth.

Ironically, throughout the "Kim Novak" manuscript Towne is never really working on *his* "Kim Novak" manuscript, but rather an assortment of other half-assed projects, most notably "The Insects Are Winning"—the title for which he has stolen from his prodigious son. As the boy explains in "Genius Baby," a published excerpt from the "Kim Novak" manuscript, "[The insects] keep multiplying and breeding and everything. . . . They outnumber all other forms of life. And they are going to win. Man is done for" (*BMB* 7). The seemingly harmless, childish aspect of this theory is significantly sobered and darkened by its nihilistic conclusion: that humans are on the way out. And the doomed meaninglessness of human experience seems to be what fascinates Towne the most. Writing in his notebooks, Garrett has Towne say, "Everybody wants to be somebody. I am just the opposite. I want to be nobody." Corresponding with his son's vision of humanity's extinction and irrelevance, Towne defines much of his own identity in terms of what he is not and what he would like to avoid doing. However, as negative and empty as this worldview may appear, it is a representative perspective rather than a Towne eccentricity. As Garrett remarked in his notebooks, Towne "like so many Americans, is not really one thing or another," drifting in an indeterminate limbo of identity and purpose. Actually, in "Exemplary Letters from *The Realms of Gold*" Garrett specifically remarks, "R. C. Alger is a nihilist. Jack Towne is a hustler and a bum, no good from the word go. The only things that interest Towne are the ephemeral pleasures of money and sex" (6). Although Alger gets the nihilism rap here, Towne's "ephemeral" interests ultimately come across as equally apathetic and empty. Like Lemuel Pitkin in Nathanael West's *A Cool Million*, R. C. Alger and Towne constitute maimed living manifestations of what Horatio Alger's American dream has become. Locked in a civilization that is devoid of meaning and dying fast, Alger and Towne mock the process with the self-satisfying purposelessness of their endeavors.

With "Kim Novak" safely unpublished and the poison pen letters temporarily ceasing, Towne disappeared from print in 1970, only to reemerge "as offensive as ever" (40) in the 1977 epistolary piece "P.S. What Is Octagon Soap: A Tale from the Tumultuous Sixties," which constituted another unpublished section from "Kim Novak" and also contained the first published information on Towne's identity and background. Many readers may be completely unaware that, following a disastrous sojourn in Hollywood, John Towne somehow managed to resume his long-interrupted academic career during the tag-end doggy days of the 1960s. Using a bogus curriculum vitae, he succeeded in finding gainful employment "as a member of the faculty at Nameless College, Virginia, a sweet and attractive little school squatting in the shadows of the Blue Ridge Mountains and dedicated to the probably laudable aim of educating sweet and attractive young women" (40). From this remote and bucolic academic perch Towne slowly, though not subtly, began revealing himself as "at once lazy and vicious and a creature of invincible bad taste" (41). Towne's seedy aesthetic meditations and careless writing as they appear in "Kim Novak" repeatedly conspire to underscore the latter declaration, and nowhere is Towne's true personal and aesthetic identity revealed more fully than in the first section of his unpublished poem "Cheerleader":

Cheerleader
Bouncer of Basketballs
Stern keeper of home plate
She ran on swift beautiful legs
across all my dreams for a full year
bright hair flashing behind her
and laughter like golden apples
daring one and all to muster

enough energy to master her
I am sorry
I was not the one.

"Cheerleader" contains all the elements of Towne's most distinctive work. It is at once awkward, sexist, silly, domineering, sentimental, and self-righteous—its imagery and language delivered with as much nuance and subtlety as a dump truck depositing a load of gravel. Towne's theory of prose is equally misguided and vulgar, imploring his young, impressionable female writers at Nameless "to get the show on the road with a big, fat, easygoing dependent clause, holding off the subject for a good while and letting your participles and your adjectives do the heavy work for you. Hold back on the verb as long as you possibly can. Otherwise it can end up being as embarrassing and disappointing as premature ejaculation."

In addition to feeding his vulnerable students a steady diet of obscene, bogus aesthetics, Towne employs much of his spare time dreaming up narratives and projects like "Cheerleader" that he believes will embody the "next big thing." However, they are almost always couched in such tasteless terms and skewed logic as to render the actual prospect of their compositions an impossibility. For example, with regard to his proposed novel "Jane Anor, Space Nurse," Towne stresses to his editor the untapped cultural relevance of nurses:

> Nurses know how to take precautions. Moreover, they are extremely unlikely to come up pregnant. And, even if they do, nine times out of ten, they won't come knocking on your door weeping and wailing. Like the mature individuals they are, they will do something about it and go back to their duty. . . . Nurses get their edge because they actually study biology, physiology, anatomy and stuff like that. When the time comes, they know what to do and how to do it. . . . In short, all the world knows that Nurses like to have a good time and they deserve it.

Almost virulent in its ability to subvert all standards of taste and decency, the raunchy unsuitability that informs nearly all of Towne's works seemed to have infected Garrett's Towne material as well in the late 1970s. Following the publication of "A Record as Long as Your Arm" (1978) Towne again would scurry away into silence and anonymity. In fact, while characterizing the story as "a remarkable tour de force," William Peden also cautiously identified it as "the swan song, I assume, of John Towne" (89). In his essay "Against the Grain" Garrett used the phrase "a record as long as your arm" in describing how poetry collections often list the prestigious magazines in which the content has appeared as a kind of selling point ("Against" 226). However, in the Towne story the technique takes the form of the numerous empty and tasteless excuses Towne employs while trying to justify his myriad betrayals and missteps to Ray Wadley, a former close friend who kills himself following his humiliating discovery of Towne's affair with his wife. Having originally composed the piece as the conclusion to "Life with Kim Novak," Garrett had envisioned the episode as a way to wrap things up with Towne's "well-deserved ruin [and] complete farcical disaster." Though "Kim Novak" still had not hustled its way into print, the publication of its final chapter suggested to many relieved readers that Garrett finally was closing the book on Jack Towne.

Reflecting back on the period of the late 1970s, Garrett once stated, "Towne was gone, I thought, for good. Not knowing how a decade later he would resurface like a killer whale in a novel called *Poison Pen*" (*WD* 130). Just as Towne had disappeared in 1970 only to return at the tail end of that forgettable decade, so his second departure, to the chagrin of many, turned out to be another episode of Towne skillfully playing possum. Adding insult to surprise, Towne's convincing feint would be followed by a devastating literary sucker-punch: *Poison Pen* (1986), a book of indeterminate genre, which Garrett's editor, Sam Vaughn, repeatedly attempted to foil and dissuade. As he explained to Garrett in a letter, "I wasn't at all sure that it would help a hell of a lot in the growth of your reputation as a serious and distinguished writer." Unmoved by Vaughn's arguments, Garrett received a final admonition from his concerned associate, which warned him that the book could "cause all the trouble you could hope for." When the contentious tome finally appeared after literally becoming hung up in Stuart Wright's presses for several weeks, it was met by a rich array of responses. Opting for safety and tactful subtlety, Ron Smith called it "controversial" (715). On the other hand, Thomas Fleming vividly evoked the book's tastelessness: "Most people I know don't admit to owning a copy and if they do they keep it in their underwear drawer along with their copies of *Nude Living* and *Mein Kampf*" (22). Perhaps the best overall summation has come from R. H. W. Dillard: "A wildly comic, sharply satirical, unkept rascal of a book" (*UGG* 163).

Containing narrative misdirection, numerous letters, and various confusing levels of voice and action, *Poison Pen* suggests the approach, though not the style, of novelists such as B. S. Johnson, a writer Garrett admires who had succeeded him as editor of the *Transatlantic Review*. To be sure, *Poison Pen* is an exercise in self-reflexive metafiction as Garrett conceives of the term: "Author and reader actively participate in making up the story at hand, and the story is told by the author-narrator" (*MSP* 148). However, because the book is wrapped in so many different levels of narration, the reader often has difficulty deciding which voice or author to trust, while also remaining completely uncertain of Garrett's intentions. For his own part, Garrett has maintained that the project was "more for my own fun and games than anything else" ("George" 77). Yet, many of Towne's details and several episodes from the book correspond with phenomena from Garrett's career. A 1964 headline from *The Cavalier Daily*, "Garrett Assays Goldwyn Future in Film World" (Omwake 1), attests that Garrett, like Towne, was a Hollywood writer for a time, only to return to the groves of academe in due course. Further, there is more than a hint of the University of Virginia's autocratic former English Department chairman Fredson Bowers in Towne's hapless employer. (Bowers also is mocked in the Garrett-coauthored film *Frankenstein Meets the Space Monster* (1965) through a minor military administrator named General Bowers.) Also, like Towne, Garrett admits that for a time he suffered from "a genuine addiction to amphetamines" ("George" 76). Although *Poison Pen* constitutes a satire more than anything else, it does in fact draw significantly on events from Garrett's academic experiences as a means of achieving what he called an "inward and spiritual liberation" ("George" 77).

Moving beyond the use of Towne as a way of working out Garrett's academic concerns and frustrations, post-*Poison Pen* Towne pieces occasionally have employed him in critiquing fictional projections of Garrett. In "A Letter to the Students of the University of Virginia" Towne lords over his authorial master, cruelly characterizing him as "disgruntled, disillusioned, and more or less dysfunctional. He is also, in the words of one of his colleagues in the English Department (a true child of the Thrilling 1960s) 'completely irrelevant'. . . . My author is an old guy and getting older every day. But being a fictional character, I can stay the same way always" (*GSE* 158). Aware of his extensive abuse at Garrett's authorial hands, Towne gloats over his perceived superiority. Yet, when Towne continues his critique of Garrett in "False Confessions," his tone is more bitter, complaining, "What I really hate, is being made the public scapegoat for the author's guilt. He heaps troubles on my head in hopes of hiding the grubby truth about himself" (*GSE* 195). Strange as it may seem, Towne appears to be correct in identifying Garrett's frequent use of him as a kind of ventriloquist dummy for his aggravation and wish-fulfillment urges, which safely spares Garrett the trouble or danger of having to insert his own genuine identity into the fray.

Although Towne argues for himself as a hapless victim of Garrett's guilt and evil, there is little doubt that he truly is an appalling person. However, his low character often appears as much a byproduct of the culture around him as it is an inherent quality. As Garrett concedes, "Towne's hydraulic law of uniform corruption—that is, corruption everywhere seeks its own level and that, thus, all aspects of our life and world, at any given instant, are equally corrupt—seems to have some real truth to it" (*MSP* 42). Supporting this idea is the fact that Towne ends up in academia, as if Garrett is implying that Towne's tastelessness and vindictive ruthlessness are ideal attributes for the environment of higher education. Garrett has hinted at this theory elsewhere, noting "I'm surprised that the world has caught up with [Towne] in a way. He was more outrageous in the 1960s. Now he seems, if he were suddenly plunged into a contemporary academic novel, a familiar figure. 'So what's wrong with him?' would probably be the reader's attitude" (Int). Nicholas Birns has observed that Towne's "undersong is a profound commitment to high standards" ("Review of *Going*" 222) and, while he lauds the virtues of the intellectual life, Towne's literal actions continually relegate him to the gutter. An unfaithful and abusive husband, father, and friend, Towne repeatedly tries to justify himself by adopting what he believes to be innovative political and intellectual positions, which really are nothing more than poorly concealed, crude existential philosophies of insensitivity and extremism. A corresponding precursor to his general style are the satirical writings of Calder Willingham, who, for example, in "What Is Rape?" urges, "Rapee, mend your ways and instead of lying in a ditch, bloody and unconscious, stand on your feet and look at the world with a courageous eye in which there is serenity and respect for your own soul" (108–9). Shocking as it is, this is just the kind of advice Towne might easily advocate (and probably will at some point) in a similar style. Although the dark, vicious humor Towne employs alternately evokes laughter and consternation, it does have a serious point. Garrett has lamented the veiled censorship of a critical climate in which "fictional characters must not be allowed to maintain views, prejudices, or, indeed, use words which offend stereotypical contemporary standards. Or if they do so, they must be known to be unredeemably wicked and must be *punished* for their sins" (*MSP* 51, Garrett's emphasis). Cheerfully waggling his tongue in the face of this accepted practice, Towne repeatedly slithers away from the crimes and offenses he has committed, perhaps slightly bruised or chastened but still bursting with inextinguishable lust and folly.

In a review of John Barth's *Giles Goat-Boy*, Garrett remarked, "Since both the form and content, the subject and its treatment, are riddled with ambiguity, doubt, and contradiction—deliberately so, for that is the essential burden of this remarkable novel—it is extremely difficult to write about *Giles Goat-Boy*" (*MSP* 223). Like Barth's novel, *Poison Pen* contains disclaimers from different people (the pathetic scholar Dr. Holmes, publisher Stuart Wright, and

Garrett himself) and the discovery of a lost manuscript (Towne's footlocker full of scribbled gibberish), all conspiring to tease and confound the reader's quest for meaning. And to a significant degree the book's overall message and effect depends on literal reader choices. For example, at one point Garrett strongly urges readers not to read his letter to Christie Brinkley. Having made the readerly decision to respect that request, I cannot comment on that section of the book. This situation also is exacerbated by the fact that Towne, like the protagonists in such memorable works as Willingham's "The Eternal Rectangle" and R. V. Cassill's *Clem Anderson*, is a highly unique writer, constantly manipulating the language and appearance of the events Garrett feeds him. In one of his reviews Garrett has asserted, "Generally speaking, novels about writers, even when produced by very good writers, leave a lot to be desired" ("Author" 6), and at least part of the reason for this is the writer-character's conflicting relationship with the author of the book. As Garrett remarks in his essay "The Lost Brother," Towne's "habit is to say what he pleases—not necessarily what he thinks" (*BMB* 196), which underscores how Towne's deceitful nature, beyond his relationship with Garrett, makes many of his assertions at odds with his genuine beliefs—a further cause for interpretive confusion.

Looking back on his experience with Towne, Garrett asserts that for all his negative qualities, "Towne has been a good and faithful companion, even if he is, like the human heart, desperately wicked and faithless to everyone and everything except for himself and his private, primitive hungers" (*BMB* 197). Abstracting the companionship theme to another level, one sometimes detects Towne's presence lurking in Garrett narratives where he is not literally named. For example, in the story "To Guess the Riddle, to Stumble on a Secret Name" (1992), a piece in a collection coedited by Garrett and Susan Stamberg, the unmistakable odor of Jack Towne surrounds a character named Mark, who is "full of misery and mischief, and he likes to share it with other people" (61). Aspects of Towne's personality also appear in the eccentric, skirt-chasing professor Moe Katz and the writer Billy Tone in the novel *The King of Babylon Shall Not Come against You*. At the outset of his review of John Updike's *Rabbit at Rest*, Garrett remarked that "When a writer lives with and writes about a character in four books and for more than thirty years, as John Updike has done with Harry ('Rabbit') Angstrom—central character of *Rabbit at Rest* and of the quartet that began with *Rabbit, Run* in 1960—author and character get to know each other, strengths and weaknesses, good habits and bad, like an old married couple" (*MSP* 298). Like Updike and Rabbit, Garrett and Towne have come to know each other thoroughly, to the point that Towne now openly talks about Garrett in pieces that begin with conventional accounts of Towne. In a remarkable twist, this technique seems to have humanized Towne in a way that was impossible while he remained imprisoned within traditional narratives. Freed to talk about his relationship with Garrett, Towne conveys, sometimes movingly, his fears and regrets to the reader. Much earlier, Garrett had attempted to humanize Towne in an unpublished story from the 1960s called "Sing Me a Love Song": "Jack Towne is, of course, not the man he seems. He is not even the man he knows and he goes to any length to hide it from himself. Behind the mask of empty-headed, smiling, garrulous, easy-going Jack is a frightened child. A primitive being in a hostile world of totem, taboo, and nameless, hostile forces." Though this dimension of Towne's character would not become readily apparent for almost forty years, it does much to reveal his true character and the interaction of his more superficial qualities and deeds with a culture and world that push individuals toward acts of genuine evil.

A figure whom readers love to hate but sometimes venerate in spite of themselves, Towne remains for Garrett "that wild prodigal whom I love" (*Luck's Shining Child* 3), straying across moral, political, and narrative boundaries with an abandon that often invites censure, laughter, and ridicule; but is accompanied, every now and again, by a vague sense of affinity and even admiration. The grand figure of Garrett's academic writings, Towne exhibits characteristics of Garrett's earlier scholar/writer figures while transcending all of them with his fully developed and highly unique persona and background. A walking, talking apotheosis of Garrett's tenuous relationship with the academy, Towne shocks us into mirth and outrage even as his shadowy subtext seriously indicts the more wanting aspects of higher education and the culture that surrounds us.

"Which Ones Are the Enemy?"

The Military Writings of George Garrett

"Which ones are the enemy?" he yelled. "Jesus Christ, Riche!
Which ones are the freaking enemy?"
—Garrett, *Which Ones Are the Enemy?*

The question "Which ones are the enemy?" is one that military personnel and their beleaguered fictional projections find themselves asking again and again, across time, in numerous scenarios—even with regard to their commanding officers. Referencing such archetypal themes, writers of military fiction like Garrett seek to abstract their narratives beyond immediate historical events and into an arena where their ambivalent underpinnings are laid bare as timeless variables of military existence and war, as relevant to the night-vision-goggled American infantryman in Iraq as to the confused, terrified helot fleeing before a Spartan advance. Garrett has said of war writing, "Clearly a crippling of some kind has taken place if it is necessary for each generation to begin at the beginning of human experience and, in spite of all previous knowledge and experience, to suffer the same series of shocks and disillusionments" ("The Literature" 509). Attempting to capture the relevant universal qualities of military life, Garrett's fiction works toward an understanding of recurring philosophical motifs rather than tunnel-visioned explanations of isolated martial experiences.

Garrett relates humanity's timeless archetypal interest in war to our most base inner urges: "It is enormously appealing. . . . People love the excitement of being at risk and the pleasure of killing other people . . . it comes with the animal, I think" (*GSE* 141). The unfortunate and sometimes perverse immediacy of war to the human experience results in its constantly having a profound influence on culture, artistic and otherwise. In *James Jones*, his biography of the popular World War II writer, Garrett observes, "The story and direction of our literature has changed, even as our national life, our *way of life*, has changed—sharply, perhaps radically—since World War II" (14, Garrett's emphasis). Though it specifically points to the powerful culture-shaping influence of the Second World War, Garrett's assertion is applicable to almost any historical conflict on some level, the repercussions of which often have formidable effects beyond the generation of those who actively experience the altercation. Meditating on the haunting quality of World War I, Paul Fussell observed the "obsession with the images and myths of the Great War among novelists and poets too young to have experienced it directly. They have worked it up by purely literary means, means which necessarily transform the war into a 'subject' and simplify its motifs into myths and figures expressive of the modern existential predicament" (321). Whether wanting for their lack of genuine experience or valuable for their more distant perspectives (or perhaps a little of both), military accounts related by authors removed from the event by a generation or more none-theless underscore the far-reaching and evolving repercussions (as much imaginary as real) of conflicts across time.

Speaking to the interrelatedness of different wars and their various repre-sentations, Garrett describes in a taped lecture the general tension between artist participants in separate conflicts and how that tension often gives rise to and is accompanied by changes in aesthetic form (*American Literature of World War II*). Having been on active duty during the Korean War, Garrett comments on this relationship with some authority and seems to have ex-perienced it himself in terms of his artistic relationship both to World War II and the Vietnam War. Writing about accounts of Vietnam in the 1990s, Garrett remarked, "[I] had logged too many hours of hearing and swapping tedious stories ('war stories,' we always ironically called them) with other G.I.'s not to be profoundly skeptical of a whole lot of what I heard from the next generation of soldier boys" (*MSP* 101). Though its specific historical variables differed from Korea, Vietnam held little fundamental difference for Garrett as an overall military phenomenon. In fact, in a 1965 notebook Garrett toyed with the idea of writing a "G.I. story" set in the context of the Vietnam War, in which the protagonist would "sense [the] decay and degen-eration of culture and [the] American Dream," a theme Garrett had earlier identified with post-World War II American culture. In abstracting universal cultural and military motifs to the milieus of different historical conflicts,

Garrett's approach resembles the technique of writers like William Hoffman, who in narratives such as "Night Sport" and *Tidewater Blood* removes
his own military experiences from 1940s Europe to Vietnam settings for the
sake of cultural relevance. As Hoffman explains, "I really feel that war is a
timeless universal. The only thing that changes are the cultural conditions
and outer accouterments: tactics, technology, uniforms, and so on. But the
central truth of it is the same in all wars. The reason I use Vietnam now is
the immediacy it has for readers, but the essence of war doesn't change"
(Clabough 85–86). Seeking to articulate the eternal aspects of war and the
military, writers such as Garrett and Hoffman have no problem with trans-
fusing their own genuine experiences and ideas into the given conflict of the
day, hoping that its contemporary pertinence will help compel readers to
delve toward the deeper truths lurking beneath it.

Even when a writer sets his story in the context of the most recent news-
worthy war, he still faces the formidable challenge of convincingly expressing perhaps the most horrifying phenomenon a human being can encounter.
As Garrett explains, "You can't duplicate the combat experience of war. The
movies can't do it. They can be noisy and scary, but that's about it" (Int). Part
of the problem with portraying war and even peacetime military life is the
fact that normal human and societal criteria rarely function. With this dynamic in mind, novelist Robert Bausch has characterized Garrett's military
fiction as a "world of lunatic order" (9). Though a regimented authoritarian
structure exists, it is one that often appears, especially to the civilian reader,
devoid of logic and meaning—a kind of method of madness: the now-pro-
verbial "catch-22." Whereas the soldier may have his doubts about the structure as well, it is an unavoidable edifice that almost inevitably takes over his
own habits and thought processes. Writing about his military service in his
notebooks, Garrett explains that it was due to "a combination of G.I. hair-
cuts, the rubbing tightness of a steel helmet, nerves and fear, bad food, dirt
and so forth . . . I lost my strength . . . and with it my interest in the church.
Any church." Influenced by the persistently numbing and banal lifestyle of
army existence, Garrett abdicated any concern for conventional religion, its
organization and customs being largely irreconcilable with the system and
rituals of army life.

The breaking down of civilian edifices of order and belief, while sometimes leaving the soldier in an interpretive limbo, occasionally affords him
a new freedom of realistic association, sharpened by the nearness of danger
and death, that enables him to imagine in great detail the lives of other military participants—comrade and enemy, enlisted man and officer, victimized
civilian, and so on. Referencing this idea of fluid identity in Garrett's work,

writer David Madden has remarked, "[T]he army stories are so memorable for me because the author could be, in the army, one of at least two; when he could not, he empathized himself into being a participant in the crowd" (48–49). Whereas many of the most celebrated novels of the American military—*From Here to Eternity* and *Catch-22*, to name but two—interpret experience predominantly from the perspective of the enlisted man, often at the expense of demonizing officers, Garrett's narratives generally are more ambivalent, presenting various tiers of the military equation with objective understanding. As Fred Chappell has noted, Garrett "is one of the few writers of military fiction who sympathizes with the officer as well as the enlisted man" (Chappell, "Fictional" 71), a quality he shares with James Gould Cozzens, who in *Guard of Honor* produced arguably the most convincing fictional depiction of officer interaction and military bureaucracy in the history of American literature. Mentioning *Guard of Honor* himself, Garrett has suggested his preference for what he calls "indirect" military narratives, those that attempt to get at the essence of military life through nuanced considerations of some of its more overlooked, unpopular, and trivialized aspects. He maintains that

> I don't know what constitutes good military fiction. I do believe that some of the finest pieces have been very indirect. One of the great novels of World War II is *Guard of Honor* and there's no combat in it. It's all about the military hierarchy. One of the best World War II films which covers the immediate post-war period is *Tunes of Glory* with Alec Guinness. It's about a regiment in Scotland and the transition from war to peace. The men are being sent home and the regiment is falling apart. At one time I wanted to do a little piece on two stories, J. D. Salinger's "For Esmé—With Love and Squalor" and one by Peter Taylor ["Rain in the Heart"]. (Int)

Salinger's memorable story follows a veteran in post-World War II New York City and Taylor's a group of pre-World War II trainees in the South. Although Salinger and Taylor both saw substantial combat during their military stints, they eschew battlefield narratives in their work for the more subtle shades of pre- and post-war dynamics of identity. Combat surrenders the stage to the complexities of people living their lives shortly before and after it, with hauntingly favorable results.

Much of Garrett's military fiction, like the stories of Salinger and Taylor, focuses on the dynamics of noncombat or peacetime military existence, suggesting some of the more universal aspects of soldiering in a very indirect manner. In one of his earliest published stories, "In Other Countries" (1956),

Garrett portrays the relationship of two enlisted men from opposite ends of the civilian social ladder: a college-educated man from New York and a barely literate Tennessean. Their relationship is best characterized by a remark Garrett makes in his notebooks: "They are the kind of curious friends the system of the Army creates, men who might never have met otherwise, men whose lives and backgrounds are utterly different." At the center of the story is a meditation on the ways in which civilian structures break down in the face of shared military rank and a jointly traumatic field experience. After the two men are nearly run over in the night by a wayward tank, the narrator recounts:

> This was the accident, the sudden equalizing force of fear and the feeling that death had been near to both of us, that made Harry and me buddies. It just happened. We didn't have to think about it or even be self-conscious about it; we were just friends from that instant. There was nothing to talk about anyway. Both of us had participated equally in an awful, incommunicable experience. Both of us, in a sense, felt that we owed our lives to the other" (293).

Having mutually experienced a traumatic, life-threatening event, the two men suddenly become brothers—beyond all considerations of civilian background, class, and education—in a way that is both powerful and "incommunicable."

Reflecting the influential though often overlooked dynamic of military bureaucracy, the protagonists of "In Other Countries" are thrown together simply because the first letters of their last names are the same. Correspondingly, in an untitled, unpublished story Garrett employs a character named David Barnstone who experiences a number of unusual experiences in the army simply because his last name places him at or near the head of most lines. In "The Other Side of the Coin" (1957) Garrett abstracts this concept of regulation-based chance to a more tragic level, highlighting the ridiculousness of military procedure in the midst of death through the doomed figure of Lieutenant Austin, a young flier whose self-destructive irrationality reflects the general chaos of World War II. A formidable pilot whose on-the-ground antics exasperate his superiors, Austin eventually earns the grudging respect of the narrator, Captain Pierce:

> In a way I began to like him, to sympathize with him because it seemed to me that we were all living strangely in what was not much more then a series of disconnected adventures. On the other hand, to be truthful, I envied him too, because I thought he had possession of something

which the rest of us had lost somewhere. I'm not sure what it was, unless (to make a guess) it was a kind of innate ability to see himself and the wide world without taking either very seriously. (25)

Possessing a youthful, boyish appearance, Austin functions as a kind of cherubic trickster figure, underscoring the absurd meaninglessness of off-duty military regulations to an individual who regularly risks death. His propensity for getting drunk, wrecking trucks, and punching out officers seems minor when he eventually meets his end in the air, and much of his erratic earthbound behavior seems to manifest itself as a kind of coping mechanism for the constant danger he faces while flying. As Pierce tells the teetotaling colonel, "Maybe the boy's crazy. I don't know. I'm almost forty now, and I've forgotten what the world looked like at twenty. I do know it would have seemed like a damned crazy world if I had to do the things these kids are doing" (26). Thrown into a milieu where people ceaselessly are trying to kill him, the young Austin often has trouble abstracting his stressful and unpredictable duty in the clouds from the mundane, rule-laden life on the ground, which appears both silly and absurd in the context of the dangers he constantly faces while flying.

One of Garrett's favorite war novels, Stephen Becker's *When the War Is Over*, is a largely factual narrative based on the execution of a twelve-year-old boy arrested for being a Confederate guerrilla. Not considered a threat by any of his captors, the boy is nonetheless executed out of malice in the wake of Lincoln's assassination well after the war has concluded. The seemingly heartless and even meaningless role of military bureaucracy and unequivocal regulations in the midst of human courage and loss that appear in narratives like "The Other Side of the Coin" and *When the War Is Over* suggest Jeffrey Walsh's observation that "[s]ince war is demonstrably the most pointless and destructive of all human activities it frequently inculcates in the front-line writer a feeling of existential loss and disorientation, a dawning awareness that the exemplary sacrifice of troops is meaningless and utterly futile" (3). Overwhelmed by the terrible relationship between strategic decisions and real human expenditure, military writers who are also veterans approach and represent concepts like courage with attitudes that range from reserved caution to outright cynicism.

Not one to ignore the horrors and ambiguities of military service, Garrett investigates a number of problematic scenarios in his fiction. In "The Blood of Strangers" (1957) an American veteran of World War II named Peter returns to post-war Austria on vacation with his shallow wife, Louise, whom the narrator describes as "pretty, petulant" (*KM* 109). Forsaking their established tourist itinerary, Peter insists that they drive out into the Austrian countryside. Although he does not inform Louise of his intentions, Peter is searching for the spot where he had raped a local girl during the war. In contrast to this buried horrific act, Louise remarks that in his army photograph Peter had looked "so young and sweet and funny" (*KM* 112), producing a confused ambience of chronology and ambiguity in the story. Louise's naive and spoiled American demeanor balances that of the victimized, war-suffering Austrian girl just as the lucrative post-war American boom that allows Peter and Louise to take grand international vacations counters the surreal hardness and brutality of the country at war. From his prosperous rational perch looking back, Peter recalls that "place and time were vague, distorted . . . nothing made much sense" (*KM* 110). Unable to reconstruct his wartime identity or even the time and place of his crime, Peter remains frustrated at his inability to reconcile his private horrific past with his identity in the present.

Similar incidents that focus on the implications of overseas military men abusing women appear in a number of Garrett's other stories. In "Don't Take No for an Answer" (1956) a surly G.I. named Stitch relates his elaborate hustle of a plain-looking, vacationing American woman while on leave in Paris. Although Stitch conveys his seduction in heartless, misogynistic terms, he remains attractive as an adept breed of story-telling antihero. In his notes for the dramatic version of the story, Garrett remarked that Stitch is "complex. He is a loner and the others don't *like* him really, but he has a kind of hold over them and people. Partly it is his ability to act and tell a story. Partly, it is his ambiguity" (Garrett's emphasis). Despite the fact that he seems to have performed a questionable act, misleading and then dumping the naive American woman, Stitch remains compelling to his male military audience, mostly because he "could always tell a good story" (*KM* 77). Any moral considerations are ignored in the face of the men's desire to hear an interesting tale related in fine detail, which breaks the overpowering monotony of their lives in the barracks. As Stitch maintains, "I felt kind of bad, not real bad" (*KM* 83), his feelings about the event being subordinate both to the apparent success of his literal actions and his skillful recounting of them.

Writing about the post-World War II American military in the 1990s, Garrett noted the fundamental shift in the role of the American soldier:

> The new thing (already old now in my lifetime) was the sending forth of American citizen soldiers all over the world where, quite aside from their duties, just by being there they came to know foreign people and languages and cultures, in bits and pieces, true, but more closely than

even they could have imagined. We had been strictly local and were now bound to be global. (*OAG* xviii)

Thrown into other cultures where their presence was met with a whole range of positive and negative reactions, post-World War II American soldiers frequently found themselves participating in intimate cultural narratives well beyond the scopes of their jobs and country. For example, in the vignette "The Art of Courtly Love"—from the short story "What's the Purpose of the Bayonet?" (1957)—the narrator, an American soldier, shacks up with a Czechoslovakian war refugee named Inge. Although he knows she does not love or even like him very much, the narrator regularly bombards her with material goods she cannot afford herself, to the point that she comes to rely on his support and allows him to live with her. Stubbornly refusing to recognize his own complicity, the narrator becomes enraged when he discovers that she is in love with a local German man, destroying everything in her apartment and threatening to report her to the police as a prostitute. Exploiting his colonizing presence in a foreign culture, the narrator preys on the poverty of Inge's local community while selfishly refusing to acknowledge her natural preference for a member of her own culture.

Not all of Garrett's culture-bearing stories center around the invasive role of the American military in a foreign country, many of them choosing instead simply to reflect the strange inner workings of a foreign local community or life on an overseas military base. For example, the vignette "Torment," the final military anecdote from "What's the Purpose of the Bayonet?," recounts the severe beating of local prostitutes by Austrian police. Unable to stop prostitution, especially with the nearby presence of the American military inevitably fueling the business, the police periodically gather together as many hookers as possible and flog them severely, brutally mauling them without any real hope that the punishment will make them change their lifestyle. Witnessing this hellish, chaotic spectacle, the story's narrator, an American serviceman, remarks, "In back rooms, in hidden corners, behind blank smiles, all over the world people are suffering and making other people suffer. The things God has to see because He cannot shut his eyes! It's almost too much to think about. It's enough to turn your stomach against the whole inhuman race" (*KM* 143). Unable to interpret what he sees in terms of Austrian society or his military background, the narrator abstracts the event to the meaningless cruelty of all humanity, a dynamic that freely and consistently crosses all cultural barriers.

The prevalence with which military culture ushers in, either directly or indirectly, casual, absurd brutality reveals itself through a number of unlikely avenues and figures. For example, in "Crowfoot," an anecdote collected in *The Old Army Game* (1994) but written much earlier, a group of men shoot up a portion of their base after having their passes pulled at the last minute. Long after the rest of the men have given themselves up to base authorities, a Native American named Crowfoot continues to hold out by himself, periodically spraying the ground with his BAR (Browning automatic rifle) when anyone attempts to advance on his position. After his sergeant, who is also the story's narrator, succeeds in persuading him to surrender, Crowfoot stands up and, despite all promises to the contrary, is promptly shot. The narrative action of Crowfoot's purposeless death, coming on the tail of an equally irrational action by his peers, is mirrored amid a Korean War setting in "Heroes." More ridiculous than Crowfoot in both his appearance and actions, the story's protagonist, Floogie, is described as "goofy looking. Clumsy as a bear cub. Couldn't do much of anything right" (*OAG* 314). The scourge and brunt of his outfit, Floogie constantly separates himself from his brother soldiers in an effort to avoid the constant hassles of ridicule and bad camp assignments. Removed from the other men, Floogie keeps sleeping when his unit withdraws from a position during the night and awakes to find a strong contingent of Chinese advancing on him. Thinking his comrades are still around him, Floogie puts up a valiant fatal fight, which the rest of his unit can hear more than a mile away. Listening to Floogie's firing, the narrator imagines "Floogie crawling around the position in the dark. Feeling for his buddies and not finding anybody" (*OAG* 319). Killed while single-handedly defending his position, Floogie becomes an unlikely hero. A modern knight in fool's clothing, he proves his mettle when death is imminent.

In the vignette "How the Last War Ended," a section from the story "Comic Strip" (1957), two opposing captains discuss "the utter absurdity of defeat" and "the marvelous shrug of the surviving" (*KM* 101). Against the accidental and incidental losses of people like Crowfoot and Floogie, military personnel who have endured such expenditures repeatedly find themselves meditating on these largely archetypal topics. Winning and losing, death and survival, are met with ambivalence and a weary "shrug," the process of achieving whatever end fate has dealt them having worn the participants to a perspective of uneasy doubt or, worse, apathy. Revealing the significance of the title "Comic Strip," Madison Smartt Bell explains, "Garrett evolved what he calls the 'comic strip' principle of narrative design as a way of arranging material that lacks conventional linear continuity. . . . the relationships between panels can just as well be imagistic or thematic" (325). With their temporal and thematic ambiguity, war and military narratives are ideal and frequent candidates for the comic strip technique, forsaking thematic closure and narrative resolution for brief and sometimes fragmented snapshots of archetypal military dynamics.

Whereas Garrett locates his military fiction in different time periods and contexts, many of his comic strips and more traditional military narratives take place against a specific backdrop: the camp of the Nth Field Artillery. A fictionalized projection of his own artillery regiment in post-World War II Eastern Europe, the Nth appears among Garrett's earliest military writings—unpublished stories such as "One More Tattoo"—in which he experimented with and practiced a number of different styles and voices as means of successfully relating the military experience. In "Hooray for the Old Nth Field," a comic strip section from "What's the Purpose of the Bayonet?" (1957), the narrator says of the outfit, "It's amazing how all the misfits, deadbeats, eightballs, VD cases, alcoholics, and walleyed, knockkneed, stockade-bait suddenly turned out to be trained artillerymen" (*KM* 127–28). Whereas figures like Crowfoot and Floogie constitute memorable individual antiheroes, the Nth seems to comprise a kind of collective antihero army, the acknowledged garbage dispenser/hotbed for all the American military's problems. However, with that identity comes a singular resignation and toughness that results in a peculiar esprit de corps. While offering up a kind of lengthy mock-prayer, the narrator gets close to the essence of his unit:

> Save me, Lord, from companies and battalions of well-adjusted, deadserious, clean-cut, boy-scout, post-office-recruiting poster soldiers. Deliver me from mine enemies, West Point officers with spitshined boots and a tentpole jammed up their rectums. . . . Save me from good people, on a piece of graph paper, percentage-wise. Give me the bottom of the barrel, men who still have themselves to laugh at and something real to cry about, who, having nothing to lose and being victims of the absurd dignity of the human condition, can live with bravado at least, and, if they have to die, can die with grace like a wounded animal. (*KM* 130)

Ridiculing the pomp of military class and appearance—neatness, West Point rigidity, paper-laden statistical efficiency—the narrator celebrates his preference for real soldiers with genuine human problems and gifts. Often down-and-out and wanting in both discipline and demeanor, the Nth nevertheless takes pride in its visceral authenticity, stubbornly celebrating its flawed, hard-scrabble humanity against the sterile regimentation of military culture.

Appearing under various names and guises in several narratives, the Nth receives its most thorough treatment in Garrett's second novel, *Which Ones*

Are the Enemy? (1961), which is narrated by a hard-luck enlisted man named John Riche, a Korea veteran and self-nominated prospect for "the Congressional Medal for Losers" (*WOE* 3) who finds himself stationed in Trieste. A kind of Nth everyman, Riche, according to Garrett, "conceals his virtue behind a screen of vices" (*GSE* 139). Like the Nth itself, Riche buries his legitimate attributes behind his half-assed practices of gambling, whoring, drug-dealing, and generally working the army system, which has led Garrett to characterize him as "a variation of the unreliable narrator. You can't take his opinion as being wholly accurate" (*GSE* 139). Yet, this is an inevitable dilemma all narrators demonstrate to greater or lesser degrees on some level. As Garrett says of James Gould Cozzens's World War II novel *Guard of Honor*, "The form of narration, with all events filtered through a single center of consciousness, creates its own pattern and its own difficulties" (*"By"* 43). However, whereas *Guard of Honor* constitutes a high-minded, intricate meditation on the concept of ethical duty, channeled through the impressions of a intelligent army officer who is also a civilian lawyer, *Which Ones Are the Enemy?* is related through the largely uneducated, enlisted sensibility of Riche. Riche's rough, conversational dialogue also possesses a peculiar air of spontaneity, possibly stemming from the fact that Garrett composed the novel in "about two weeks or so" (*GSE* 139). In fact, when Garrett submitted the manuscript, one editor accused him of having pilfered someone else's work, its tone and appearance being so radically different from his previous stories or his highly descriptive, meditative first novel, *The Finished Man*.

The ambling, colloquial narrative style of a delinquent narrator that Garrett chose for the book was not without precedent, suggesting a variation on Mac Hyman's technique in his wonderful picaresque World War II novel *No Time for Sergeants*, which anticipated such memorable World War II satires as William Hoffman's *Yancey's War* and Joseph Heller's *Catch-22* in its hilarious indictment of military culture. Yet, the action of *Which Ones Are the Enemy?* is more traditionally dramatic than it is satirical, and Riche's rough comparisons often convey his own situation and that of the proverbial military outcast with a clarity that outshines highly refined, descriptive narratives. For example, when Riche explains his fondness for the cuckoo bird, he remarks, "They say it's a dirty bird and a thief and all. I couldn't have cared less. What he does with himself is his business. It was his cry or his song or whatever it was that seemed like it was my language. And you never saw one. At least I never did. You could only hear him, here, there, and then gone again like a ghost" (*WOE* 29). Simplistically rolling up his own difference, independence, and remoteness into the personality of the bird, Riche reveals much about himself, especially in relation to "they," the military and the world at large which view beings like the bird and himself as "a dirty bird and a thief and all." Although Riche has plenty to worry about and consistently makes his situation even more precarious, he views the adversity of life with a resigned, happy-go-lucky attitude, maintaining, "Whenever I feel like putting the blame on something I can always blame my good luck" (*WOE* 79). In a preface to an early unpublished version of the book Garrett remarked that "soldiers tend to make 'mistakes' that a more rational man in a more casual society would not." Deprived of freedom and many of the other pleasures of civilian life, military personnel often find themselves pressing the boundaries of regulations and good sense in an effort to make their lives more bearable and humane.

Although Riche's personal dilemmas remain front and center throughout the book, they often serve as springboards for deeper observations concerning military history. When Riche has a conversation with Fishbein about World War II novels, he not only reveals a deeply concealed penchant for self-education but an engagement with military experience beyond the scope of his own enlistment. Fishbein maintains that between their contemporary comrades and the soldiers in World War II novels "there's one big difference. All those characters in the old prewar, peacetime Army were different in one way. None of them had been in a war. Almost all of you guys have been shot at. Some of you, like Ryder and Mooney and Loller, say, have been in *two* wars. That makes a hell of a difference" (*WOE* 189, Garrett's emphasis). Referencing the large-scale deployment of World War II and Korea veterans in the post-war era, Fishbein contrasts their own more jaded and realistic perspective on combat and service versus the naive outlook of personnel just before the Second World War. In fact, the novel's title serves as a kind of reference to this shift in the American military. On the verge of an engagement during the Korean War a green officer character named Lieutenant Huff is unable to tell the difference between northern and southern Korean soldiers, frantically asking Riche, "which ones are the enemy?" (*WOE* 124). Of course, the implications of his question go well beyond Huff's imminent engagement and the Koreans. As George Core has pointed out, "The enemy is everywhere" (xii), pervading the opposing combatants, fellow soldiers, chain of command, and even oneself—a metaphor for the ambiguity and senselessness of war. For Garrett's part, he conceptualizes the "enemy" as the abstract historical phenomenon of peacetime military: "There is no real enemy. There is only the Cold War. There are the inescapable facts of routine, training, spit and polish and boredom, the hurry up and wait of peacetime army duty." Perceived as being devoid of any legitimate meaning or identity, the general military becomes the enemy. In fact, Riche experiences an unusual cross-rank affinity with his captain since he thinks of him, like himself, as "another loser in the old army game" (*WOE* 14). Garrett elaborates on "the old army game" in a story of the same name which appeared the same year as *Which Ones Are the Enemy?* Following two recruits who come to outrank their cruel, hard-army drill instructor, the tale mocks military rank and identity while also portraying the powerful hold it establishes on certain individuals. As Sachs tells Sergeant Quince, the army is "just a game, a stupid, brutal, pointless simple-minded game" (*CG* 16). Sachs gloats since he believes he has won the game, but Quince, for whom the army provides his only sense of identity, begins to cry, since Sachs has taken "everything away" (*CG* 16) from him through his belittlement of the system of being to which Quince has dedicated his life.

As Sachs's behavior demonstrates, the occasional cynicism and humor that inform the old army game often are of a perverse variety, and Garrett pursues this idea further in a number of stories that interrogate domestic military cultural issues and the tension between civilian and military mores. In "The Wounded Soldier" (1964) a veteran with a horribly disfigured face attempts to readjust his identity in the context of civilian American society. Seeing his disfigured face for the first time in a mirror, he feels as if he has just been "born again" (*CG* 37). Mindful of the soldier's impact on civilian perceptions about the military, a high-ranking officer attempts to bribe him to stay in the hospital, fearing that his appearance in society might cause, in the soldier's words, "a considerable cooling of patriotic ardor" (*CG* 39). From the point of view of military culture, the soldier presents a serious problem of representation. The soldier rhetorically tells the visiting officer, "It would have been so much more convenient if I had simply died" (*CG* 40). Yet, the soldier is curious about life beyond the military hospital and eventually re-enters the civilian world, albeit with a mask to cover his face. As the soldier discovers for himself, there is no place in society for a person with his variety of wounds and background, and he resigns himself to one of the few professions that celebrate grotesque difference: the circus. Only in that arena is his appearance acceptable and the people are free to laugh at him, since it is what they are expected to do. Yet the audience's laughter is not that of warm, genuine humor but rather a nervous reflexive mechanism against something they cannot fully confront or absorb. As the narrator points out, "[A] man is just as likely to giggle when he meets his executioner as he is to melt" (*CG* 41–42). Unable to account for the soldier's wound, the civilian audience dismisses it with laughter, even as the emotion that triggers their thin merriment points to something darker and more disturbing within themselves.

In "Unmapped Country" (1964) a more subtle conflict between military and civilian methods of interpretation emerges when an officer drives out to the eastern Tennessee backcountry to give a father the details of his son's death. Standing as a roadblock to this task is the difference between the officer's acute military language and the father's uneducated, agrarian culture. An even more marked cultural conflict informs "Texarkana Was a Crazy Town," (1964) which focuses on the friendship between Mooney, an African American soldier/character who also appears in *Which Ones Are the Enemy?*, and the unnamed narrator. In *Which Ones Are the Enemy?* Riche describes Mooney as "naturally pissed off about being born black" (*WOE* 45), which on the surface appears racist but actually turns out to be a form of gentle teasing, since Mooney is one of the few people in the book Riche genuinely admires as a soldier and a person. The narrator of "Texarkana Was a Crazy Town" also has a high opinion of Mooney, who seems to know the narrator's mind better than the narrator. When the speaker resolves to leave the army, Mooney prophetically tells him, "You don't know anything else but the army" (*CG* 127). Mooney also has affected the narrator in more subtle ways. When he discovers that his new civilian employer and coworkers have assaulted a mildly retarded African American man named Peanuts, the narrator beats up his boss and returns to the army—actions that have larger cultural connotations. As Garrett explains, "Service was already the destiny of the poor even before, again out of pure political fear, the American Army was returned to its earlier status as Regular. But before all that, from the days of World War II through much of the time of the Cold War, the service, the Army, even with all its elaborate hierarchy and rank and privileges, was the great democratic equalizer" (*OAG* xviii). Conceptualizing Mooney and Peanuts as human beings without reference to their race, the narrator of "Texarkana Was a Crazy Town" embodies the post-World War II army's practice of "democratic equalizing," lashing out against the racially motivated beating. At the end of the story, when he returns to the room that he and Mooney share, he asks his friend, "[H]ow come you're so black?" (*CG* 144), to which Mooney responds with laughter, their friendship being devoid of many of the tensions that would inform a similar relationship in civilian life.

Following his flurry of military fiction published between the late 1950s and mid-1960s, Garrett would move away from definitively military narratives, his references to martial life appearing in small anecdotes such as Moses's service flashback in *Do, Lord, Remember Me* (1965), Jojo Royale's war stories in *The King of Babylon Shall Not Come against You* (1996), and various sections from Garrett's Elizabethan novels. However, although the references to military life generally are spare, they often are character-shaping and carry with them repercussions for the larger work. As Moses relates:

> Lucky or not, I am alive and am still breathing. I learned then, knew
> and know still a few things worth knowing. I know that pain is bad
> and life is precious. I grieve not for the fallen any more than I ask
> them to grieve for me. . . . over those wide fields, through trees and
> deadly streets of villages, towns and cities I ran and I run still, bent
> low, forward, not backward, holding my weapon, until my time comes.
> (*DLR* 174)

For Moses his past life and the value of his existence in the present are irrevocably wedded by his experiences in the army and the memory of his dead comrades. Just as the specter of his life-changing past continues to haunt Moses, so Garrett eventually began moving away from fictional military narratives toward autobiographical accounts of his own time in the military. In "The Tanks," a piece from *Whistling in the Dark* (1992), this transition becomes altogether palpable as Garrett describes a story he would have written about a forced march by reservists. Relating the details of the piece, Garrett's memory and his planned fictional elements blur as he articulates an autobiographical march he endured while serving as a reservist.

In the title narrative of *Whistling in the Dark*, perhaps Garrett's most powerfully intimate piece of military writing, fiction is forsaken altogether for the autobiographical recounting of Austrians who fought for Germany during World War II being returned from Siberia in the 1950s. A young enlisted man in Austria, Garrett listens to a *Gasthaus* owner's own internment account beforehand but remains unimpressed—"young and strong and (as yet) undefeated," he cannot "seriously imagine surrendering to anybody" (*WD* 13). However, the ironies and hard lessons of history are closer about him than he initially imagines. As it turns out, it is to the very same *Gasthaus* where he is drinking that a young Adolf Hitler, only a boy, would come to fetch beer for his father. In the poem "Some Enormous Surprises," the young Garrett/soldier figure reflects on Hitler as

> this little pale-faced boy,
> for whom [God] has arranged some enormous surprises,
> beyond any kind of imagining, even myself,
> drunk in this place, years from home, imagining it
> (*WD* 15)

Initiated into the place-bound complexities of history beyond his own time and country, the narrator can only wonder at its strange relation to himself.

Later, the immediacy of the connection becomes unavoidable and overpowering when he witnesses the Austrian prisoners of war returning from Siberia:

> I stand there knowing one thing for certain—that I am seeing our century, our time, close and truly. Here it is and, even among strangers, I am among them, sharing the moment of truth whether I want to or not.
>
> An American sergeant stands in the swirling crowd with tears rolling down his cheeks. He will be gone from here soon, first miles, then years and years away. But he will not, because he cannot, forget this movement or himself in it, his share of this world's woe and joy, the lament and celebration of all living things. (*WD* 17)

Moving from a position of youthful, present-bound indifference to one that recognizes the individual's irrevocable connection to human history everywhere, the young Garrett/narrator powerfully discovers his own tenuous relationship to time and human events, the crushing epiphany of which will stay with him forever.

The recognition of one's relationship to universal and timeless historical forces segues, almost inevitably, into an interest in one's family history. In "Uncles and Others" (1992), another autobiographical section from *Whistling in the Dark*, Garrett recounts his family's military involvement over the centuries as "usually paradoxical. Which is to say, even the most innocent and inexperienced of us, thanks to Tribal history, arrived wherever we were sent, that is wherever we had to go, almost without expectations or illusions. Which, in turn, means that we were usually spared the common experience of disillusionment" (*WD* 34). Citing the skepticism and resignation of other Garretts who have served, Garrett matches it to his own—a kind of cross-generational sensibility that recognizes history's ironies and contradictions, but does not inhibit Garretts from dutifully continuing to take part in them. Abstracted to another level, the Garrett family's historical relationship to military service is not unlike George Garrett's own identification with history. In "A Story Goes with It" (2002) he recounts several contrary historical perspectives on a group of World War II German saboteurs before concluding, "Based on official United States government documents and data, the actions taken (or not taken) by the FBI, the Coast Guard, the Justice Department, et al. are shown in the most favorable possible light" (677). However, Garrett ultimately gives greater credence to the largely undocumented version of Eddie Weems, who recounts blunder after blunder on behalf of the Germans and the American government, culminating in a shootout in which contingents of FBI agents fight it out, each believing that the other group is made up of Nazi spies. Which ones are the enemy? For Garrett, Weems's interpretation of history is closer to the reality he has experienced and knows. Furthermore, it is this very paradox of history and people's wide-ranging interpretations of it that continues to make Garrett's military fiction relevant. As Garrett once recounted in an interview, military writing is

> still applicable because of these last couple wars. Before they came along a lot of editors had a distinct dislike for military fiction. They might think you're endorsing military life or something. Plus, I've had younger editors tell me that they're not into doing historical fiction since my military stories take place before 1960, which is before they were born. I guess they are historical although I've never thought of them that way. (Int)

Recognizing the unintentional historical legacy of his own fiction in a genre that unfortunately regenerates its popularity and publishability with the arrival of military conflict, Garrett confirms his archetypal perspective on both the military and the writing that portrays it. Though the face of the enemy may change (and occasionally even resemble our own), we can be sure there always will be one, and for writers like Garrett the complexity and value of that lamentable eternal narrative is greater than the finite dynamics of a single conflict or campaign.

Time and Historical Fiction

The Elizabethan Novels

*The man who lives in the present—in his own present—lives to that ex-
tent in both the past and the future: the man who seeks to live elsewhere,
both as an artist and as a man, has deceived himself.*
—Wright Morris, *The Territory Ahead*

Much still remains unsettled with regard to how historical fiction constitutes a meaningful literary form. Andrew Lytle once criticized the term *historical novel*, since he believed it "implies that if the book is not all it ought
to be as fiction, the reader can fall back upon its history" (410). Lytle saw
historical literature as having its own built-in, double-tiered safety mechanism: should the writing and characterization disintegrate, readers may still
at least scan the pages for entertaining allusions to cultural fashions such
as the funny-looking clothes of the period at hand. Sharing Lytle's disdain
for this frequent practice, Lukács urges writers of historical fiction to avoid
it at all costs in his influential book *The Historical Novel*: "The historical
novel of our time, therefore, must above all negate, radically and sharply,
its immediate predecessor and eradicate the latter's traditions from its own
work" (350). Rather than employing tired historical methodology or piling
on quaint ephemera as means of salvaging literary value, Lukács's ideal work
of historical fiction should aspire to accomplish something new and different
with regard to its antecedents, as well as the period it has chosen: attempting
to move the genre forward by doing something "radically" distinct.

Part of the problem with the term *historical fiction* lies in the very nature of its two words, *historical* traditionally implying factual events and *fiction* carrying with it the connotation of a compelling, though ultimately made up, story. However, as Garrett points out, this dichotomy is not so neat as we would like it to be:

> Sometimes imaginary history, and at its heart an imaginary sense of place, not only haunts our lives with ghostly voices and echoes but is, finally, stronger, even more accurate than the cut, shuffled, and dealt world of hard facts. Having lived long enough, I have inevitably witnessed things, *experienced* them, that later, in the hands of others, as past history, were rearranged to suit the pleasure and purposes of "objective" observers, historians who, never deviating from factual "accuracy," nevertheless have turned the truth completely upside down. (*SE* 12, Garrett's emphasis)

Most historians, not unlike most literary scholars, are given to theories (polemics of their time) which seek to organize the events they confront into tidy, fashionable packages of meaning that may then be filed away among other events and/or under more general headings. In arbitrarily placing frameworks upon events, as opposed to allowing the events themselves to dictate the interpretive approach, many historians end up generating histories that strongly resemble polemical, narrative fiction. Bearing this in mind, it is important to note that "the model for [Garrett's] historical writing is Shelby Foote, who wrote what's probably the single biggest piece of prose narrative of our lifetime: the three-volume history of the Civil War" (Easton 40). Although Foote did not employ a conscious theoretical exegesis for his history, his prowess as a writer of prose, both nonfiction and fiction, was sufficient to make his work a model for Garrett's attempts at historical fiction. Furthermore, since he is a novelist as well as a historian, Foote constitutes a kind of fascinating, self-contained exemplar of both historical nonfiction and historical fiction. In fact, Garrett considers Foote's novel *Shiloh* "for my money the finest work of *fiction* of our time set in the Civil War" ("A Literary" 22, Garrett's emphasis). Elsewhere, in an essay on *Shiloh* and Mary Lee Settle's *All the Brave Promises* Garrett lauds the way in which the books' "blending of fact and fiction becomes a kind of alchemy, a gold model for other writers" ("The Best" 450, Garrett's emphasis). Conceiving of history and literature as important components, the volatile sulphur and quicksilver, in a formula that has the potential to produce a powerful aesthetic, Garrett believes in merging the two in an effort to get at the essence of experience, both historical and artistic.

If we agree with Lukács's assertion that historical fiction must strive to do something new in relation to its predecessors, we must then ask the question: what makes Garrett's historical writing distinct from the work of writers he admires, like Foote and Settle? The short answer to this question is: himself. As Garrett explains, "One of my reasons for thirty years of writing about the Elizabethans was to get away from writing autobiographical stuff. And I find, just by living long enough, that the man behind that curtain is, in fact, more revealed in those works that are nonautobiographical than in the stories when I was telling things that had really happened to me but could have happened to anybody" (*SE* 264). Looking back on his career, Garrett believes that the more he has shunned personal experience for historical abstraction, the more he actually has revealed of himself. He is not alone in this assumption. The writer Kelly Cherry has observed that Garrett's fiction "projects itself *into* time, as if time is a kind of space. What we are employing here is, of course, the powerful metaphor of incarnation. To assume a body and by means of it penetrate time is an act of love—it can't be performed by someone who is afraid or unaware of time" (16, Cherry's emphasis). For Cherry, Garrett's skillful ability to manipulate and authenticate fictional time is tied irrevocably to his visceral construction of time as a space and himself as a body. This successful technique of imagination, the joining of the abstract and the physical entity, results in a loving "incarnation" of genuine fiction.

Taken slightly further, Cherry's observation might work toward an articulation of Garrett using time, participating in it transcendentally, as a metaphor for the self. When asked about his treatment of history in *Death of the Fox* and *The Succession*, Garrett elaborates:

I think what I really meant to say there was something about time— something which is more evident in the second novel than in the first, although the first one is involved with memory. The second one has less organized memory than it does the kind of simultaneity. In both of them I was trying to deal in different ways with a variety of characters, some of whom really don't cause large things to happen in history but are a part of the whole picture. (quoted in R. H. W. Dillard, "George Garrett" [1983], 158)

Although Garrett is talking about the relationship between his characters and temporality, his point is also self-reflexive, indicting himself as both a weaver and participant in time, inside and outside of the novel. From the heart of Garrett's Elizabethan books, temporality subtly asserts itself, much as an author does, as the organizing force for meaningful action, and in taking the Elizabethan period as his historical milieu, Garrett embraced a culture uniquely given to the art of recounting and portraying human experience, both of its own time and others. As Garrett summarizes, "The Elizabethans left us a great imperishable gift of language—a language renewed, brightened and sweetened, richly decorated as never before or since" ("Daily Life" 231). An extraordinary era of rich language and innovative writers, the Elizabethan period, with its unique historical and aesthetic elements, helped to fuel Garrett's imaginative representation of it in the twentieth century. While writing *Death of the Fox*, Garrett came to the conclusion that "the proper subject and theme of historical fiction is what it is—the human imagination in action, itself dramatized as it struggles with surfaces, builds structures with facts, deals out and plays a hand of ideas, and most of all, by conceiving of the imagination of others, wrestles with the angel (Wallace Stevens's 'necessary angel') of the imagination" (*SFC* 34). In the midst of his grand scenarios, exhaustive historical details, and large casts of characters, Garrett's struggle essentially was reduced to one of the artistic self. For after all, the successful portrayal of huge masses of facts and events still hinges on the writer's successful establishment of an appropriate aesthetic.

When the writer Wright Morris warns that "The man who seeks to live elsewhere, both as an artist and as a man, has deceived himself" (230), he suggests the dangers of imaginary identity and historical fiction. This is also a pitfall Garrett recognizes and articulates at great length:

Beyond knowing, yet built on the foundation of it, is the challenge of imagining the past, giving back life and breath to the ghostly shapes of it that endure. To resurrect the past and to restore some life to it, we must first of all believe (and act on that belief) that those ghosts were once as alive as we are here and now, that they were, and therefore are, as we consider them, much the same as we are with all our aches and pains, joys and sorrows. Like us and yet . . . Perhaps the gravest temptation, leading directly to the gravest fallacy, arises from the paradoxical requirement; for we must, likewise and simultaneously, not allow ourselves the illusion that the ghosts of our own past, when alive and kicking, were really much like ourselves, like ourselves dressed up in funny costumes. Explorers of the past, to see it as truly as can be, must unburden themselves of many assumptions and concentrate on the differences, outward and visible, inward and spiritual, between themselves and ourselves. Failure to honor this obligation allows the past to become nothing more (or less) than a funhouse of mirrors replicating

in a multitude of grotesque and simplistic forms not our ancestors but
ourselves. ("News" 586)

On the one hand, historical writers must imagine as closely as possible the
culture and lives of their characters; on the other, they must possess enough
humility to realize that there likely will remain something essentially different and unknowable about people of that time and the largely alien world in
which they lived. To bring one's own cultural and philosophical predisposi-
tions to the historical period at hand is to stray into Morris's area of self-de-
ception, which usually results in caricatures and clichés rather than accurate
characters and meaningful revelations.

Garrett also realizes that another problem with writing historical fiction
stems from some of its more unfortunate popular associations as a genre. He
notes that

One minor problem is the continuing, if modest popularity of the
historical romance which is, after all, a kind of fantasy fiction, often
straining common credulity even more than either pure fantasy or science fiction. Essentially, and at its very best, the historical romance is
really about contemporary people, ourselves and our neighbors, all
decked out in funny costumes, talking an odd lingo and, no matter
whether set in sixth-century Constantinople or pre-Columbian Mexico, being aptly relevant to our own immediate crises and concerns.
("Young" 26)

Abstracting our own theories and fashions into the past, writing of this kind
accomplishes little beyond mocking our own culture and the unfortunate
historical civilization into which it is thrust. In an effort to make our stale,
culture-specific dilemmas seem both exotic and universal, they are removed
to an alien milieu. Garrett wished to avoid at all costs writing "relevant"
historical fiction, by which he meant fictional texts that choose and treat
their subject in terms of a contemporary socio-political issue or point of
view. For his representative type of this kind of writing, Garrett cites William Styron's *The Confessions of Nat Turner* as "a superb example of the cult
of 'relevance,' of timeliness" (*SFC* 23), its concern with racial unrest in 1830s
Virginia consciously designed and cleverly marketed to speak to and correspond with the controversial popularity of the issue in the 1960s. Garrett's
respect for the authenticity and even sacredness of past cultures also ruled
out satire as a vehicle for his historical fiction. He explains, "The firm assurance in either myself or the values of my own time necessary to satirize

another time was lacking" (*SFC* 25). Wary of the blindness and interpretive shortcomings of late-twentieth- and early-twenty-first-century culture, Garrett resolved to learn as much as he could about Elizabethan culture and to place himself there imaginatively with as much open-minded seriousness as he could muster—learning and interacting with the phenomena of that time on its own interpretive grounds.

Although Garrett realized he could never become an Elizabethan or imagine their time as it truly was, he aimed to capture what he identified as a "shared sense of authenticity, the mysterious collaborative process between writer and reader whereby fact and fiction come together, hand in glove, in a credible, if alien (sometimes fantastic) reality" ("The Survivor's" 5). If he could not bring real Elizabethans to the reader, Garrett at least hoped to present a "credible" vision of them, a task made more difficult by his "collaborative" relationship with the readers of our contemporary time. Foreseeing that his readers would struggle with comprehending an attempted authentic Elizabethan worldview, Garrett sought to couch his story in readable twentieth-century terms while also doing his best to remain as true as possible to the spirit of the historical times he was portraying. In his review of Ron Hansen's novel *The Assassination of Jesse James by the Coward Robert Ford*, Garrett says of Hansen, "Rather than waiting around a decade or two while a subject came looking for him, he found the subject of his first two novels—a late twentieth century view of the late nineteenth century (old) west" ("Review of *The Assassination*" 607). Like Hansen, Garrett found that he would have to pursue his project actively, learning all he could about his historical period and then bringing it convincingly to readers with little or no familiarity with it. Readily apparent here is the archetypal dilemma of the historical novelist, who at once must appear aesthetically and historically authentic, yet clear in the light of his own culture. He must live both in his own present and the present of the past, ranging across both times with an eye toward interpreting history for readers in his own time, while not reducing or explaining its complexities in the context of an alien present.

In his preface to an early version of *Death of the Fox* called "Stars Must Fall," Garrett employs a stream-of-consciousness section to portray his authorial self or a fictional projection of that self as "trapped I thrash against time and space dreaming a light long gone lost spent a time gone by hoping to summon up a company of ghosts and strangers." As Fred Chappell has noted, Garrett's feelings of confinement are passed on to his characters, who—not unlike novelists—are both victims of their times and ambassadors of its culture:

[N]one of Garrett's characters—none at least that I can remember—ever assents to the essential worthiness of the present order. It is merely the best thing, the only thing, that they know. They had no hand in creating present order, and they are powerless to change it in any significant degree. The toll that its guardianship exacts from them is excruciating, and their normal emotional states are those of overburdened weariness or, more rarely, searing outrage. They have been yoked to the heavy dung cart of history, sentenced by inner feelings of responsibility to pull it through the Slough of Despond before them, and they are always painfully aware of the injustice of a situation which they were born into and which they are deliberately defending in order to pass on to others. (Chappell, "Fictional" 74)

Trapped in their time and haunted by an awareness of their condition, which frequently waxes tragic, Garrett's Elizabethan characters nevertheless live their lives to the best of their relative abilities. Like the figures he imagined, Garrett too was struck with the task of living his aesthetic life—writing his historical books—even as history sought to spoil his invitation to its "ghosts and strangers." Garrett's feelings of entrapment also may have helped guide him toward the elderly biographical figure of Ralegh, imprisoned in the Tower with only his memories and the assurance of an imminent death. In fact, in one of his notebooks Garrett confessed that before he could know Ralegh, "first I acknowledge I must come to terms with myself," linking his own artistic dilemmas to the personal dynamics and circumstances of his protagonist. Fortunately, Ralegh also was in many ways representative of his age. As Garrett explains:

A complex, often enigmatic, roundly dimensional character, Ralegh teases and challenges our imaginations even as his story, in its large outline of bright rise and sad fall, and in its details of adventure and war on land and sea, of life at the Elizabethan court and among the great men of both Elizabethan and Jacobean times, seems to embody the best and the worst of those times, both in familiarity and in alien fascination. ("New" B4)

Having found a figure who spoke to him personally while also meeting the necessary historical requirements of relevance and scope, Garrett arrived at a way of connecting his aesthetic intentions and experience with Ralegh's historical variables as a possible means of escaping the prison of history.

Although Garrett had discovered his protagonist for *Death of the Fox*

(1971), he possessed hardly any real connection with England, which forced him to leave much of the places and topography he described in the hands of historical descriptions and his own imagination. As Garrett remarked shortly after the book's publication, "I have spent one week in England in all my life. I took everything I could in those seven days and then spent a lot of time on Ralegh biographies and books on the Elizabethan period" ("Ralegh" 3).[1] Garrett's reference to spending "a lot of time" reading about Ralegh is an understatement. As early as the first years of the 1950s Garrett was studying as much Elizabethan material as he could with an aim toward writing a scholarly biography of Ralegh. Having experienced various fits and starts, Garrett relates that the "final writing, myself committed by then by contract and obligation, began in 1964 and continued until the fall of 1969, interrupted sporadically in this second stage only by mundane conditions, not by other work" (*SFC* 21). He spent nearly twenty years conceptualizing, researching, and writing *Death of the Fox*, a period of time that seems lengthy on the surface but appears increasingly reasonable when one considers the sheer volume of historical information Garrett believed he needed to master in order to render the kind of authentic narrative he had in mind. To be sure, the varied interests and expertise of Ralegh himself contributed to the amount of material Garrett was forced to address. Writing in a 1964 notebook, the year he began composing *Death of the Fox* in earnest, Garrett arranged a "Breakdown for Ralegh Research," which listed: "1) Ralegh; 2) General History; 3) Elizabeth; 4) Sailing and Nautical; 5) Military; 6) Life and Times; 7) Literary; and 8) Exemplary." Having already amassed nearly all of the necessary information on Ralegh's life, Garrett still found himself struggling with a means of breaking down and expressing the extensive significance of its various dimensions.

The problems accompanying the complexity of Ralegh's character also seemed to spill over into Garrett's attempts to locate the appropriate genre and stylistic vehicle for telling his story. Garrett recalls that originally his Ralegh biography became a play, which in turn "became four or five versions of a novel that then collapsed into themselves and became one novel" (quoted in Howard 21). At one point Garrett also had thought to write the entire novel in the form of a letter from Ralegh to his son. These numerous variations are significant, since they do not seem to have been so much discarded as retained and transformed into various sections of *Death of the Fox*. Furthermore, much of the unique brilliance of the novel seems to stem from the fact that Garrett knew very little about established methodologies for historical fiction and thus stumbled upon and created several erratic ways of presenting events. As he explains:

At the time of writing it, I knew so little about the genre of the historical novel, having read very few of them myself and never really thinking about my own work as belonging to that category, that I suspect it
took me much longer to write the book than it should have, certainly
than it would have if I had known where I was conforming to tradition
and conventions and where I was going off on my own, departing into
thin air. (*SFC* 6)

Beyond the more general concerns of overall form, the project's stylistic vehicle also presented an assortment of options and problems for Garrett. In a
1964 notebook entry Garrett jotted down a reminder to "remember that for
economy, both of my own time and for the purposes of more imaginative
evocation and involvement, must (a) resist temptations of antiquarianism
and (b) *organize method* as soon as possible" (Garrett's emphasis). Having
become a self-made expert on the Elizabethans, Garrett faced the dilemma of
how best to convey his extensive knowledge of the time without making his
novel resemble an Elizabethan document or a deadening scholarly tome. As
he explains, "The writer must invent a new language, not pedantically of the
period, yet not of ours either, a tongue invented for the characters to speak
and for the telling of their stories" ("Young" 26). Garrett had read a host of
Elizabethan and Jacobean writers in order to be "physically in *touch* with the
language, rhythms, the styles of the times" (*SFC* 29, Garrett's emphasis), yet
he found himself increasingly attempting to relegate those influences to the
background as he grasped for a style that would attract contemporary readers while also reflecting the genuine spirit of the historical period.

At least one aspect of the style of *Death of the Fox* owes itself more to
the vagaries of the composition process than any conscious decision. As
Garrett explains, "Look at the short paragraphs in *Death of the Fox*. They're
short because I can cover a page in forty or fifty longhand words" (Israel
46). Garrett's varied historical, organizational, stylistic, and unconscious
decisions for the novel resulted in a diverse array of readings from initial
reviewers. Writing in 1971, Frank McCullough offered the banal claim that
"*Death of the Fox* is a Vietnam book, written during the long bitter years of
this war" (18). Although McCullough's reading appreciates the novel as a
historical allegory, its reduction of the book to a single contemporary conflict overly simplifies Garrett's complex intentions for the dialogue between
past and present. More accurate was Walter Sullivan's astute comparison of
Death of the Fox to Thomas Mann's *Doctor Faustus* in an unpublished letter
to Garrett, pointing to the "the way in which the main figure is both image
of and subordinate to the grander theme." As Sullivan suggests, both works

use complex, single characters to capture elaborate, sweeping historical moments. Later readings have succeeded in further articulating Sullivan's point. Writing in 1998, Monroe Spears abstracted Sullivan's interpretation to a more universal level, identifying Ralegh's central theme as "the triumph of time and the meaning of time and history" (51). For Spears, Ralegh and *Death of the Fox* do not speak to specific historical events or periods, however grand, but rather to the very nature of history itself. As Irving Malin has said of Ralegh, "*Now*—the present moment—is the time. Not the past. Not the future. But, of course, now moves quickly, so quickly that it becomes the past" (19, Malin's emphasis). Malin's point about time distinguishes itself from Spears's reading in remarking that Ralegh's concerns are not so much historical but temporal. History is not past events but rather "now-moved-on." Everything has the immediacy of the present whether it is happening or has happened. Such unique temporal distinctions have led John Carr to summarize that "Ralegh stands within history and seeks to both live within it and rise out of it, and Garrett has caught this delicate balance in the man's character perfectly" (24). For Carr, *Death of the Fox* becomes a meditation on Ralegh's personal and symbolic struggle with time—with the events of his life and his place both in and across them.

William Robinson has asserted that "Ralegh's death is [Garrett's] subject, but he writes to turn that death into a new life. To do so, he strikes out to reconstruct in its living oneness what Ralegh by an act of reason willfully set asunder and thereby removed from the created world of time and space" ("Imagining" 34). Robinson's point identifies the intersection of Ralegh's now-time existence and Garrett's authorial intentions for him. Casting him into different roles and various periods from his life, Garrett offers a timeless composite of Ralegh in all his incarnations. As Fred Chappell explains, "It is almost as if these complex, life-engulfing vocations are but poses for him, roles that he plays in carrying out a large design he has in mind. If he needs a sailor or courtier, he makes himself into one, instead of hiring another man as his agent" ("Introduction" xix). Offering now-time reflections on various aspects of his life, Ralegh works toward a "large design" concerning his own experiences and the very nature of existence. Writing to his son, Ralegh remarks, "[I]t is the prerogative of the old to inflict upon the young a tedious celebration of the past, spent seasons, festivals, and holidays of lost time" (*DOF* 516). Yet, Ralegh's recorded exploits and recollections to his son are neither senile murmurings nor sentimental yearnings. Instead, he offers up events from his own life as disposable, humanized samples of how life should and should not be lived.

What adds tragic dramatic weight to Ralegh's musings and the novel as a whole is his courageous knowledge of his own imminent demise. At one point he ruminates, "*Time will bleed away, an inward wound, until I truly bleed.* If time were blood and the executioner struck my head now, there would be nothing left in me for a crowd to see" (*DOF* 517, Garrett's emphasis). A historian (among many other things), Ralegh is aware of and infinitely involved in history, both personally and in the abstract. He reflects this dynamic in likening his letter to his son to his composition of the *History*: "Following an appraisal of the peculiar follies of ambitious worldly men, based upon authority, reason, and experience; demolishing the idols of riches and honor. Only to take a turn, as if to reconstruct something else from the jagged shards he had made" (*DOF* 519). Possessing a unique blend of irony and, at long last, hard-earned humility, Ralegh recognizes that the historical follies of others and his reasoned judgments of them have been and will be visited upon himself. In fact, that is precisely what is happening even as he utters it, the irony of which could not have been lost on Garrett as he sat composing the words. However, for all his knowledge of history and his recognition of his inevitable role in it, Ralegh realizes that he can never fully contextualize himself or human events. As he says in the *History*, "[T]he world's bright glory has put out the eyes of our minds" (*DOF* 550), meaning that the shiny vanities of life dull our rational ability to interpret properly either it or ourselves. Such knowledge might easily lead one to a very cynical perspective on history, yet Ralegh's view of time and his fallible place in it is humane. Reflecting on Elizabeth's rule, he remarks, "All memory is vain and foolish and all history compounded of many memories, therefore all the more vain and foolish. Yet a man could do worse than to remember such times" (*DOF* 555). Although he possesses a rare, acute knowledge of history, Ralegh recalls certain times and periods with fondness and warmth, even as he realizes such memories are selfish illusions. Yet, in knowingly giving himself over to the frailties of vain remembrance, Ralegh humanizes himself all the more, demonstrating his preference for the human experience—shortcomings and all—as opposed to the cold corridors of history.

As he hurries to complete his letter to his son, which he writes "in love and for the sake of the fellowship that time has denied us" (*DOF* 563), Ralegh feels that "time has claimed his consciousness," likening it to "a hard sound of hooves on a dry road in summer" (*DOF* 559). Knowing that his life is drawing to a close, Ralegh attempts to construct himself outside of time for the benefit of his son. Yet, for all his brilliant understanding of history, Ralegh struggles to see and articulate his role in it. As the narrator explains, "Nor can Ralegh, though a student of the ironies of time and capable as any man of comprehending the turns and counter-turns of future time, imagine the satirical ending of his won chronicle" (*DOF* 687). Even the wisest of humans, even Elizabeth in *The Succession*, becomes wrought with doubt when considering their time of passing and the effect, or lack thereof, it will have on future individuals and events. Yet, as Ralegh movingly summarizes, there is no shame in this lack of foresight:

> Faith is the understanding that past, present, and future can be possessed by the imagination, but only in a coinage of questions.
>
> Wisdom is, then, the knowledge that if any of these men, from King to hangman's son, could, by signs and portents, come to imagine part of the truth of the future, he could not believe it.
>
> To believe would be to be turned to stone or into swine, as in the old myths. And he would no longer be able to live as a man, not able to feel, and therefore unable to care.
>
> To be a man alive, awake or asleep, darkness or daylight, is to feel and to care.
>
> Best, then, that none of the living can read the ciphers of the future.
>
> Which are vanishing with the rising of the sun. (*DOF* 699)

To read the future accurately would be to sacrifice one's humanity. However, whatever shortcomings Ralegh experiences in addressing the future need not apply to his actions in the present, especially those with reference to the past. Speaking his last words on the scaffold, Ralegh

> in one step dismisses trivial present time, like a magician with a wand of words, banishes the present to reappear in and from the past, a younger past, himself sharing and partaking of that youth, summoning out of memory a glory which has been lost forever and, being lost, is now valued as priceless, calling up ghostly figures dancing to a music of which even the echoes have faded to the absolute purity of silence. (*DOF* 731–32)

Standing on the precipice of death, Ralegh halts the present on the authority of his past, a vanished past made all the more powerful by its utter absence from the present. In this way, Garrett not only skillfully conducts the death of a man, but the final obliteration of an epoch and the stunning birth of that time (and Ralegh) as history.

In "Traces of the Elizabethans" Garrett identifies the term *enchanted ground* as an expression stemming from "standing on the very spots where they stood, walking on the old stones and the ground they walked on" (*MSP* 4). Although Garrett began thinking about his second Elizabethan novel,

The Succession (1983), shortly after the publication of *Death of the Fox*, he would also take time during the 1970s to work on a play entitled *Enchanted Ground* (1981), which—as the title expression suggests—is not so much a historical play as it is a meditation on how history is imagined. As the play's male reader remarks, "The world we're in, the times we are living through, are wildly different from any kind of past that any of us can possibly imagine" (7). Suggesting Garrett's composition process for historical fiction, the female reader replies that, despite the barriers of time and culture, they must still attempt the task of "speaking of and for others—the voices of men and women out of the dim past. Giving over our voices to be the voices for ghosts, known and unknown, real and imaginary" (9). Whereas these musings on the nature of historical representation sound familiar, *Enchanted Ground* offers something new in its epicurean quality—that is, its focus on the importance of inanimate objects (artifacts) in history: "These things— these old and often beautiful things, left over and now preserved for us—all are haunted with spent energy. When you think about it, when you dream it and let it be, you can only feel that even the ground is enchanted. That even the rocks have memory" (10). Beyond human experience, Garrett invites the "place" of experience, the physical qualities of which may have helped to shape events in the past and may do so again.

The importance of physical place in *The Succession* was to become much more important for Garrett than it had been in *Death of the Fox*, the geography of which was based on a combination of scholarly descriptions and Garrett's imagination. By contrast, in his essay "Traces of the Elizabethans," Garrett chronicles his own slow, winding journey north toward Scotland, which literally sets the narrative pace for *The Succession* through the figure of the messenger who bears news of Elizabeth's death. As Garrett recounts:

> I spent a good deal of time, by car and on foot, following in the footsteps of my characters, looking not so much at the houses and buildings and artifacts, though I certainly looked at them where I could, as feeling the ground under my feet, walking and wondering how this may have felt for those for whom (the times as well as the places) it was home. It was a foreign place, to be sure, but it was *my* foreign place. (*SE* 14, Garrett's emphasis)

Garrett's wanderings across England and Scotland afforded him a visceral base for his imaginative events that his first novel had lacked. However, despite this advantage, his actual composition process was mired by a different kind of wandering: that of the nomadic, academic variety. As he summarizes:

So, for a decade writing my book I had to earn the money to buy the time to do it. Had to hustle—give nickel-and-dime readings, wherever they would have me, write nickel-and-dime pieces about anything for anyone who wanted one, work at conferences and part-time teaching jobs whenever I could with, occasionally, the good fortune of filling in, replacing some more desirable and distinguished writer who became ill or just cracked up or whacked out or bugged out. Coming off the splintery bench like George Blanda in his old Chicago Bears days. ("The Year" 92)

Hopping from job to job, Garrett was plagued by a constant barrage of mundane interruptions and distractions. However, just as the aging Blanda left Chicago to achieve new levels of success with the Houston Oilers and Oakland Raiders, so Garrett emerged from years of peripatetic toil with an excellent new novel.

Whereas Ralegh had functioned as the dominant figure in *Death of the Fox*, a number of different characters conspire to inform the central historical event of *The Succession*. As Garrett explains, "It is a more difficult book to read, for several reasons, than *Death of the Fox*. It's not organized the same way at all: It's built more around an idea than it is a single character" (Ruffin 25). Because the novel revolves around an idea based on a historical event, Garrett was forced to account for more numerous perspectives and implications. He asserts, "*The Succession* had to be more diffuse, wide-ranging. More layers of language had to be suggested, because there were so many characters acting over such an expanse of time. Here I move further away from literary reading—to letters, to Robert Carey's great autobiography, to jest books and the like" (*MSP* 15). In other words, Garrett was attempting a more conceptually ambitious novel, complete with a larger cast of characters, heretofore untapped dimensions of Elizabethan culture, and, by necessity, many different styles and forms. Yet, these concerns are not wholly restrictive to historical fiction. Garrett once characterized *The Great Gatsby* as "a complicated composite of several distinct kinds of prose, set within the boundaries of a written narration, a composite style whose chief demonstrable point appears to be the inadequacy of any single style (or the means of perception, point of view), by itself to do justice to the story" (*SFC* 66). Just as *The Great Gatsby* uses different stylistic vehicles to convey a number of class, gender, cultural, and philosophical differences among its characters, so *The Succession* lets its players speak for themselves in their own voices, allowing them to collectively guide the overall narrative to the inevitable conclusion of a historical event. However, in uniting the abstract march of history with an ambitious stylistic agenda and the colloquially mundane aspects of its participants, Garrett points to something much larger. As R. H. W. Dillard has astutely noted, "What enabled Garrett to write *The Succession* is what enabled Shakespeare or Tolstoy to write at the level they did: a religious belief that gives them awareness of the presence of the eternal in the temporal, of the universal in the particular; the Word in words" (*UGG* 158). Ultimately, Garrett's end product constitutes something that goes beyond the sum of its content and form, disrupting conventional notions of time, event, and expression through a transcendent rendering of them.

Although the book has large universal concerns, at its most basic level *The Succession* literally is about the uneasy shift of royal power from Elizabeth to James. Like the messenger in Garrett's poem "Fragment of a Tragedy," the emissary in *The Succession* "guiltless and eloquent arrives / to speak in rhythm of catastrophe" (*DOL* 55). Although many characters in the novel fear revolution and a number of other unfavorable scenarios, the clever Robert Cecil reminds us that the succession is "no new question" (*SUC* 52), the lack of "newness" in the issue, as well as the book's title, highlighting the importance of temporality and history in the book. As Richard Betts relates, "Perhaps the most important aspect of change in the novel involves the succession of time, the continuous alteration of the present as the unrealized future is transformed into the recollected past. Thus the characters live in an ever-changing present which has a problematical relationship to both the future and the past" (74). In spite of using a much larger cast of characters than *Death of the Fox*, *The Succession* shares the earlier novel's temporal preoccupations with memory, present action, and historical sequence. Yet, because the central event that binds these themes involves a nationwide transfer of power, Betts believes "[i]ts version of history is characterized, at least on the surface, by chaos and discontinuity and dominated by change" (74). However, although its literal events may appear chaotic, the novel succeeds in presenting them in a lucid, albeit complex, manner. As Dillard observes:

> The brilliance of the novel is not that it has so many characters and covers so much time, but that out of all this apparent disorder and disconnection such a coherent and orderly and meaningful whole takes shape. It does not have a modernist preoccupation with fragmentation, but rather a thoroughly postmodernist awareness of interrelatedness and interdependence. ("George Garrett" 156)

Whatever inconsistencies the book may possess in terms of individual characters and events are resolved by Garrett's collective arrangement and portrayal of them, which repeatedly manipulate time even as they ultimately reconcile it.

A symbolic manifestation of this temporal manipulation practice reveals itself in the novel when Queen Elizabeth enters Kenilworth Castle: "[T]he clocks were stopped in her honor. There could be no more past or future until her departure" (*SUC* 161). Like Ralegh in *Death of the Fox*, Elizabeth is a master translator and manipulator of history and time. Although much of her extensive influence and understanding stems from her position of power, Elizabeth realizes that everyone, including herself, willing or unwilling, ultimately functions as time's pupil and servant. Very early in the novel, Garrett reveals that for Elizabeth time "is a birch-rod schoolmaster, and she knows the tunes and melodies, all the conjugations and declensions, by heart" (*SUC* 3–4). Though time may be her lord and instructor, Elizabeth has learned his habits and lessons exceedingly well, and, for the most part, avoided his punishments and reprimands. She expresses, for example, later in the book her knowledge that both her pretty Maid and herself are destined to become "no more than a glitter of dust in a shaft of light" (*SUC* 533), the finite appearances and intellects of both inevitably passing, one slightly before the other, into lost shadows.

Of course, there are few characters who possess Elizabeth's wisdom in recognizing their role in time and history, and Garrett often employs young people like the Queen's Maid to capture the blind vanity of existence in the present. Robert Carey's young companion, speaking for many of his generation, is described as musing, "If the Earl wants to believe that England was peopled by fallen angels in the times of Queen Elizabeth, then let that be his pleasure. But, as far as this young man can care, angels or devils, they have all turned to dust" (*SUC* 154). Caught up in the issues of his own life and times, Carey's companion has little genuine interest in the stories of a dead age or his elderly master, who soon will be taking his place among his departed contemporaries. Although Garrett gently mocks the archetypal youthful vanity of Carey's associate, he is equally wary of the sentimental memories that plague the aged Carey. The Messenger reminds us that "memory of pleasure, and even of the hope that humbly attended it, is always near enough to be called forth like a benign, obedient spirit. For as long as memory will last" (*SUC* 283). However, countering the gentle joys of recollection is the "time of dreams when any kind of ghost can rise. When ghosts are savage and unruly. Where Time is the fearful teacher whose punishments are endless" (*SUC* 283). Balancing the practice of fond remembrance, the dream world visits upon us the darker aspects of personal experience, cured, repackaged, and made potent by the specter of time. Dillard resolves much of this tension between memory and time when he notes that in the novel, "[M]eaning accrues to experience from its relationships in time (past and future and present) and in consciousness, individual *and* shared" (*UGG* 146, Dillard's emphasis). Temporality and apprehension among others and the self results in a measure of knowledge that at least approaches understanding. Appreciating time in relation to others and oneself gives one the feeling, however illusory, of context with regard to existence.

Temporal considerations with regard to one's functions were not far from Garrett's mind after the publication of *The Succession*, as he began to dwell on the dynamics that would accompany the composition of his third Elizabethan novel, *Entered from the Sun* (1990). In 1983, Garrett said of his book plans, "I'm going to do a quite short, skinny one—like one of the sections in *The Succession*—which has to do with the murder of Christopher Marlowe, and then that's it—I'm done with historical fiction" (R. H. W. Dillard, "George Garrett" [1983] 156). Although the novel ended up both taking and being longer than he originally had hoped, Garrett was serious about establishing a much sparser narrative. Among some notes entitled "Novel Concerning the Murder of Christopher Marlowe," Garrett revealed, "My model for this story is (indirectly) the work of Raymond Chandler." In the very conception of the book then, Garrett practiced a kind of temporal displacement, abstracting a particular style of mystery writing to the Elizabethan era.

Garrett's practice of time manipulation was not lost on reviewers. As Steven Kellman argues, "The novel derives its urgency from conscious oscillation between the end of the sixteenth century and the end of the twentieth" (134). Yet, there is much more to the book than the transfer of stylistic and cultural variables across centuries. As Monroe Spears remarks, Garrett "creates living characters who represent both their own time and the universally human in any time" ("A Trilogy" 128). Constituting more than a dialectic between the complexities of a historical period and our own, *Entered from the Sun* is also about time, in and of itself. One way this may be glimpsed is in the book's structure. As Tom Whalen observes, "*Entered from the Sun* has no beginning. We begin, as I said, *in medias res*, already immersed within the text, within the texture of the times" (99). Not following a conventional narrative sequence, the reader is immediately thrown into the sights, smells, and other ephemera of the era at hand. Furthermore, this process of immersion is accompanied and partially wrought by an unusual textual commentator both of and not of that period. Not unlike Anthony Burgess in *A Dead Man in Deptford*, Garrett introduces a kind of self-reflexive ghost, a voice that directly addresses the reader. Not surprising in light of the first two historical novels, one of the enigmatic speaker's dominant concerns is the nature of time. He remarks, for example, that "the lost time of living and being, our brief time to suffer and to rejoice, is now and always an eternal February. It can be summer again only in your memory" (*EFS* 25). Such dialogue, spoken with an abstract awareness of time's impartiality and a warm appreciation of humanity, could well have fallen from the lips of Ralegh or Elizabeth in the previous two books. Contextualizing the book's epoch and the very nature of temporality, the voice of *Entered from the Sun* is not unlike the voices of Ralegh and Elizabeth in *Death of the Fox* and *The Succession*, shaping their time in one regard while acknowledging both its and their own imminent tragic passing.

Mortality and the nature of existence are also much on the mind and in the experience of *Entered from the Sun*'s central character: the rough, good-hearted mercenary, Barfoot. As the narrator explains, Barfoot is "rich beyond his years . . . so many things are vague and timeless, outside of all accurate measurement and definition" (*EFS* 76). Having stared death in the face on a number of occasions, Barfoot has acquired a measure of suffering and human experience far beyond his age in years, something the flawed and untrustworthy narrative voice may speak of with some authority. The utterance articulates itself as existing both in our time and the time of its story, which is to say, outside of time. Thus, when the voice remarks, "[*T*]*hese are ages*, yours and mine, given to . . . every kind of nightwalking false knaves" (*EFS* 163, Garrett's emphasis), it relates the narrative present and past to each other, while stressing to the reader that history has not altered the essence of humanity much beyond our outer accouterments and cultural fashions. Also central to this statement is its suggestion of our own finite roles in history. There have always been knaves, saints, and any number of other human archetypes who, like unknowing players, perform their functions in the given society of their time, before all eventually succumb to death and surrender their parts to others. This concept is revisited near the conclusion of the book, when the narrator notes that the characters of the story will vanish, only "[n]ot into history" (*EFS* 325). Perhaps the most tragic element of *Entered from the Sun* stems from its repeated insinuation of the fact that none of the major characters will be remembered beyond the spans of their own lives, despite their wisdom, brilliance, and foolishness. (There are minor ones who will: Marlowe, Ralegh, etc.) As Emily Dickinson says in the poem upon which the book's title is based, "Doom is the House without the Door," and when each of these characters enters that house their lives and stories are lost forever, save through the imaginative vehicle of historical fiction.

At the conclusion of *Entered from the Sun*, the author (whether or not this is supposed to be Garrett or a projection of him seems unimportant) remarks, "I have been happy for a time, living among Elizabethans. Happier, I do believe, than I could have been living only in our own century. Our bitter shiny century" (*EFS* 347). Whoever the speaker is, his declaration likely speaks for Garrett as well. Having created three extraordinary historical novels, the research and writing for which spanned four decades, Garrett's time spent on and imaginatively in the Elizabethan period was employed with great ingenuity and achievement. Writing in a notebook in 1965, Garrett remarked to himself, "If I can ever just finish the Ralegh book, I want to try one on Ovid in exile." Little could he have known at the time that his book would not be published for another six years and that it would be followed, over a period of two more decades, by companion novels that both are and are not sequels. Literal time, as well as imaginative temporality, was much on Garrett's mind and a great deal of it would remain dedicated to an imaginative existence among the Elizabethans. Projected historical works based on Ovid's time in exile and the relationship between Alexander Hamilton and Aaron Burr would be forced to wait, and in time other writers would take them up. In a sense, Elizabethan history had mastered Garrett as much as he had mastered it. In fact, in his essay "Traces of the Elizabethans," Garrett remarks that his reading and thinking spent on that period have "consciously and unconsciously influenced all my work in every form I have been able to work in ever since in both poetry and prose. Including this paper. Including, yes, the screenplay for *Frankenstein Meets the Space Monster*" (*MSP* 13). In his notebooks from the 1960s Garrett repeatedly had urged himself to finish the Ralegh book and even lamented that "the Ralegh thing stands between me and a new way." However, it seems now that the Elizabethan work was the "way"—the route that enabled him to discover and study history and experience in a manner that eventually would lead to a masterful wedding of the two in his work. Over time, it became apparent that Garrett was not so much spending time among the Elizabethans but that they had come to be with him, inexplicably whispering their wisdom across centuries. Fortunately, George Garrett was present in our time to attend their forgotten words and translate for us their strange and wonderful tales.

part III

Costume Change

The Striptease in Poetry and Criticism

Recent Seasonal Fashions

The Striptease in Poetry

I will write words words words,
as you do, and will sign my name,
naming my new poems like children,
calling them home from the dark.

—Garrett, "Postcard"

George Garrett's more recent poetry—as it appears in his new and selected poems, *Days of Our Lives Lie in Fragments*, and a few places hence—evinces many of the strengths of his earlier verse while also voicing some of the subjects and concerns that often come to interest or plague the mature retrospective poet. The dominant themes of Garrett's later poems include literary legacies (or the lack thereof), personal mortality and the passing of literary mentors and contemporaries, elements and contemporary applications of the Christian worldview, biblical figures (albeit not always aligned with a Christian worldview), contemporary values (or the lack thereof), loneliness, acceptance, and those isolated and unusual natural occurrences that sometimes constitute signs and symbols by which to live (especially those manifested by different varieties of birds). Garrett's verse sports a number of different outfits and styles yet is unwaveringly consistent in its presentation of experience. His is a spare poetry that draws on prior successes while evolving all the while toward an end that appears both unpostured and natural. Many of the lines ring with the suggestion of inevitability. Whatever else it may be, it is a poetry that has been earned.

Writing in 1989, the poet and critic Henry Taylor asserted that Garrett's "much larger achievement and reputation as a writer of fiction seem at times to have obscured the fact that his poetry is among the treasures of contemporary literature" (73)—an assessment that registers both high praise and critical neglect. All the more curious in the general oversight of Garrett's work as a poet is the fact that his verse output is both generous and consistent in its quality over a half-century's span of time. His oeuvre includes five entirely original volumes (*The Reverend Ghost* [1957], *The Sleeping Gypsy and Other Poems* [1958], *Abraham's Knife and Other Poems* [1961], *Welcome to the Medicine Show: Flashcards / Postcards / Snapshots* [1978], and *Luck's Shining Child* [1981]), a midcareer collected poems (*The Collected Poems of George Garrett* [1984]), and a pair of books separated by three decades that select and collect previous work while also introducing new material (*For a Bitter Season: New and Selected Poems* [1967] and *Days of Our Lives Lie in Fragments: New and Old Poems, 1967–1997* [1998]).

As a body, it is a poetry that is difficult for a critic to package or make cohere in its entirety. Writing on Garrett's verse in 1970, when the complete output consisted of only four volumes, the poet Richard Moore found it impossible to convey the nature of his appreciation, ultimately throwing his arms up in the air with the declaration, "There is so much variety of tone and feeling in it that I can find no general statement that will apply to all of it" (49). Most others who have discussed Garrett's work have followed suit in deed if not confession, usually focusing on three or four poems, or perhaps just one. Though they generally remain tight in focus, many of the assessments are adeptly orchestrated and valuable. Not surprisingly, the best of the critical material on Garrett's poetry (including published reviews, entries, and essays as well as a number of excellent unpublished papers, lectures, and panel discussions) arrives mostly from fellow poets (Neal Bowers, Fred Chappell, Kelly Cherry, James Dickey, R. H. W. Dillard, Brendan Galvin, Henry Hart, David Slavitt, Ron Smith, Richard Wilbur, and others) and focuses almost exclusively on Garrett's verse up through the 1984 collected poems.[1] Little may be added here to the extraordinarily perceptive and thorough readings of the earlier work, though a great deal remains to be enumerated with regard to the somewhat neglected poetry published since that time.

In his 1988 study *Understanding George Garrett*, R. H. W. Dillard accurately summarized the collective concerns of Garrett's earlier verse as follows: "He strives in his poems to understand that lost world of heroism and faith, the traditional realm of poetry, and to accommodate it to this age of anxiety, shattered hopes, and pandemic phobias" (*UGG* 198). A skilled poet himself, fully cognizant of the challenges of realizing one's subject, Dillard evokes Garrett's "striving" rather than a settled and complete achievement. Though he identifies the primary concerns of Garrett's verse through the late 1980s—the core of which announces a preoccupation with the place and relevance of values (literary and otherwise) in an afflicted, fragmented present—Dillard conceptualizes the collective body as existing in the midst of an ongoing process, leaving the hatch fully open for new directions and understandings. A decade later, Louis McKee's review of *Days of Our Lives Lie in Fragments* suggested not only that the poems were still evolving but that the fresher material was every bit as provocative as the old: "Dedicated readers will find many familiar pieces, and all can delight in the new" (82).

On the surface Garrett's poems, new and old, usually appear formally tight yet simple, possessed of a very accessible and conversational syntax and diction. Many refined contemporary critics coming to Garrett's poems with little or no knowledge of his intentions or his extensive learning might simply dismiss them as plain and unsophisticated. However, housed within these unassuming lines are a number of very unconventional qualities and unexpected epiphanies. In fact, if anything Garrett's unpredictability appears to have increased with age, which has led to more than one observer suggesting that his later poetry may be of superior quality. Reviewer John Piller, having specifically cited the thirty new poems in *Days of Our Lives Lie in Fragments*, asserted that Garrett "is now producing the best work of his career," Piller's appreciation stemming primarily from Garrett's measured deployment of "a world view that embraces popular culture, gains vitality from a bemused edginess, and conveys a much richer sense of the world's moral textures" (187). Although the traditional concerns identified by Dillard may be detected here, Piller's assertion of a "richer sense" is telling and noteworthy in its comparative subordination of the old to the new.

In delineating the qualities of Garrett's newer work it is perhaps most productive to begin with one of his traditional concerns, taking as an initial traceable example his preoccupation with the place (or lack of place) of historical values in the present. As his highly praised Elizabethan novels and numerous critical essays on history (literary and otherwise) testify, Garrett is well-versed in the complexities of history and its tenuous applications in art, as well as (more generally) the present. His expertise includes an extensive knowledge of the history of English poetry (especially the Renaissance period), which he sometimes, as in the poem "Free Card Draw, Jacks Are Wild," sets within and against the concerns of our time, the telling representative Elizabethan figures of which are Lucio and Iago:

> alas, poor Lucio, my lad,
> it's you, after all, who comes
> closest to us in this shameless
> day and age, you and ole Iago
>   (33)

When the dynamics of our own era are abstracted into the context of Renaissance literature it is chiefly through negative manifestations and figures that associations and relationships are created. For Garrett, contemporary American culture has no Prince Hal populating its otherwise wretched hive of scum and villainy. To his eyes, gazing as they are in this poem through the filter of an Elizabethan worldview, ours is a thin, pitiable culture of amoral duplicity and empty manipulation.

Garrett continues to associate the pervasive and often underhanded evils of our own time in terms of English history in "Duplicity," a short poem based on an epigram from Sir Thomas More. More observes that when the prince is good "he is the dog who guards the flock," yet when he is not he is the "wolf who takes us for his food" (35). More's early-sixteenth-century political wisdom easily applies to almost any of our current politicians on the national scene, and the moral weight of his words is intensified by his own well-documented and rigorous adherence to his personal values. As one of two undersheriffs of London, More was known for his legal impartiality and goodwill toward the poor. Executed for his unyielding religious and political beliefs, the last words attributed to him on the beheading scaffold were, "The king's good servant, but God's first." More's real-life integrity bestows upon the poem a historical and biographical dimension that strengthens both its message and its application across the centuries in our own shameless era.

Another poem concerned with history, "Main Currents of American Political Thought (The Latest Version)," demonstrates Garrett limiting himself to American figures in making thoroughly iconoclastic associations across time. In the process of demystifying several U.S. presidents he references Washington's wooden teeth and Lincoln's manic depression before concluding with Clinton: "a spoiled country boy / with bad temper and unquenchable appetites, 'not tough but / ruthless'" (43). Here, the historical message is different than in either "Free Card Draw, Jacks Are Wild" or "Duplicity," the flaws of Clinton, though perhaps more pronounced and depraved, set alongside the embarrassing and debilitating qualities of his historical predecessors. As R. H. W. Dillard has remarked, "Garrett is a poet of the postwar years, the disillusioned years of the continuing cold war" (*UGG* 198). As such he sometimes adopts the position of a harbinger of skepticism and doubt, the institutions and concerns of our own time either paling in comparison to those of the past or, just as bad, merely furthering and repeating the worst human crimes and tendencies of earlier eras.

Garrett's cynicism can be biting to the point that it occasionally flirts with despair, but it never forsakes hope or humanity completely, especially in the newer poems. Many of them are haunted by a kind of humane archetypal inevitability, a generous wisdom of maturity bent upon giving and sharing. To make a most uncritical association, they are friendly and paternal—they mean well, and in doing so almost always earn our trust. There is, however, a possible downside to such a poetic approach. Writing in the *Sewanee Review*, Neal Bowers, citing the newer poems' various dedications to the literary deceased, detected "an elegiac tone" (xliii), which on occasion flirts with inviting poetic weakness through the vehicle of nostalgia ("Hail to the Chief," the birthday poem for John Ciardi, may waver a bit while walking this tightrope). However, the poetry generally saves itself from seeming overly sentimental or "old-timerish" both through the genuinely earned quality of the emotions and praise evoked as well as (and perhaps more importantly) the frequent and skillful deployment of shocking narrative surprises.

One of the best of the newer poems, "Some Enormous Surprises," achieves this technique of unexpected misdirection explicitly, imagining a pale-faced, six-year-old Adolf Hitler whistling in the night as he totes a pail of beer from an Austrian *Gasthaus* for his father's supper. The poem begins with a catalogue of why people thought Hitler was insane during the 1930s: he was a vegetarian, believed smoking led to cancer, and was convinced the Volkswagen would continue to be driven in the distant future. From this unorthodox depiction of Hitler's madness, the poem moves to an Austrian bar Garrett once frequented while serving in the U.S. Army during the 1950s. It was to this *Gasthaus*, the local elders recall, that the childhood Hitler would come every evening:

for a bucket of beer for his father's supper.
Would stand there patiently waiting where
you are standing now, then, pail in hand,
set off under the early stars along a lane
towards the lights of home, whistling in the dark.

Juxtaposing Hitler's ironic adult eccentricity (ironic in the sense that his "madness" with regard to some phenomena turned out to be both accurate and prophetic) with the manner in which he performed one of his mundane boyhood chores creates a strange effect in the poem, keeping the reader thoroughly off-balance. When Garrett finally situates us we are moved, yet what has moved us remains disconcerting:

> And invisible and implacable, always
> the wide smile of God upon His creatures, one and all,
> great and small, among them this little pale-faced boy,
> for whom He has arranged some enormous surprises,
> beyond any kind of imagining, even myself,
> drunk in this place, years from home, imagining it.
>   (6)

Offered the peculiar image of a childhood Hitler extended the same divine love as all other living things, the reader marvels at the poem's powerful depiction of human existence even as the discomfort produced by the identity of its central figure lingers in the mind.

To a notable degree, Garrett appears to take impish pleasure in employing this sort of unsettling juxtaposition and does so frequently. Moreover, everything is fair game: from the widely acknowledged arch-villain of the twentieth century to the old biblical events out on the desert wastes. In "David (Again)," for example, we are offered an arresting and unorthodox image of the young Hebrew monarch, not unlike a scene out of one of Robert E. Howard's Conan narratives, holding up Goliath's "head by the snarled hair" and then, later, as a feeble old king, "taking young bodies to bed" (39). Uninterested in adjusting his possibly controversial depiction to the sensitivities and idealizations of our time, Garrett, as he had done with the American presidents in "Main Currents of American Political Thought (The Latest Version)," offers a vision of his historical figure that is both authentic to the extent of his imaginative capabilities and completely unapologetic.

Perhaps the most outrageous and entertaining of Garrett's surprises appears in "The Long and the Short of It" in which he imagines a wild bear suiting up to play football for the University of Virginia. Appearing in Garrett's backyard, the enormous animal eludes local animal control personnel before vanishing into a grove near the practice facility of the university's football team. It is at this point in the poem that Garrett ceases to record an event (for a bear did in fact enter his yard) and plunges into the realm of the fanciful as the prodigious animal practices with the team, attends classes, and suits up for the big game against Virginia Tech, mauling the opposition and forcing one of the rival linemen to complain:

> "Hey, coach, that guy
> across from me, he's the ugliest

dude I've ever seen.
Got hair all over, head to toe,
red eyes and something like claws,
too; and I'm not going back
out there without a gun."
     (14)

The manner in which the poem shifts gears from unlikely occurrence to impossible fantasy reminds one of James Dickey's more outrageous and successful poetic yarns: the plummeting stewardess of "Falling," for example, or the house-wrecking fish in "The Shark's Parlor." Yet Garrett's poem is potentially more explosive in its development than either of those pieces, since it evolves from an altogether mundane, domestic scenario. As Garrett explains to Brendan Galvin, the reader to whom the poem is specifically addressed:

I don't know what it means,
Brendan, except that maybe
even an ordinary back yard
can yield up a share of
surprises
     (14)

And this is as at should be in that the most enormous and unlooked-for surprises, those in which meaning gives way to marveling, often proceed from the most regular and unlooked-for circumstances.

What is extraordinary about most of Garrett's poetic surprises—including those pertaining to the young Hitler, the alternately barbarous and licentious King David, and the elusive gridiron bear—is that they arise from actual or at least plausible occurrences, a significant portion of their startling quality stemming from the fact that they are not wholly fictional. Garrett's visceral settings can be destabilizing as well. Some of the poems take place at his home in Charlottesville, but there are those that unfold at his summer house in York Harbor, Maine, en route on a train between Tuscaloosa and Charlottesville, twentieth-century Austria, the strange deserts of the old biblical tales, and even indeterminate shadow regions (possibly not even of this life or dimension). More often than not, all of these places appear in the form of snapshots, postcards, and other microcosms, the brevity of their sometimes cinematic cuts and fades never inhibiting their authenticity or lifelike qualities.

Perhaps because he works extensively in prose and produces more fiction than poetry, Garrett does not embrace longer forms in his verse. Yet he is a

deceptive poet in that the spare, truncated quality of many of the poems be-
lies an archetypal depth that nevertheless almost always manages to appear
original. Henry Taylor has identified one of Garrett's main powers as "the
constant and paradoxical tension between the present and the past, between
memory and imagination" (89). And for Garrett revisiting the old subjects
and ideas, and relegating them to the context of his own constantly evolving
memories and creative abilities, is not so much a choice but a directive. As
he remarks at the beginning of "Whistling in the Dark":

> What has happened, my friends, is this:
> we are saying the same things over and over again
> because we have to, because there is no other choice.
>   (44)

Garrett refuses to flee tradition, humbly revisiting and embracing the old
tales, yet usually succeeding in somehow making them his own. In doing
so he ultimately sets a very high bar for himself, perhaps one that is even
impossibly formidable, since it inhabits the rare air of the masters.

In retreading the old poetic paths Garrett leaves behind his own distinct
blazes while carving out a few detours as well through the originality of his
voice and wit. As Taylor aptly put it, "The mundane and the exotic meet" (80).
Although Garrett enjoys employing sudden, dramatic changes in his poems,
both with regard to style and subject matter, frequently (dis)organizing even
his familiar materials in unconventional ways, his subjects almost always are
conveyed as visceral, real, and humane. This mode of conveyance also serves
to situate Garrett among an increasingly rare and perhaps dying breed of
literary artist: the democratic man-of-letters poet, whose verse nearly always appears open and accessible to the (nonliterary) educated general
reader. Despite the current crisis in literary theory, obscure allusions, formal
eclecticism, and fashionable political dogmas often continue to dictate the
measure and degree of praise bestowed by many reviewers. Ignoring such
critical preferences, Garrett maintains his open accessibility while usually
managing to present or attain something distinctive.

Garrett often achieves newness or uniqueness in his poetry through the
effect of employing/rubbing a rough vernacular in/against a tight, formal
context. In addition, his recent work demonstrates a more pronounced degree of relaxation in its use of rhyme and meter. It is also possessed of a
deeper personal dimension, evincing a frequent and partially self-reflexive
(perhaps inevitable) preoccupation with literary legacies. In "Anthologies,"
for instance, Garrett addresses the fate of his and his contemporaries' life-
long, yet ongoing, poetic achievements, inquiring:

But what of all the unfamous others, ourselves
I mean, still alive and on fire and in love
With the taste of words and the making of poems?
Who will come here afterwards to blow the dust away
and disturb the peace and oblivion we have earned?
(16)

Though it speaks to autobiographical concerns, "Anthologies" is less a plea for critical attention and more a meditation on the legacy of the poet's work amid the immense bottomless void of the world's collective literary output. It is a poem that questions how to "preserve the anonymous dignity of the unfamous" (15)—the remnants of a long life spilled out in bondage and service to poetry.

It should be pointed out here that Garrett's more personal poems—those that apply to his own life and concerns—are hardly ever confessional in nature. As Neal Bowers wryly notes, "It is remarkable that he wrote and published poems throughout the 1960s, 70s, and 80s without once denigrating his immediate relatives or offering up his self-palpations as something worth a reader's attention" (xlv). Indeed, even Garrett's poems that draw on personal experience the most remain ultimately universal in their philosophies and implications. Often they do not even identify or lend clues to their narrators' and characters' genders. In fact, many of the poems' speaking and listening figures could be either women or men. This apparently purposeful omission and ambiguity serves to deepen their collective archetypal effect, as well as the powerfully distinctive humane element identified by reviewers.

Also evident in the autobiographical material is a distinctive brand of self-deprecating humor, aimed at both Garrett and other poets, utilized in a manner that would be anathema to most confessional scribblers. For example, in his rollicking excerpt "From *Lives of Our Poets: A Satire*," Garrett has the figure Palaemon, baseball cap backwards on head, steer his "dusty pickup" to a drive-in where the 1965 B-horror film *Frankenstein Meets the Space Monster* is playing. Not only is the poem irreverent and humorously unassuming in its juxtaposition of classical-sounding figures with American popular culture, but also in its use of that particularly vile and ill-reviewed film, which Garrett holds the distinction of having cowritten. As Garrett once replied to Hollywood writer-director Lawrence Kasdan, who satirically had asked him if he was proud of the movie, "Well, Sir, come to think of it, I guess I am proud of it. Of course all is vanity, but it is something really special to have had a small part in the creation of the worst picture ever made"

("The Crossover" 27). So goes a typical Garrett response when confronted with haughtiness or pretension, and it is a perspective that allows him to laugh heartily in his poetry both at himself and the cult of artistic success. How else might he—with characteristic humor—define, as he does at the end of "From *Lives of Our Poets: A Satire*," literary failure as the realization that

> death will do nothing
> to enhance or advance you,
> when even suicide would not be
> a good career move.
>   (23)

As in so much of Garrett's work, the irony of this poem is biting, macabre, and dead-on, yet so is its underlying and all-too-serious truth.

Unlike *Frankenstein Meets the Space Monster* (at least as things stand now), "Anthologies" has a sequel. In "Anthologies II" Garrett attempts to reconcile the tenuous balance between an authentic life- and career-shaping love for poetry and the often unhealthy preoccupation with reputation and legacy that accompanies that career. For the mature Garrett, the eighteen-year-old Garrett's 1946 anthology of forgotten poets that so captivated and inspired him remains

> a buried treasure of shining words,
> a safe house assigned to all the dead poets
> he loved and cherished at first sight.
>   (18)

Accepting the fact that "all but a precious few of them / are long gone to glory or oblivion" (17), Garrett honors and celebrates the neglected poets from his obscure 1940s collection of verse by emphasizing the powerful, far-reaching effect they had on his late-teen self. Forgotten by others, buried in a book no one reads, their evasive location and achievement remains known to him—a remote source of truth and inspiration for the life he has chosen.

The mature poet may justify to himself and others his long life of letters, but the fear of losing or witnessing the diminishment of the gift that led to that life remains an excruciating prospect for all writers. Such is the underlying concern of the Salvatore Quasimodo-inspired poem "Dead of Winter":

> What became of the starving birds?
> They fell into a waste of snow.
> So it is with words.

They flash like sudden angels, go
Away like ghosts.
   (37)

Buried here is a fear of forfeiting the gift and vision to experience the "flash of sudden angels," of starving amid a barren cold. The emphasis is on the creative process—the glorious feast of insight that is poetry. It is worth pointing out that Quasimodo joined the Italian Communist Party after World War II only to resign in protest when he was asked to produce disingenuous political poetry. For him, as for Garrett, the artistic concerns always came first, though he remained acutely interested in social issues (his 1959 Nobel Prize lecture was entitled "The Poet and the Politician"). Like several poems in Garrett's recent verse, much of the material in Quasimodo's later poetry is retrospective in nature.

Many of the recurring objects and symbols of Garrett's later work evoke eddies and migrations, deep currents and fanciful flights—among them, Maine's York River (as it appears in "Days of Our Lives Lie in Fragments" and "Inch by Inch") and a wide assortment of birds (geese and gulls in "Days of Our Lives Lie in Fragments," the blackbird in "Good as a Gold Watch," a martial bluejay in "First Bluejay," the cawing sentinels of "Crows," and the nocturnal, multilingual mockingbird). The birds sing for the love of singing, because they have to, while the river flows on. So too Garrett expects the true poet to keep at his craft even as time exacts its price. As he comments in "Inch by Inch," a poem addressed to John Ciardi:

Better (and you knew it and said so,
so well and so many times)

to spend our skin and bones, to pay
out blood and breath upon
a wholly unimportant poem
   (7)

Though the rewards and even the significance of the achievement may turn out to be small, a body and life spent on poetry remains one richly lived and well spent.

The conviction and assurance of poetic practice ultimately arms the poet with the necessary dedication and toughness to withstand the potentially career-crushing politics and ephemera of his profession. When Garrett personifies and gives utterance to Ambition in his poem "The Seven Deadlies Plus Two," the entity holds forth with the following promise:

I will dazzle you with sleights
of hand. And if and when
you finally and fully reward me,
I will offer the contempt you so richly deserve.
   (28)

So goes the pervasive scrabbling and operating—both in the literary world
and elsewhere—the design of which is to raise the self at all costs while
endeavoring to crush the opposition: be they true enemies or even recent
supporters and rewarders. From a poem like "Memorial Service," part of
a three-poem sequence in the July 2002 issue of *Poetry*, one gets the impression Garrett likely has been the victim of another's ambition more than
once. The poem's narrator, an invited speaker at a remembrance event for an
old enemy, flirts with the desire to urinate metaphorically on the deceased's
grave, belittling his life, before changing his mind:

And so it is that pissing on your grave
doesn't please me as much as it ought to.
Now that you have passed beyond
All blaming and shaming, what can I do
but rise and proclaim sincere admiration
when my turn comes around to speak?
   (191)

Accepting of his rivalry's evils within the context and continuum of life and
death—and mindful of his own turn to come at the podium, as well in his
inevitable role as the central figure of a similar service—the speaker refrains
from embracing the tempting specter of disparagement and articulates a
genuine praise that is true in spirit if not fact.

The last of the three poems published in the July 2002 issue of *Poetry* is
"Another Version," a piece in which the speaker instructs his child how to go
about greeting the boatman on the shore of the River Styx: "And if he should
break the silence to speak / smile and say nothing in reply" (192). One of
the important implications here is that if a person has lived his or her life
admirably and wholly, spoken it completely, then there can be nothing more
to do or say when death beckons—the end may be greeted not with fear or
resentment, but with a smile of acceptance and goodwill. What more is there
to say for the poet who has spoken his existence?

Garrett's poetry, and especially the newer verse, regularly greets experience and fact—be it cultural, religious, historical, literary, natural, or personal—with a hearty skepticism and humor that in no way inhibits its ability

to create genuine human feeling. His poems conspire to evince poetry not only as a life but as life, a breathing and functioning phenomenon that exists. As such, Garrett's ultimately is more a poetry that instructs and lends itself to delight and appreciation than it is a complex, highly theoretical body to be unraveled, charted, and delineated by academics. It is an archetypal creation, a torch in the cave: it shows us ourselves. Like the figures in one of his older poems, "A Bargain," Garrett's separate pieces constitute "the gifted few who in the daze / of glory have risked nothing less / than everything that can be lost" (52). Garrett's best poems, "the gifted few," make us an offer we cannot refuse or risk losing. We might discern them most accurately as figures of light, dancing with the joy of existence, against a black absence of meaning. Even in the darkest places they illuminate our world.

Scholarly Threads

The Striptease in Criticism

You are a rare creature given to us by friendly oceans, or something.
—Letter from Barry Hannah to Garrett

Narrow critical appraisals of writers often overlook their relationships with and opinions of other scribblers. Such an oversight can easily become a shortcoming, since writers, in considering the work and careers of their peers, usually reveal, consciously or unconsciously, their own aesthetic and professional concerns. Barry Hannah's above assertion is significant for its vague acknowledgment of Garrett's benevolent uniqueness—his strange and marvelous arrival from a convivial point of origin. Although we are not explicitly told what exactly Hannah admires about Garrett, the comment appears particularly applicable to the elder author's writing and, especially, his criticism. In his numerous critical pieces over the past half-century Garrett repeatedly has delivered considerations of an eclectic range of books, nearly always with the aim of benevolently instructing the general reader as opposed to furthering or attacking the cause of a specific theory or school. In donning his unique scholarly threads, Garrett presents us with a shifting, singular image beneath which resides a writer who cares genuinely and unwaveringly both for the state of literature and the profession of writing.

Although Garrett's career as a published critic and scholar began in 1957 with the essay "An Examination of the Poetry of William Faulkner" and has continued in the form of uncollected reviews and essays for decades, he would not produce a book-length work of scholarship until the 1984 literary biography *James Jones*.[1] While Garrett's critical writing admittedly (and appropriately) took a backseat to his highly successful work in fiction and poetry, it never was far from his mind, and the long, consistent output proves he was determined to be a well-rounded man of letters from the beginning of his career. In the spirit of that tradition and the art of quarterly writing, Garrett's critical work is highly accessible and remained so when he began producing book-length literary criticism in the mid-1980s: *James Jones*, as well as *Understanding Mary Lee Settle* (1988). The former study is a short, albeit penetrating, critical biography, while *Understanding Mary Lee Settle*—though equally brief—constitutes one of the best books in a long important series edited by Matthew J. Bruccoli at the University of South Carolina Press and dedicated to introducing educated general readers to a writer's life and work. Within the genres and publishing parameters in which they are situated, both texts are balanced in their literary considerations, generous and sympathetic in their praise, and apparently altogether devoid of gratuitous theoretical and political framing or special interest. They also are visceral and pragmatic in their treatments of the writing life and American publishing. A writer himself, Garrett knows what is at stake in the creation and development of a creative book—a knowledge that affords his firsthand observations both vividness and depth.

It is probably true that only a writer would have chosen the following quote from James Jones as one of the epigraphs for a biography about him: "Writing has to keep evolving into deeper honesty, like everything else, and you cannot stand on past precident [*sic*] or theory, and still evolve. You remember that" (1). This perspective is significant not only for its focus on aesthetic truth and the uselessness of prior frameworks but for the emphatic manner in which it is driven home. Although he does not invoke an explicit theory, Garrett employs a similar general philosophy of "deeper honesty" while discussing the books of Mary Lee Settle: "[H]er work has always set the values of courage, compassion, and integrity against hypocrisy, indifference, and above all lack of charity" (24–25). Such an observation constitutes a curious, perhaps even rustic, form of ethical criticism, already rare in the theory-dominated end years of the 1980s, in which the truthfulness of art—the strict and sincere faithfulness to the imagined character, story, and theme—takes precedence over excessively clever cuteness and hyperbolic formal pyrotechnics. The years during which the books on Jones and Settle were written are important, too, in the sense that we are able to discern Garrett's individual perspective on the literary writing game of that time:

[T]he most trendy postmodern fiction has turned away from characterization altogether, and even more traditional writers have by and
large accepted the widespread, and often selfserving, sociopolitical
notion that they are not free to imagine and write outside their own
superficial experience. . . . Fiction, like confessional poetry, becomes
interesting and engaging depending, more or less, on the facts of the
life, the author's life, behind it. (*Understanding* 16)

Lamentable to Garrett is a perceived retreat from the immediacy of character and the visceral narrative, accompanied by an apparent polemical censorship of subject matter and unnecessary focus on artist autobiography. To
Garrett's acute critical eye such practices appear both gratuitous and generally debilitating to writers and their art. Considered by Garrett in the mid to
late 1980s, the outputs of Jones and Settle conversely function as examples
of serious and truthful literary practices in an age of thin characterization,
subtle political censorship, and general absence of meaning.

The Jones and Settle books notwithstanding, Garrett's criticism predominantly develops its ideas in miscellaneous essays, reviews (long and short),
and lectures—within and across various scholarly threads—rather than in
sustained one-idea/single-subject monographs. And the collected pieces,
taken together, demonstrate just how bewilderingly diverse and numerous
his interests are. Garrett works from the basic assumption that if one is truly
interested in literature one needs to take in a lot of it, and that a serious
interest in literature involves an extensive concern with other cultural phenomena. In 1992 he published two separate collections of essays and reviews
with different university presses: *My Silk Purse and Yours* and *The Sorrows
of Fat City*. In tandem the books constitute a sound and provocative general
introduction to his critical topics and concerns across several decades. Reviewer Charles Nash characterized *My Silk Purse and Yours* as a "lively collection" in which "refreshingly independent-minded pieces celebrate daring,
honest writing, wherever Garrett finds it" (86). Nash's general observation,
whether consciously intending to or not, echoes the primary approach of
Garrett's 1980s single-author studies in announcing the "integrity" of the
new collection. Moreover, as in *James Jones* and *Understanding Mary Lee
Settle*, Garrett's primary professional role as a creative writer dominates
and enriches his perspective and position as a critic. As the book's opening self-reflexive epigraph from Joyce Cary's preface to *The Horse's Mouth*
reads, "He is himself a creator, and has lived in creation all his life, and so
he understands and continually reminds himself in a world of everlasting
creation there is no justice. The original artist who *counts* on understanding

and reward is a fool" (*MSP* ii). Implicit in the Cary epigraph is a statement on the writer's relationship to publishing and literary politics. Because success is as much a byproduct of accident and manipulation as skill, the true dedicated artist—she who faithfully lives in creation all her life—should know to accord such phenomena as little attention as possible while wholly focusing her intellect on the work at hand.

The Cary epigraph functions as an opening salvo to be followed by a number of Garrett's own specific observations on the strange and perplexing state of the late-twentieth-century literary world. Privy to the insider views of writers and critics, and the unholy alliances they frequently form, Garrett notably laments the attempt by literary and academic operators "to keep dog fashion, the limits of their little territory somehow defined and exclusive" (*MSP* 17). To Garrett's practiced eye, literary trends and reputations are less a byproduct of genuine artistic brilliance and more the result of a carefully coordinated process executed by the industry's dominant hustlers. Innovation may be welcomed, but usually it must in some way further the concerns and ambitions of the established literati and/or the dominant interpretive theories and fashions of the day. For Garrett, the prospect of judging written art on a single set of discerning assumptions, however sweeping or clever, ultimately functions as a disservice to literature. As he proclaims in *My Silk Purse*, "I don't really believe at all in the favorite American literary parlor game of literary *ranking*" (*MSP* 18, Garrett's emphasis). This perspective is as much (perhaps more) a declaration of Garrett the writer (who alternately has suffered and triumphed at the hands of literary prognosticators) as it is of Garrett the critic. Elsewhere, commenting on literary awards and reputation-building, he has confessed, "I'm not competitive. What would be the point? It's unhealthy. The whole system of publishing and academe is set up to encourage competitive living and it's usually not worth it. You're competitive with yourself in terms of doing and making something better" (Int). This declaration, with its emphasis on and dedication to the craft, bears a strong resemblance to the Cary quote at the beginning of *My Silk Purse*—it is uttered by one who lives in creation.

As *My Silk Purse* and *The Sorrows of Fat City* both demonstrate, Garrett is in a uniquely appropriate position to make sweeping generalizations about the landscape of contemporary American literature, since he claims to read "more fiction, at all stages of its development, than anybody else in this country . . . and . . . more novels and story collections than the entire professional staffs of the *New York Times* (Sunday and daily) and the *Washington Post* (ditto) put together" (*MSP* 20)—a declaration that, significantly, no one ever has attempted to challenge. Garrett brings up this fact less to underscore his extensive reading—which is truly stunning in its consistent high volume and broad scope—than to criticize the comparative lack of literacy among hugely influential reviewers. According to Garrett the combination of ill-read critics and the profit-driven nature of the publishing industry ultimately means "[a] whole lot of very good fiction is overlooked each and every year" (*MSP* 21). Drawing on his substantial knowledge as a reader and working writer, he laments the challenges of publishing and locating good books in such a climate. As George Core has said of Garrett's expertise in this area, "No writer today knows the pressures of the literary marketplace so thoroughly" ("Critical" B8)—a depressing form of knowledge in this troubling literary era, yet one that makes Garrett's insights all the more unique and in-demand.

Detecting and lauding Garrett's role as guide through the drab world of contemporary literary publishing, reviewer Irving Malin conceptualized *My Silk Purse* as a jab at those "corrupt, stupid, and trendy" books created in the literary marketplace "for fast, easy consumption" ("Review of *My Silk Purse*" 278). The accuracy of Malin's reading perhaps is embodied best in a single sentence from one of Garrett's late-1980s book reviews: "[L]iterary silliness is spreading faster than AIDS or herpes II" (*MSP* 209). This declaration, while characterizing the contemporary state of affairs as a kind of virulent disease to avoid contracting, also is notable for its grim humor. Indeed, reviewer J. A. Bryant Jr. proclaimed that the pieces in *My Silk Purse* are "as witty as they are perceptive" (438)—a welcome quality without which parts of the book would read not unlike a doom-and-gloom jeremiad.

Though portions of *My Silk Purse* are saved through humor (usually of the dark, biting variety), its underlying messages remain serious and possessed of a curious virtue: amid such a bleak and hopeless publishing landscape Garrett valiantly plods onward, producing carefully attuned criticism on anything and everything that crosses his path. In fact, one of the most impressive aspects of both *My Silk Purse* and its companion book *The Sorrows of Fat City* is traceable to the wide range of variant works they address: collections (of short stories, poems, and essays), novels, biographies, autobiographies, criticism, and histories. And it is surprising, if not astonishing, that Garrett appears correspondingly adept and equally knowledgeable in discussing all of them. Considering the early-twenty-first-century climate of specialization in the academy—in which most scholars slip on their tunnel-visioned funny-glasses and limit themselves to one historical period or a single political/theoretical manner of constructing both their work and the world—one can only marvel at Garrett's daring ability to leap dexterously across genres, paradigms, and centuries in addressing—in all their complexity and diversity—the grand narratives of writing and publishing. And throughout all of them he stubbornly refuses to cling to a specific theory or philosophy, since he realizes that each worldview remains subject to a process in motion, the paradigms of today inevitably destined to take their turns (decades? a century down the line?) at the whipping post currently inhabited by the New Criticism and other "outmoded" schools of interpretation. A highly accessible critic, writing profusely and well in the literary quarterly tradition, Garrett has produced a body of work that almost certainly is more likely to be read in the distant future than the output of his more narrowly academic and theoretically faddish colleagues.

The resonant universal and archetypal qualities that permeate much of Garrett's criticism are traceable to his extensive knowledge of history and various literary traditions across time. Having spent decades researching and composing three historical novels of Elizabethan England, he occasionally summons that period in his criticism. In fact, it is that very era which links the separate collections *My Silk Purse and Yours* and *The Sorrows of Fat City*—both books opening with sections on Elizabethan culture. Writing in the *Sewanee Review* Walter Sullivan offered that much of the wisdom of *The Sorrows of Fat City* stems from Garrett's "knowledge of the connection between Elizabethans and modern Americans" ("Where" 667). One might just as easily say the same of *My Silk Purse*; and the true nature of what Garrett received—and what we might potentially gain—from his voluminous research on the Elizabethans is best described at length in that collection:

> I greatly admired their ceaseless interest in and ability to articulate characterization. Pre-Freudian, pre-Jungian, sometimes working with equally improbable and much simpler theories, they could go as deep into human beings as anyone before or since them—this included, by the way, the self-reflexive characterization of speakers and narrators.
>
> Above all, though, I believe that then as now I was wholly overwhelmed by the range, openness, and vitality of their language, all the layers of it, from the most coarse and vulgar to the most highfalutin, the often indecorous joining of the vernacular with the rhetorical, all welded together somehow without any visible cracks or seams. Simultaneous with this richly various language, probably part and parcel of it, was the bringing together of an equal variety of images, of tones and moods, of subjects. (*MSP* 13)

Delineating the Elizabethan's broad and unlikely literary gifts, Garrett offers them to us in the context of the late twentieth century. And the time closer to our own does not come off well in the comparison, having produced mostly

a literature of inferior quality despite the ostensible progress of psychological theory and the rich exchanges between numerous multilingual, verbally
varied societies.

In the face of unceasing historical and literary change the writer, according to Garrett, is best served—and achieves the greatest honor—by performing her craft faithfully, without reference to marketplace realities or the
venue, prestigious or wholly obscure, in which she works. Garrett elaborates
at the beginning of *The Sorrows of Fat City*, "All the writers I admire, some
of them openly admired in these pages, have in common the habitual fact
that they always wrote as well as they were able to, holding back nothing,
in everything they did, major or minor, heavy or light. I have tried my best
to follow their good example" (*SFC* ix). This declaration constitutes both
the confession of a writer and the preference of a critic—it is what Garrett
practices as well as what he looks for and admires in the work of others. As
in *My Silk Purse*, theory does not play a part in Garrett's critical approach,
though it also does not escape his notice. In fact—in a very humorous and
roundabout manner—it constitutes the very catalyst that provided him with
the title for his collection. While serving as chair of creative writing at the
University of Michigan, Garrett attended a lecture by Harold Bloom entitled
"The Sorrows of Facticity," after which he confessed to Bloom that his mild
dyslexia had led him to believe that the lecture was entitled "The Sorrows
of Fat City." Believing Garrett to be poking fun at his weight, the immense
critic (whose girth did in fact match his considerable reputation) was outraged. Yet Bloom's term may be more appropriate than Garrett, who admits
to having daydreamed through much of the critic's lecture, may have realized, its dominant intention being to provide a name for those various works
we never actually have read or studied firsthand but assume we know—a
phenomenon prevalent in the United States in the late twentieth and early
twenty-first centuries, even among academics.

As in *My Silk Purse*, the reviewers and academics discussed in *Sorrows
of Fat City* do not escape responsibility or censure for the deplorable state
of things in the literary world. Among the book's many epigraphs is a back-
handed comment on critics from Faulkner: "All that is needed for admission
to the ranks of criticism is a typewriter" (*SFC* 12). This is an opinion Garrett
ultimately seems to share, for he says of the contemporary critic, echoing a
similar assertion in *My Silk Purse*: "I am familiar with more writers and more
and various texts than they are, even the most, and most justly, celebrated
among them. They cannot be much help in refining my appreciation of and
for new texts and old verities. And they are no help at all in the endless

wrestle with my own words" (*SFC* 12–13). What may come across as misplaced crowing to people unfamiliar with Garrett's heavy, unceasing reading becomes more plausible when one takes into consideration his extensive reviewing, judging of literary prizes, and intermittent composition of the *Dictionary of Literary Biography*'s comprehensive "Year in Fiction." As Muhammad Ali once stated matter-of-factly, "It's not bragging if you can back it up," and Garrett's documented responsibilities have, in fact, forced him to read and comment upon, either in print or informally, literally hundreds of books per year for several decades. Simultaneously, one detects somewhere in his comment the large and heavy footprint of 1980s and 1990s literary theory, which, among many other things, succeeded in replacing countless novels and poetry collections on graduate English department reading lists with various (and often completely nonliterary) cultural studies titles. Acknowledging this historical phenomenon makes Garrett's comment far less surprising. Indeed, it easily might have come from a writer half his age.

Although publishers, academics, and critics are Garrett's favorite mushy punching bags in *Sorrows of Fat City*, he is not averse to pointing out problems and shortcomings among his fellow writers. For instance, he believes many of them are complicit in succumbing to the pressures of the marketplace and/or resorting to sensationalism while apparently possessing little knowledge of their readerships. Garrett describes the manner in which they populate their stories with

> criminals, antiheroes, wise children, schizophrenics, clowns, and, of course, plenty of professors and artists.... Which is strange. Because if we are to understand what has been happening in America in this century, we have to understand the professionals.... It is also a simple fact that almost all of the actual and potential 'reading public' in America, throughout this century and no less now than earlier, is composed of mature men and women of the professional class. (*SFC* 86)

Sensing a peculiar cultural and artistic disconnect between writers/readers and the subject matter they most frequently embrace, Garrett identifies yet another potential barrier in the production of more authentic literature in the contemporary era.

Although many of Garrett's observations come across as brutally frank in their criticisms, his work as a whole is mediated by a recurrent element of humility, perhaps captured best in *Sorrows of Fat City*, when he sums up the process by which he hit upon, or rather fell upon, a way of reading the novels of Saul Bellow:

> [H]aving duly warned everyone, admitted some premeditated and ac-
> cidental faults, confessed to a lack of proper credentials, and no doubt
> already driven off a country fair number of readers with an undeniable
> display of a serious lack of high seriousness, I seem to have stumbled
> upon a banana peel myself and landed smack upon—a method. (*SFC*
> 152)

Listing his shortcomings and relegating his arrival at an avenue of interpretation to a clumsy accident, Garrett sketches a portrait of himself recognizable to and akin to that of the general literary reader who, doubtful of meaning and untrained in theory, stumbles about in the novel at hand to the best
of his ability. It is a rhetorical strategy that symbolically places him among
readers rather than at a podium, telling them what to think.

Garrett's extensive stumbling (or feigned stumbling)—his unpostured
and unorthodox, yet comprehensive, knocking about in whatever subject he
comes upon—collectively allows him to achieve broad and highly personal-
ized perspectives on a substantial array of large subjects. Not surprisingly, he
is especially remarkable in his ability to perceive the big picture with regard
to identifying problems in contemporary writing and publishing. He does
not, for example, limit his critique of polemical writing to the literary realm,
taking the time and space to point as well to the death (if it truly ever was
alive) of objective journalism:

> It needs to be noted that contemporary journalistic theory, denying
> the possibility of any truly "objective" reportage, allows that all good
> reporting is, in a sense, "advocacy journalism." Thus, though journal-
> ism may (or may not) seek to be fair, it nevertheless takes moral and
> political and social stands and choices. (*SFC* 216)

As fascinating a topic as this may constitute on its own terms, Garrett does
not leave it isolated in space or to its own devices. Instead, he develops and
expands the observation, offering that literary concerns and journalism are
wedded irrevocably through the function of book reviewers, who, according
to Garrett, inhabit a very problematic role:

> Unquestionably, the salaries of the professional book reviewers, earn-
> ing them far more than all but a small handful of the serious poets
> and novelists they review, make them, together with the employees of
> commercial publishing houses, among the very few who actually *profit*
> directly from contemporary literature. They have a considerable in-
> ducement toward the preservation of the status quo, if possible. (*SFC*
> 218)

Viewed in terms of salaries and profits, contemporary literature begins to take on a form of industrial production in which writers are more workers than owners, and the publishers and reviewers have as their primary concern the sustainability of a system that benefits them materially.

Though all but a few academic literary folks miss out entirely on the economic advantages of the corporate publisher-reviewer system, they still manage to influence what is read and studied beyond the published moment through their syllabi, research, and the gradual, collective practice of canonization. However, as Garrett points out, canonization and the appearance of certain works on reading lists usually has more to do with the structure of higher education than the intrinsic value of a given literary work: "Within the boundaries of classroom times and academic calendars, it is feasible to deal only with certain significant, representative and *teachable* examples" (*SFC* 223). Concerned with advancing their theories and careers, academics most often choose only those works that fit and highlight their interpretive frameworks while either discrediting or, worse, ignoring those equally substantial artistic achievements that do not.

Garrett's skepticism of academics and their theories partially explains why he refrains from working in the mode of the academic article, his pieces, as demonstrated here, embracing varied topics and approaches to an astonishing degree while keeping the educated general reader firmly in sight as an ideal audience. This practice continues in his regionally focused, third book-length collection of criticism *Southern Excursions: Views on Southern Letters in My Time* (2003), the essay section of which is introduced with the following qualifier:

> These are not strictly essays, I suppose, not in the conventional sense of the term, anyway. They are representative pieces of essay length, originally written for various books and magazines—reviews, lectures, critical pieces, and even a travel article—where I was allowed a little more space and elbow room than one can usually expect. (*SE* 1)

Up front, without even making it to the first piece, we are greeted by Garrett's imaginative versatility, which—as was the case in the two earlier critical collections—proves by book's end to constitute the text's primary value and strength. Poet David Middleton accurately listed the book's broad yet often converging preoccupations as follows:

> Southern literature as being regional and unique yet also universal, Southern respect for individualism and the literary vocation, Southern writers as teachers of creative writing or pursuers of other ways

of making ends meet, the state of Southern publishing, the role today of the literary quarterly (especially the Southern quarterly), the place and importance of book reviewing, the lust for—as opposed to the just bestowal of—literary fame, and the joys of the literary life as lived by the honest and dedicated craftsman. (133–34)

These are familiar concerns abstracted into the specialized, yet somewhat elusive, realm of southern literature. Rather than focusing on a single facet of that regional discourse, Garrett plunges into it headlong, taking on the various phenomena that make it up in all their exclusive and interlocking complexity.

Irving Malin, who had also reviewed *My Silk Purse*, accurately said of the newer collection: "Garrett defies convention, constructs real arguments, and remains a true ghostly presence in the 'south'" ("Review of *Southern Excursions*" 149). Malin's curious description is nonetheless an accurate one. Working here and there, commenting in a number of modes in a wide assortment of venues, Garrett's presence occasionally appears "ghostly"—a disembodied voice capable of drifting across boundaries into numerous subject areas. However, when gathered together, manifested as one, the pieces come across as real, defiant, and relevant—undeniably present in the South they scrutinize. Indeed, the book's wide-ranging quality gives it an authority lacking in all but the rarest and best regional academic studies. The gathered reviews—as varied as those in *My Silk Purse and Yours* and *The Sorrows of Fat City* despite the reduced geographical canvas—concern themselves with topics as broad and seemingly disconnected as William Byrd II, George Washington and the Dismal Swamp Company, intellectual orientations of the Civil War, lesbian fiction, and—the recurrent standby—Elizabethan history.

Although Garrett believes southern writers continue to play a vitally important, differentiated role on the contemporary literary scene ("If, as so many critics have gleefully predicted, the novel falls over dead, it won't be the fault of the southerners" [*SE* 6]), he uses significant portions of *Southern Excursions* to articulate the dangers and challenges—most of them shared with American writers everywhere—that confront them. He specifically warns of the sometimes necessary, though problematic, relationship between writers and the academy, expressing his concern that an art that takes its cues from the ideals of higher education administrators "is in danger of being grotesquely crippled and is very unlikely to be part of any valid literary tradition" (*SE* 52). A cofounder of the now-thriving and enormous Association of Writers and Writing Programs (AWP), Garrett worries about the possible over-institutionalization of writers and artistic concerns in general. Poets, with their meager book sales and incessant pressure to win awards, are especially susceptible: "Most of our celebrity poets, all but a very few, are institutional (corporate) creatures, working for colleges and universities, by and large happy institutional campers" (*SE* 151). Understanding the allure of reliable salaries and benefits, Garrett nonetheless expresses concern over the inevitable political conflicts and unfortunate artistic capitulations that often emerge out of the relationship.

Beyond the academy, Garrett again—as he had in his two previous collections—criticizes the immense and generally debilitating power of trade publishers, warning that they "are able to make of southern literature whatever they please by publishing only those things that please them and conform to their preconceived views" (*SE* 109). Beleaguered by the pressures of publishing and the academy, the contemporary southern writer struggles with authenticity both in her art and her persona, since it is the separate corporate behemoths of trade publishing and higher education that are most responsible for creating writers' public images. As in his other critical books, Garrett does not lead us into such dark and despairing scenarios without eventually offering some hope and instruction. For example, he holds up Fred Chappell's principled literary criticism for its obliviousness to literary celebrity, overall evenhandedness, and willingness to "cheerfully (and fairly) kick ass when that is in order" (*SE* 152). There are glimmers in the darkness, moments of light, that suggest one still may practice her craft with high-minded seriousness, responsibility and integrity.

As opposed to Chappell, Garrett, as a critic, admittedly is less willing to swing the steel-toed boot, even when it is deserved: "I can't see any good reason to review a book that I really don't like" (*SE* 133). This difference in critical perspective appears more a result of Garrett's and Chappell's divergent strengths and personalities than anything else. Chappell most often brings the penetrating and objective perception of an electron microscope to the formal underpinnings of whatever attracts his attention, whereas Garrett usually is more interested in the celebration of a work's strong points within the context of its genre and the visceral publishing scene. The approaches, yielding as they do very different results, are equally valid and valuable in a literary era that could do with a lot more of each. As Garrett says of contemporary southern literature in general:

> What seems to be missing from our newly peaceable kingdom is the critical cutting edge so evident in the generation of masters. They may have been often wrong, both in judgement and in advice and counsel,

but their act of questioning the prevailing modes of thought in America was of great value in the national debates of the twentieth century. There is a sense that the present generation of southern writers would rather be safe than sorry. (*SE* 296)

Beset by the agendas of the academy and publishing, and perhaps intimidated by the unpredictable dangers of taking critical stances, most contemporary southern writers simply resolve to steer clear of the responsibility.

Such a current state of affairs only serves to make the critical work of Garrett, Chappell, and a few others all the more crucial to southern letters. In a climate in which it would make all the sense in the world to either adhere to the publisher's/reviewer's ground rules or stop writing criticism altogether, Garrett stubbornly refuses to play it safe, regardless of the consequences. The sole bumper sticker on an old car he once owned read "No Regrets," and we well might affix a similar label to the covers of his critical books. As Barry Hannah perceived, accurately and enigmatically, Garrett is indeed a rare creature—a critic possessed of an unusual combination of good taste, extensive and unorthodox learning, broad and deep experience, and an unwavering ability to achieve clarity. He nearly always engages the reader's sympathies, since he says what he means and arrives from a position of almost unquestionable artistic integrity. Guile, sarcasm, and cynicism often come into play, but they always are employed in favor of the writer and the practice of free-minded art. At the end of a 1959 essay entitled "Faulkner's Early Literary Criticism" Garrett listed the earlier southern writer's strengths as a critic:

[A]n emphasis in all literary forms on artifice to distinguish art from life, a concept of complete fidelity to character, a devotion to the American scene, a sense of the vitality of language, and, finally, a position that art, however truthful and tragic, must be a positive statement against anarchy and chaos. Few of his professional critics can show as much consistency. (*SFC* 254)

Nearly half a century later, with innumerable essays and reviews behind him, Garrett might easily apply the same qualities to himself. Driven to explicate the crippling plights of real writers and the abstract state of literature in his time, Garrett has administered his criticism consistently and well. It is to the advantage of all that it is as deep and as varied as it is long.

part  **IV**

The Writer Laid Bare

An Interview and Unpublished Fictional Excerpt

"The Outer Limits of Probability"

An Interview with George Garrett

That's what an interview essentially is, isn't it? A couple of people kidding
each other to the outer limits of probability and then joining together to
kid the readers, if any.

—George Garrett (the fictional character), *Double Vision*

The following interview took place July 9, 2003, at Garrett's home in Charlottesville, Virginia.

CC: In 1990 you told Richard Easton, "Artists, I think, by definition are more explorers than exploiters. The one thing that artists who are still alive and growing are most anxious to do is this: not to recall a series of habitual gestures."[1] Do you still agree with that and is it getting harder to do?

GG: Yes. I don't go around thinking about it a whole lot. It is in part a self-justification for what I've been doing in that I don't seem to be able to repeat myself too much. Maybe I would if it was easier and, yes, it's harder to do because you have a harder time finding, not readers, but publishers who are sympathetic to a radical change. There are exceptions. Just in the last few days, I've been reading, catching up on, the work of an African-American writer I admire a lot named Percival Everett. No two books of his are alike at all. They're all different from each other in style and subject; more different in many ways than anything I've written. And I think Madison Bell is that way a little bit too. But the more successful writers in commerce, in the sense of publishing and money, have every temptation after succeeding to continue doing more of the same thing. It's the same principle as Brand X or rock bands that develop a particular sound that's instantly recognizable. There are lots of pressures to do this and they've increased over the last few years. By the same token, it's so difficult for literary fiction anyway that you might as well do what you please and then try to find somebody. There is less incentive for the writer to compromise. So that's a help to somebody who's trying to do something a little different. Pushing the envelope and so on.

CC: Many of your early published stories, stories in *King of the Mountain* such as "The Rivals," "The Lion Hunter," "A Hard Row to Hoe," and "The Sea-coast of Bohemia," may be read as initiation narratives. Do you think there is a relationship between this theme and a young writer attempting to find his voice?

GG: Yes, I think that's inevitably the case. I probably did not think so at the time, but looking back on it: yeah, I would think that, no matter how you did it or what you did—sci-fi, fantasy, et cetera—the initial drama of early published fiction is the drama of finding your voice. There are many different ways of doing it; the stories are quite different. That's probably the main theme, at least overtly, that young writers have: who am I and what is my voice? So the initiation story becomes the primary story.

CC: In one of your recent short stories, "My Adventures in Fantasy Land (A Story Full of Sex and Violins)," you seem to have returned to a meditation on the youthful initiation theme. Do you approach it differently now?

GG: Yeah, I think, particularly with that story, it's less urgent. There are a couple of elements. One is that you are more apt to see yourself as comic, if you have survived long enough. It was not comic at the time but essentially you are working with a recapitulation of a certain point of view in which it is now possible—and I've done several stories of this kind—for the elder version of the same person to be more tolerant of youth and its foibles. That story has changed a little bit since its publication.

CC: Is it part of something larger?

GG: Yes, it was going to be part of a novel called "Double Vision." But it was stretching it a little too much I think. It made for a much harder book. Even my best friends said, "I don't understand this," and they're smarter than I am [*laughter*]. So I focused in on the central story and am hoping to get a short book out of it instead of a big, long book that nobody understands. Really it's just about, as I call it somewhere in there, "the shotgun marriage of fact and fiction." Stuff that's real and stuff that's made up, and the blending of the two. Essentially that's double vision anyway.

CC: That sounds very promising.

GG: Well, I don't know. One day I think it's O.K. and the next I don't. But I've put a lot of work into it.

CC: In your poem "Four American Landscapes" you describe how the Florida wind "shuffled the palm fronds like new money."[2] Florida has been an important milieu in your fiction from your earliest published stories and *The Finished Man* on up through *The King of Babylon Shall Not Come against You*. How have Kissimmee and Orlando changed for you as aesthetically imagined places?

GG: Well, they're not there anymore. Orlando was a town, the whole time I was growing up, of twenty-five thousand people. It didn't change any then. The big change came during World War II when they sent fifty thousand soldiers to Orlando and it never got small again. I don't know the population now. I do know that I went there not too terribly long ago with my two grandchildren. We were over at the beach, an hour away. I think they wanted to see Mickey or something but they had to put up with me driving around Orlando. I could see, at one point, the house where I grew up, but I couldn't figure out how to get there. They have these sprawling overheads, highways, interstates.

CC: So you were just kind of circling around over it.

GG: [*laughter*] Yeah, I would point and say, "There's the house." From that distance it was about the size of a model and that's as big as it ever got. Of course, I used to be able to find my way blindfolded around Orlando. Kissimmee was basically a transplanted western town, a cowtown with cowboys and ranches. It hit right up against Disney World so it totally changed too. Those places were just destined for change. But in writing I imagine them as they were. I can't reverse the changes and, in fact, I may exaggerate some of them.

CC: I might ask the same question about the South as a whole. In an essay called "The South," you remark, "Change and decay have always been primary subjects in southern literature. Because it is characteristic of the southern writer (especially in prose fiction) that he feels compelled to capture in words and describe things as they are before they crumble and vanish forever."[3] Do you think this is true of your fiction?

GG: Yeah, I think there's not so much a sense of nostalgia as there is something akin to the urge to fill a photograph album before everything has changed. Change is such a strong part of it. All over the South, perhaps Faulkner is the only one to deal with it in prose, a kind of delayed change was there. Just as the South was beginning to get its head out of the water, the Great Depression arrived, which really didn't end for the South until after World War II. In the 1930s I used to visit my grandfather, who lived in a place called Naples, North Carolina, which doesn't exist anymore I'm told. It was between Asheville and Hendersonville. All around there were developments that never got off the ground: street lamps and sidewalks without houses or buildings. That was the norm growing up: that you would see things that came to nothing. Very surreal. I didn't even know what a development was. I would get on my bike and go out in the woods and suddenly come upon an area with driveways, sidewalks, beautiful street lamps, and sometimes an old abandoned hotel. I thought, naturally as a child does, that's the way the world is: it's full of abandoned places and buildings. Then everything changed radically and I began to feel, as many others do, the need to preserve some memory of that earlier version of place.

CC: In 1995 you wrote, "The southern novel has gradually become a genre, every bit as formulaic as science fiction, the thriller, the historical romance, or the old-fashioned western. [. . .] The southern novel advances through a minefield of habitual gestures and conventions, edging closer and closer to the pure and simple status of irrepressible cliché."[4] What's the status of the southern novel? Is your opinion the same?

GG: [*laughter*] That's really laying it on, isn't it? Well, I would have to say that in part my opinion is the same, except that's what happened is a large number of very good writers have worked out in different directions from this. People like Lewis Nordan, Jim Grimsley, Barry Hannah, or Richard Dillard. All these people have worked away from and played with the expectations of audiences and publishers of what a good southern novel is supposed to be.

CC: That's What I Like (About the South).

GG: Yeah, that was the whole thought behind putting together that anthology. But you know we still have a problem, chiefly with the expectations of other people. Let's say, for the sake of argument, that the southern novel is a genre like romance or any of these others. They keep cranking those out and they're all different from each other in some way or another. So there's nothing unusual in that. I think we have an extra problem in that the publishers in the critical world have a distinct idea now of what they think it is we should appropriately be writing about. You watch the careers of some writers: they'll be championed for a while for the very things they are then chastised for later. But the primary subject matter of the southern novel will never go away. Right now the commercial world is not real interested in southern points of view but that's not very meaningful. We have such a strong tradition, I suspect it'll just go on.

CC: Do, Lord, Remember Me and its various other manifestations and *The King of Babylon Shall Not Come against You* are both southern novels with overlapping characters, events, and stylistic techniques. On the one hand *King of Babylon* appears self-reflexive and postmodern—the writer making veiled but detailed references to things in his other works. On the other hand, it appears to add something and somehow flesh out the earlier novel. What is the relationship between those two books?

GG: That's a complicated kind of story. You were talking earlier about one's attitude toward initiation stories and how that changes once you've been pretty thoroughly initiated. You sort of look back on it and realize how you didn't see the pattern as it was developing at the time. *Do, Lord, Remember Me* and *The King of Babylon Shall Not Come against You* are like two sides of a coin. Ironically, I guess—sort of in the sense of a joke, one of them has a gigantic guy as the powerful preacher character and the other one has a midget called Little David. They're different versions of each other if you reverse things around. In that sense, things overlap, although one story takes place in the mountains of North Carolina and the other in Florida. There are other elements involved. The whole thing began as a story in *The Girl in the Black Raincoat* called "To Whom Shall I Call Now in My Hour of Need?" I tried it that way and a few others, and eventually it developed into *Do, Lord* and was revisited in *King of Babylon.* One person reviewing *King of Babylon* in Lakeland, Florida, hated it and complained about getting the same story over and over again. When's this guy going to think up something new? [*Laughter*]. That was embarrassing but it had a point that I hadn't thought about up until then. If hardly anyone's reading your work, maybe you can repeat yourself.

CC: Those are probably the only two books of yours he's read.

GG: Yeah, anyway, he was annoyed. And then I had to be in Lakeland for something and the folks there tried to keep it from me even though I already knew. It's a story I doubt I go back to. Really for *King of Babylon* I was looking for a story that would be at ease in Florida and that would allow me to talk about the kinds of changes that have happened. Also, for both books the conventional ways of telling stories were put aside in favor of looking for more fun ways to do it. They are very much byproducts of the intense time I spent working in movies. Writing for films allowed me to discover certain things that can't be done in prose, but also things that can't be done in film. I believe Faulkner benefitted and learned from his experience in Hollywood as well. He was a good screenwriter. He incorporated things from film into his writing but also learned to accentuate in his work things that movies can't do.

CC: You've got a good essay on that.[5]

GG: So anyway, I think the same thing applied to me with this stuff. There is some jumping around in time and point of view. Basically things to keep it lively and interesting in terms of the way stories happen and the way in which the past is always spontaneous and always there.

CC: For people to reassemble.

GG: It's a puzzle with missing pieces.

CC: I also think it's interesting that some of the missing pieces have shone up in other places. *Bad Man Blues*, for example.

GG: Yes, there I did it very deliberately, changing slightly some of the names and circumstances. It's something that's happened before, with John Towne. There are a bunch of pages that don't cohere at all of "Life with Kim Novak Is Hell." Just a bunch of pages in a box.

CC: William Peden once said, "George Garrett's house of fiction has as many dark rooms as sunny ones, and there are maggots in the basement."[6] How do you conceive of the grotesque and do you think your applications of it changed over the years?

GG: Well I'm rather fond of maggots [*laughter*]. You know they used to use them for wounds, since they only eat dead flesh. Now what they would be doing in the basement, I'm not so sure. They like sun [*laughter*]. We're doing a lot of laughing here but with the flip of a coin the grotesque can turn serious. I think that's part of the fun: not knowing when that coin is going to be flipped.

CC: Speaking of the concomitant humor and seriousness of the grotesque, John Towne's low-hitting, apathetic tactics still seem very appropriate for the calculating way in which universities and their administrators function. Is Towne a byproduct of backstabbing academic business or a backlash against it?

GG: A little of both, I would think. I'm surprised that the world has caught up with him in a way. He was more outrageous in the 1960s. Now he seems, if he were suddenly plunged into a contemporary academic novel, a familiar figure. "So what's wrong with him?" would probably be the reader's attitude.

CC: You appear to receive periodic interest from Hollywood producers who want you to adapt your work for film. Southern writers like Faulkner, James Agee, and James Dickey all poured significant energy into Tinsel Town projects, and you had your own Hollywood stint working for Sam Goldwyn Jr. in the early 1960s. What's your attitude toward doing that kind of work now?

GG: I'm too old for the aggravation right now. That's really what it's all about and why they pay you so much. But it's not enough for the aggravation. It's possible to beat the system: I think Faulkner did. Shelby Foote was going to go to Hollywood and work with Stanley Kubrick on a movie called *Paths of Glory*, and Faulkner told him this: don't take the work seriously but take the people very seriously. They know they've got you in the sense that you want your work to be good. If you ever invest your pride in a script or film you're dead: you're totally at their mercy. But they can't hurt you if you don't care. They want a scene where flight attendants come down in parachutes, no problem. It's their money and no pride is involved.

CC: At one point, after completing *Death of the Fox*, you had thought to write historical works based on Ovid's time in exile and the relationship between Alexander Hamilton and Aaron Burr. You've said that your work among the Elizabethans has probably concluded. Do you have any plans in the vein of historical fiction?

GG: Well. Ovid's exile has been pretty well covered now in a couple of novels. Also, David Slavitt was the first person in a hundred years to translate the poems Ovid wrote while in exile. The poems really do a wonderful job of covering his exile, so what could I add? So I just dropped it. I never really dismissed or got over the Hamilton-Burr duel, although it's something that's been done a lot. However, there's a lot of story left—I don't have time to deal with it—in terms of Burr. There's something there but I'll leave it to someone else. I've kind of boxed myself in in terms of the kind of historical fiction I do, which requires my knowing my way around in the period before I can do it. I greatly envy people who can hop onto one or two things and re-create the world of, say, eighteenth-century London. It might take me every day of the rest of my life just to get a sense of what eighteenth-century London was like. I've been thinking seriously about doing a book on Robert Greene, who was a playwright and poet, and one of the earliest bashers of Shakespeare. My most recent novel manuscript, "Double Vision," ends, for various reasons, with the first chapter of a book about Robert Greene as a kind of epilogue. It ends with the beginning of something else that is historical. Whether or not I'll go on and write some more chapters, I don't know.

CC: You have written a respectable body of military fiction and taught interesting classes on war literature. What constitutes good military-based fiction and is it still important today?

GG: I don't know what constitutes good military fiction. I do believe that some of the finest pieces have been very indirect. One of the great novels of World War II is *Guard of Honor* and there's no combat in it. It's all about the military hierarchy. One of the best World War II films which covers the immediate post-war period is *Tunes of Glory* with Alec Guinness. It's about a regiment in Scotland and the transition from war to peace. The men are being sent home and the regiment is falling apart. At one time I wanted to do a little piece on two stories, J. D. Salinger's "For Esmé—With Love and Squalor" and one by Peter Taylor. The Salinger story has basically two scenes: a pre- and post-war one. There's no war in it but it's all there. Someone told me—a woman who used to go out with him at that time—that the story's the first and last scene of a six-hundred-page war novel. Salinger saw a lot of combat, more than most. The story's interesting because you're left to imagine your own war and the effect it's had on this guy. Peter's story is rather like that in that it never gets beyond this training camp in Chattanooga. There's only one scene that makes a reference to combat but it's very somber in that you know everyone's about to go off to war. There's this scene after a day of drill in the rain. The men have been dismissed and the sergeant looks at their footprints and thinks about what may lie ahead in combat. You can't duplicate the combat experience of war. The movies can't do it. They can be noisy and scary, but that's about it.

It's still applicable because of these last couple wars. Before they came along a lot of editors had a distinct dislike for military fiction. They might think you're endorsing military life or something. Plus, I've had younger editors tell me that they're not into doing historical fiction since my military stories take place before 1960, which is before they were born. I guess they are historical although I've never thought of them that way.

CC: Over thirty years ago you told Caroline Cross, "My end purpose has never been to make a living or to be a rich, famous author. It's not very sane; any success is accidental, anyway."[7] In one of your Towne stories, you write that a colleague at the University of Virginia once labeled you "completely irrelevant." Does your literary success or legacy trouble you at all?

GG: Less than it used to, probably less than it ought to. No writer that I know of wouldn't admit, in a moment of truth, that they were not troubled by their lack of success or reputation. It doesn't matter who. I've known writers who've been draped in every honor and award and there's still no satisfying them. They still feel slighted, which is sometimes almost comical. There are more important things. When I was very young I didn't expect anything. I thought we would all be dead by the time we were forty anyway. I couldn't imagine that we weren't all going to be nuked. It was there and it was gonna happen sooner or later. Now that we seem to be beyond that, it's still not on my mind as much as it might be. I'm not competitive. What would be the point? It's unhealthy. The whole system of publishing and academe is set up to encourage competitive living and it's usually not worth it. You're competitive with yourself in terms of doing and making something better.

On the occasion of my seventieth birthday my friends, as a joke, presented me with a brass trophy that bears the inscription: Floyd Dell Award. At one time Dell was thought to be destined for success along with Faulkner, Fitzgerald, and Hemingway. He wrote some good books, but ultimately was forgotten. I guess I'll make do with that.

"No Novel Today"

Fragments from "Life with Kim Novak Is Hell"

In the late 1960s Garrett began composing a partially epistolary, highly satirical book-length manuscript called "Life with Kim Novak Is Hell." The
project's narrator and "hero" is John Towne, a sleazy, recurring academic
figure who is described in Chapter 5 as reporting his exploits in a "ridiculously elevated and clumsily hyperbolic, life-affirming tone." Garrett's manuscript eventually swelled to over 1,500 pages, and most of its sections are
now hopelessly out of order. However, the following three segments are significant in that they record Towne's articulation of the "magic striptease"
concept (an idea that would appear again in the title novella from *The Magic
Striptease* and which informs the scholarly approach of this study), his skeptical view of aesthetics, and his (now ironic) plans for writing and completing his novel(s).

"Magic Striptease"

I believe *realismo* has seen its day. Seen better days anyway. Now when I
think of *serious* writing I find myself almost as if by instinct converting the
raw & rude & crude material into fable. Fable without fear or worry of veri-
similitude. Frankly clothed in the motley of artifice.

For example, Ray, I found myself thinking in the hushed dreamless moments before sleep, moments ruffled and moving yet not moving like the
waters of an inlet just as the tide is turning, thinking a story which would be
my story and say what I want to say neatly & economically.

I imagined a character. An impersonator who by practice and obsession
raises his art to the *nth* power, that is [a single mild intrusion of the improb-

able or supernatural à la Marcel Ayme] he goes one step beyond imperson-ation and is finally able to *become* anyone else, any shape or form or sex. Consider that a moment. He can wear these shapes & forms as one would wear costumes, but of course he remains himself, retains his original identity which is as much or more mysterious than it was before. Whatever he finds, whatever he does with this marvelous gift brings him no closer to the truth of the magic mirror where he can see—*himself.*

Already it is becoming not *my* story, but a kind of American story. Is not possibly the fact that we are always *becoming* rather than being, the most singular burden of our experience? That since we can or believe we can change everything, including ourselves, for better or worse we are at once curiously *responsible*, burdened beyond our means, and at the same time desperately, urgently ignorant of who we really are or if, indeed, we are anything. . . .

A problem. If I weren't so damn lazy, I'd write it up. I can see the general shape of it. I even have a title to work with & from—*The Magic Striptease.* Ironic, for this peeler can never get down to flesh & bones. Each layer reveals yet another enigma.

Dig?

ART

If you don't think *Life With Kim* is art, Ray, you better reconsider. And consider the 33rd Biennale at Venice [Italy] where all the Artists & Leaders of the Art World gather. Look what the world brought to that great occasion, as described in *Newsweek*: From Belgium came some cat who makes insect-men out of bread & casts them in silver. From Brazil came "sound-sculpture." From Italy a large packing crate entitled "Sistine Crate." For my money, here's the best of the bunch: "Japan showed Ay-O's 'Tactile Chamber,' a canvas dotted with holes into which viewers inserted curious fingers, which were then shocked by a gentle electric current, or delicately smeared by strange colored liquids."

Thank God Genius Baby isn't interested in Art!

"No Novel Today"

The way things are going, Ray, you're just going to have to wait for *Insects* for the real nitty gritty, the naked truth about what happened *after* the last time I saw you. I haven't even been able to tell you anywhere near enough about what happened *before* I met you, the kind of a person I had been, what my experiences had been, etc.

I don't have enough time and you don't have enough patience.

I can almost hear the sound, he'll call them irrefutable arguments you would use. For one thing there's the lack of unity. Lack of unity in my protagonist, this Jack or John Towne who is and isn't me. Lack of unity in his character & in his experience. I mean, if you were doing it as a novel, how would it be done? He moves in and out of too many worlds & groups. His *life* doesn't make much sense, have much order or unity of design or direction. He has a purpose: to make, as fully and complete as possible, a confession to a good friend whom he has wronged grievously. Yet it appears to be an odd sort of confession. Sort of like Tricksy Dicksy Nixon's famous "Checkers Speech." Maybe, it would seem, not in excess of sorrow or unbearable grief. Maybe, it seems, not so much out of a deep need & desire for absolution as an attempt to "set the record straight." Which may be true to life, in a crude sort of way, but doesn't necessarily become Art, especially since I toss aside [a peel as swift as Georgia Southern at her peak & prime] such basic rhetorical tease-tools as sympathy with the protagonist, concern with his present & past problems, and thus reasons for caring if he slips on a banana peel or not. Nor can I let go so completely as to make him an unmitigated scoundrel all the way. [Scoundrels can make for fascinating reading, provided they are doing interesting evil things and with minimal regret or self-consciousness. Frankly, though, I'd be lying if I tried to claim I was all that bad]

My last rhetorical refuge might be to claim I was typical—or anyway that *Towne* is typical and therefore a kind of living & breathing sociological *exemplum*, worthy of study & consideration on that account. Now that may be true. The country, maybe even the whole world, may be crawling with types like me & Towne. Maybe so, but I don't want to think about it. Even if it's true. Because like every other individual, I like to think I'm unique. It keeps me going. And in some of my more rational moments, I get bugged thinking there may be other guys out there right now just like me and more on the way, too, kids who don't even know it yet. Bugged by the competition? A little, it's true. Makes you have to stay awake & watch your step all the time. Also, from time to time, morally outraged. I mean, I've worked out various ways to live with myself, one day at a time like an alcoholic, but I get angry at the thought of also having to live with a multitude of selves just like me. I'd rather simply quit, give up, become *one* thing *or another*, a familiar type, taking on an acceptable role, even if it was Skid Row Bum, rather than to discover that my every act and purpose, i.e., taking any role seriously, was in and of itself a most typical role. Ergo, I can't claim my protagonist is typical, if only for my own peace of mind.

Instead of making it easier, it looks like this warm-up is going to make *Insects* exceedingly difficult to write. More and more problems arise.

I know what you'd have to say about that. Maybe it shouldn't be written, then. Maybe I would be wiser to break it up, isolate segments, for instance academic life, small town southern boyhood, the war in Korea, Hollywood, marriage, etc., and make something out of each one separately. Different books with different characters etc. that would be sensible. Only Ray, I don't relish the role & label of "writer" any more than any other.

And you know me Ray that's too much like work. And not the quickest or likeliest method to achieve my worldly goals, which, might be briefly summarized as broads in the bed & money in the bank

And even if it were the way, the road to glory in the sack & honor on the street, where would my whole idea of making a confession to you be? If you'll pardon an unfortunate image, it would be out the window in its skivvies.

So, all I can say is that I'm going to write *Insects* this summer. I will it & it will be done. You can count on that. It's a promise.

Meanwhile, until I can get around to it, you'll have to be patient some more and make do with this, these fragments I have shored against my ruin.

John Towne

Redress

A Conclusion

In truth I move along as naked as the fairy-tale emperor
in his new clothes in everything I have ever written.
And that is the measure of the truth of what I write.
—Garrett, *Contemporary Authors*

Having marched Garrett's work onto the runway in all its various colors, guises, and layers—having viewed his output biographically and regionally, grotesquely and academically, militarily and historically, poetically and critically, before finally offering his words in their own naked clarity—this book closes with a redress, which is less a rectification and more a readjustment: a final contextualization of a writer possessed of a dizzying and dazzling wardrobe.

The book's first part, "Undergarments: The Autobiographical and Regional Writer," identifies the fundamental autobiographical and regional narratives that lie closest to Garrett's lived experience and constitute the foundation upon which his forays into numerous genres often are built. Even in his mature years, Garrett remains fascinated by initiation narratives of the self and regional identity (his southern and, particularly, Florida roots). Moving beyond the identity mode, the four chapters that make up Part II, "Styles of Dress," demonstrate Garrett's vagabond talent in extensive action, illustrating the various ways in which his fiction tackles the diverse traditions of the grotesque, the academic narrative, military writing, and historical fiction with unique and successful results. The distinctive, far-reaching quality of Garrett's work becomes even more evident when we take into account his forays into other genres, and the book's third part, "Costume Change," traces the value of his relatively recent poetry and criticism, establishing that many of the qualities underlying his identity interests and fictional modes are revisited and elaborated upon, albeit in different contexts and forms. In the study's final part, "The Writer Laid Bare," criticism and scholarship give way to the unfettered voice itself, and we witness Garrett's variable interests, the striptease of artistic meaning, on and in their own terms.

The unfolding of this book is recounted clearly enough, yet there remain a few loose ends and wayward threads. As Garrett might say (as he often is fond of saying), "There's a story that goes with it." When Shelby Foote visited the University of Virginia in the early 1960s, a student asked him "what Faulkner was really like." Foote, learning that the student had read Faulkner's books, replied, "That is all there is." In terms of his own literary career, Garrett had hoped and sought to write books "into which 'the real me' (whatever that might be) could vanish forever, wholly transformed, leaving only ghost and flesh, finally mere shadows behind" ("George Palmer Garrett" [2002], 104). He dreamed that the artist might become his work, that the underlying body might lose itself in the inner folds of the various outfits it elected to wear. Yet, in the end, the work only served to augment the personality and concerns, as various as both were capable of being, of the artist and the man. The work contains the man but the man also bears the burden—the heavy, packed suitcase—of the work. As Guido says at the end of *Fellini 8½* (a film of which Garrett is very fond), "All the confusion of my life has been a reflection of myself." The work, however strange and powerful, remains, in a very important sense, both only an image of and a secondary phenomenon generated by the artist.

The striptease theory at the heart of this study has sought to trace the various images Garrett has projected through his art. It illustrates how his work and appearance shift dramatically and skillfully depending on the discourse, genre, or tradition he confronts. And therein lies his chief strength and enormous uniqueness as an artist and writer: the ability to say so much, to produce work of a consistently high order, in so many different ways. Yet, it is just this very talent that probably is most responsible for the fact that his work is not better known. Hopping around from form to form, leaving his clothes scattered about the room, Garrett creates a wardrobe wondrously varied, yet probably also diffuse to the eyes of many critics and scholars. Add to that a deep and unwavering biographical dimension of humility, rare among writers and other artists, and his underdeveloped literary reputation becomes understandable. As an anonymous reviewer of this study at the University Press of Florida accurately summarized, "Part of [his] neglect probably results from the fact that Garrett has been so active for so long as an unselfish promoter of other people's writing—people have tended to take his own accomplishments somewhat for granted." Richly diverse in his literary concerns and wholly dedicated to addressing the challenges confronting novice contemporary writers, Garrett, to a significant degree, has created the very conditions that have made the underappreciation of his work possible.

Though perhaps detrimental to the reception of his own work, Garrett's long service to writing and writers is singular and extensive to the point of demanding a book-length consideration of its own. He taught at a number of very different institutions (among them Alabama, Hollins, Michigan, Princeton, Rice, South Carolina, Virginia, and Wesleyan)—creating or fine-tuning writing programs at some of them—and everywhere he went he was a champion, both on-duty and off, of writing and literary culture. In addition, accompanying Garrett's institutional successes are a seemingly endless list of seminars, readings, conferences, and individual consultations and correspondences—nearly all of them documented across the more than three hundred boxes of personal papers in the special collections libraries of Duke and Virginia—through which he has fought for the same principles, usually without any direct benefit to or financial compensation for himself.

Garrett's published meditations on literature, his numerous essays and reviews (collected and uncollected), perhaps are most useful in beginning to establish his relationship to and locate his place within the landscape of contemporary American literature. Unlike scholars and writers who reserve their publications for obscure and specialized journals, Garrett has produced a large amount of writing aimed at the educated general public. Fueling this body of work is a strong, uncompromising belief in teaching the value of the arts to the everyday reader and citizen. Avoiding polemical readings and convoluted theoretical terminology, Garrett often attempts to demonstrate why a poem, novel, or historical study works or doesn't work, and why its achievement or lack thereof is important to our collective literate culture. At work here is what we might call an "open aesthetics," a practice which treats the nonspecialist reader as a democratic equal in discussing and celebrating the value of the arts and writing. Far from embracing pure formalism or some other culturally irresponsible method of reading, Garrett repeatedly stresses the place of art in our society and daily lives. Perhaps most notably bringing this dynamic into focus are his essays on the techniques and business of publishing. Investigating with naked honesty the successful benefits and buried evils of the publishing world, Garrett's essays on book making (and breaking) attempt to instruct the public on how literature is created, while identifying, too, the problematic elements of the industry.

Considering Garrett's work in the continuum of American literary history, it is perhaps most profitable to place him in the tradition of the now exceedingly rare southern "man of letters"—he (or she) who embraces and produces literature in all its complexity and multiple forms (novels, short stories, poems, plays, criticism, translation, editing, and so on). This kind of southern writer, stretching back to Poe, perhaps finds its best modern examples in the Nashville-based writers of the 1920s and 1930s (most notably Davidson, Ransom, Tate, and Warren). Whatever the ultimate value of their literary outputs, the sheer variation of what each of these writers produced is astonishing and almost unheard of in our own era of narrow specialization. Chronologically, Garrett (born in 1929) probably was the most variously gifted southern writer to arrive on the scene following Warren (b. 1905). However, there are a handful of southern writers slightly younger than Garrett among whom he appropriately may be placed: Reynolds Price (b. 1933), Wendell Berry (b. 1934), Fred Chappell (b. 1936), R. H. W. Dillard (b. 1937), Kelly Cherry (b. 1940), and Robert Morgan (b. 1944). Each of these writers (and there may be a few others we could add) has produced work of a high order in fiction, poetry, and criticism, as well as in other genres. And there are connections among them that suggest the remarkable variation of their output is something more than accidental. Price and Chappell studied under the great writing teacher William Blackburn at Duke, Berry is a second-generation Nashville Agrarian, Dillard and Cherry benefitted under Garrett's influence at Virginia, and Cherry and Morgan profited from Chappell's teachings at North Carolina-Greensboro—where, incidentally, Chappell earlier had developed a friendship with Allen Tate.

Though the comparative value of the highly differentiated work produced by these immensely gifted writers is endlessly debatable, in sheer bulk and variation Garrett's collective output eclipses those of his variously gifted peers and the Nashville writers who served, consciously or unconsciously, as models for them. Yet, Garrett's achievement strays even beyond that of the Nashville icons in a number of respects, and perhaps most notably in his Hollywood writing. His best script, *The Young Lovers* (1964), based on a novel of the same name by Julian Halevy (New York: Simon and Schuster, 1955), would be Peter Fonda's first film and recounts a college relationship between Eddie Slocum (Fonda) and Pam Burns (Sharon Hugueny). Of dubious distinction but more lasting fame is the script for *Frankenstein Meets the Space Monster* (1965), cowritten with University of Virginia graduate students R. H. W. Dillard and John Rodenbeck.[1] In his essays, Garrett has written extensively about the experiences of literary writers in Hollywood, most notably Faulkner, and his own tour of duty in the West Coast film world afforded him yet another creative medium to work in while also making him grateful for and appreciative of the qualities of high art so obviously lacking in commercial film culture.

On a fundamental level, Garrett's unique, swashbuckling style of variable artistic creation stems from an inherent ability to assimilate highly structured knowledge and artistic forms while simultaneously remaining skeptical of and detached from them. Such phenomena take the form of outfits that may be tried on, cast aside, put away, or thrown out entirely. For example, writing in his notebooks in the 1960s Garrett objectively gauged the impact of his Princeton education and his accompanying reaction to it:

> [A]s a result of an expensive education, I was unprepared to know and almost unable to learn. Which may say something about the teaching and study of contemporary literature. Absence of the kind of scholarship necessary. Treat books as if they just happened, matter of fact miracles, not related to a complex system of commerce which includes publishing, distribution, and, yes, citation and the academy.

Suspicious of what he was taught and stubbornly refusing to be molded by his undergraduate and graduate years at Princeton, Garrett chose instead to formulate his own vitally alive method of reading—an approach that would stay with him and serve him well in his own work for the rest of his life.

Two more unpublished notebook entries from the 1960s bring us to a stopping place, which is as much an ongoing mantra as it is a conclusion. The first highlights Garrett's supreme dedication to art—the fact that beneath all the layers lies the persistent naked impulse to create, no matter the circumstances:

> Today the disappointment of a further rejection slip + admonitions not to be clever. I see it is perfectly evident that I have no real talent at writing. I can never be professional. Yet it is such a challenge that I must stick to it, hoping always that I shall learn and grow. Consistent failure is rather disconcerting and causes me to despair. But so what? I have nothing but time, my life. I will continue to study and work and try to achieve the integrity, harmony + radiance which are requisite to any work of art.

Still early on in his career, Garrett is stung by criticism and rejection, yet frustration and doubt are accompanied and eclipsed by a confession of heartfelt dedication to the writing life. And over the course of his literary existence that very thing has proven to be the wellspring from which emerges the measure of the truth of what he writes. Perhaps most telling, this dedication—this unwavering commitment to art at all costs—informs the good and the bad times alike. Completing the final proofs for his novel *Do, Lord, Remember Me*, Garrett is less satisfied by his accomplishment than he is excited at his newfound availability to explore—to try on new aesthetic garments once more: "Having finished (actually finishing today) final writing + reviews of Do, Lord, Remember Me, now a world of possibilities is open for me. What next? Many things + little time. Little time." Alternately a friend and a foil in Garrett's quest for literary knowledge and production, time, as literary history, remains an essential variable in evaluating a writer's success. Taking his uniquely woven and sometimes far-flung outfits into consideration, it is difficult to argue that Garrett's use of his literary time was not prodigiously well-spent. Producing incessantly, believing there is always something to be said hereafter, he remains ever eager to embrace and express the next imagined phenomenon—to wrap and button it about himself like a new suit of clothes.

Notes

Introduction. "Art of the Magic Striptease"

1. Unless otherwise noted, all unpublished quoted material comes from Garrett's papers in the Special Collections Library, Duke University.

Chapter 3. Garrett's South

1. For a cross-section of formative interdisciplinary scholarly dialogue on the uneasy relationship between globalization and regionalism, see Helge Hveem, "Explaining the Regional Phenomenon in the Era of Globalization," in *Political Economy and the Changing Global Order*, edited by Richard Stubbs and Geoffrey Underhill (Oxford: Oxford University Press, 2000), 70–81; James Mittleman and Richard Fall, "Global Hegemony and Regionalism," in *Regionalism in the Post-Cold War World*, edited by Stephen C. Calleya (New York: St. Martin's, 2000), 1–22; Jan Aart Scholte, *Globalization: A Critical Introduction* (New York: St. Martin's, 2000); and Sandro Sideri, "Globalisation and Regional Integration," in *Regions and Development: Politics, Security and Economics*, edited by Sheila Page (London: Frank Cass, 2000), 7–43.

Chapter 4. "Maggots in the Basement"

1. Alan Spiegel, "A Theory of the Grotesque in Southern Fiction," *Georgia Review* 26 (spring/winter 1972): 426–37; William Van O'Connor, *The Grotesque: An American Genre and Other Essays* (Carbondale: Southern Illinois University Press, 1962); Patricia Yaeger, "Beyond the Hummingbird: Southern Women Writers and the Southern Gargantua," in *Haunted Bodies: Gender and Southern Texts*, edited by Anne Goodwyn Jones and Susan Donaldson (Charlottesville: University Press of Virginia, 1997), 287–318; and Sarah Gleeson-White, *Strange Bodies: Gender and Identity in the Novels of Carson McCullers* (Tuscaloosa: University of Alabama Press, 2003).

2. Appearing in a number of novels, stories, poems, and songs by numerous writers, the image of the girl in the black raincoat grew out of the mysterious midsemes-

ter departure of Kelly Cherry from one of Garrett's writing classes at the University of Virginia. Haunted by her disappearance, her fellow students began composing stories and poems about her—a practice that eventually was adopted by Garrett and writers and scholars across the country, ultimately resulting in the publication of the "antianthology" *The Girl in the Black Raincoat*. As Garrett recalls:

> Kelly came to my creative writing class, shy and soft-voiced and quite beautiful, and more than a little mysterious in the long buttoned-up raincoat she wore always and everywhere, its hem barely revealing the blue sneakers she also always had on. Long before punk, her hair was an extravagantly artificial red. And, needless to say, all of the young men in my class those days, still coat-and-tie days (though some of them affected early signs of rebellion from dress codes and other authoritarian impositions by going barefoot or, anyway, without socks), all of them were madly, possessively, irrepressibly in love with her. So was I, I reckon, a little. So was everybody. ("Introduction II" 15)

Chapter 5. Life in the Academy Is Hell

1. A fictional cinematic exposé on the squalid, pathetic backstage lives of pill-popping Hollywood starlets during the 1960s, *Valley of the Dolls* was based on Jacqueline Susann's best-selling 1966 novel of the same name.

Chapter 7. Time and Historical Fiction

1. Garrett also benefitted from the research acumen of Ruthe Battestin, who periodically performed fieldwork for him in England (Robinson, "George" 182).

Chapter 8. Recent Seasonal Fashions

1. A number of published references to Garrett's earlier poetry may be found in the special Garrett issue of the *Mill Mountain Review* as well as the scholarly collection *To Come Up Grinning: A Tribute to George Garrett* (both listed in the Works Cited section).

Chapter 9. Scholarly Threads

1. *Princeton Library Chronicle* 18 (spring 1957): 124–35.

Chapter 10. "The Outer Limits of Probability"

1. Easton 33.
2. Garrett, *CP*, 41.
3. Garrett, "The South," 33.
4. Garrett, "It's the True South," 167.
5. "The Man Who Wrote the Movie: Faulkner and the Public Arts," in *Southern Excursions: Views on Southern Letters in My Time* (Baton Rouge: Louisiana State University Press, 2003), 86–93.

6. Peden 65.

7. Cross 4.

Conclusion. Redress

1. The movie, rereleased on DVD by Dark Sky Films in May 2006, ultimately proved a more advantageous accomplishment for R. H. W. Dillard, likely fueling his appointment to the board of governors for the Count Dracula Society, known later as the Academy of Science Fiction, Fantasy, and Horror Films.

Works Cited

In regard to primary and secondary sources, I list those works from which I quote in my consideration of Garrett's fiction. As a result, many of Garrett's works and a substantial number of scholarly articles about them are not included. For the most comprehensive published bibliography of Garrett's work, see Stuart Wright, "George Garrett: A Bibliography, 1947–1988," in *To Come Up Grinning: A Tribute to George Garrett*, edited by Stuart Wright and Paul Ruffin (Huntsville, Tex.: Texas Review Press, 1989), 116–84.

Works by Garrett

"Against the Grain: Poets Writing Today." In *American Poetry*, edited Irvin Ehrenpreis, 221–39. London: Edward Arnold, 1965.
American Literature of World War II. Videocassette. Eminent Scholar/Teacher Series. Omnigraphics, 1988.
"Another Version." *Poetry* 180, no. 4 (July 2002): 192.
"Author of His Own Death." *Washington Post Bookworld*, September 8, 1996, p. 6.
Bad Man Blues: A Portable George Garrett. Dallas: Southern Methodist University Press, 1998.
"B. S. Johnson." In *Poets of Great Britain and Ireland since 1960*, part 1: *A–L*, edited by Vincent B. Sherry Jr., 277–82. Detroit: Gale, 1985.
"The Best Way Home: Fact and Fiction in *Shiloh* and *All the Brave Promises*." *Sewanee Review* 110, no. 3 (summer 2002): 437–50.
"*By Love Possessed*: The Pattern and the Hero." *Critique* 1, no. 3 (winter 1958): 41–47.
Cold Ground Was My Bed Last Night. Columbia: University of Missouri Press, 1964.
The Collected Poems of George Garrett. Fayetteville: University of Arkansas Press, 1984.
"Con Game." *Richmond Mercury* 1 (December 6, 1972): 9.

"The Crossover Bear; or, the True Story of Frankenstein Meets the Space Monster (Among Other Things)." *Virginia Quarterly Review* 81, no. 1 (winter 2005): 4–39.

"Daily Life in City, Town, and Country." In *William Shakespeare: His World, His Work, His Influence,* edited by John F. Andrews, 1:215–31. New York: Scribner's, 1985.

Death of the Fox. Garden City: Doubleday, 1971.

Do, Lord, Remember Me. London: Chapman and Hall, 1965.

"Don't Make Waves." In *Man and the Movies,* edited by W. R. Robinson, 227–60. Baton Rouge: Louisiana State University Press, 1967.

"Don't Try and Sell Me No Pink Flamingos: An Introduction." In *White Trash: An Anthology of Contemporary Southern Poets,* edited by Nancy Stone and Robert Waters Grey, xi–xii. Charlotte: New South, 1976.

Double Vision. Tuscaloosa: University of Alabama Press, 2004.

Empty Bed Blues. Columbia: University of Missouri Press, 2006.

Enchanted Ground. York Harbor, Me.: Old Gaol Museum Press, 1981.

"Ending Badly in Commerce." *Richmond Mercury* 1 (December 6, 1972): 17.

Entered from the Sun. New York: Doubleday, 1990.

An Evening Performance. New York: Doubleday, 1985.

"Exemplary Letters from *The Realms of Gold* (An Excerpt from an Upcoming Novel)." *Rapier* 1, no. 2 (January 1967): 6–7, 26–28.

The Finished Man. New York: Scribner's, 1959.

"Foote's *The Civil War:* The Version for Posterity?" *Mississippi Quarterly* 28 (winter 1974–75): 83–92.

"The Function of the Pasiphae Myth in *Brother to Dragons.*" *Modern Language Notes* 74, no. 4 (April 1959): 311–13.

"George Garrett." In *Sudden Fiction: American Short Short Stories,* edited by Robert Shapard and James Thomas, 257–58. Salt Lake City: Peregrine Smith, 1986.

"George Garrett." In *The Fugitives, the Agrarians, and Other Twentieth-Century Southern Writers,* 21–25. Charlottesville: Alderman Library (University of Virginia), 1985.

"George Palmer Garrett." *Contemporary Authors,* 202:97–132. Detroit: Thomson-Gale, 2002.

———. *Dictionary of Literary Biography: 1986.* Edited by J. M. Brook, 71–90. Detroit: Gale Research, 1987.

Going to See the Elephant: Pieces of a Writing Life. Edited by Jeb Livingood. Huntsville: Texas Review Press, 2002.

"A Grim Farce from Beginning to End." *Richmond Mercury* 3, no. 18 (January 8, 1975): 15.

"Here Is Heartbreak, and Here Is Laughter." *New York Times Book Review,* July 4, 1993, p. 8.

"In Other Countries." *Prairie Schooner* 30, no. 3 (fall 1956): 292–98.

In the Briar Patch: A Book of Stories. Austin: University of Texas Press, 1961.

Interview. Cassette. Audio Prose Library, 1984.

"Introduction." In *Gulliver's Travels,* by Jonathan Swift, xii–xv. New York: Harper and Row, 1965.

"Introduction II." In *The Wedding Cake in the Middle of the Road: 23 Variations on a Theme,* edited by George Garrett and Susan Stamberg, 14–19. New York: Norton, 1992.

James Jones. San Diego: Harcourt, Brace, Jovanovich, 1984.

The King of Babylon Shall Not Come against You. San Diego: Harcourt, Brace, 1996.

King of the Mountain. New York: Scribner's, 1957.

"Literary Ladies of Dixie." *Virginia Quarterly Review* 79, no. 1 (winter 2003): 161–66.

"A Literary Letter from George Garrett." *Richmond Mercury* 3, no. 1 (September 11, 1974): 20–23.

"The Literature of the Great War." *Sewanee Review* 84, no. 3 (summer 1976): 496–509.

Luck's Shining Child: A Miscellany of Poems and Verses. Winston-Salem: Palaemon, 1981.

The Magic Striptease. Garden City: Doubleday, 1973.

"Memorial Service." *Poetry* 180, no. 4 (July 2002): 192.

"My Adventures in Fantasy Land (A Story Full of Sex and Violins)." *Five Points* 7, no. 1 (2003): 13–35.

My Silk Purse and Yours: The Publishing Scene and American Literary Art. Columbia: University of Missouri Press, 1992.

"New Book on Sir Walter Is Exceptionally Fine Work." *Charlotte Observer,* February 24, 1974, p. B4.

"News of the Renaissance." *Sewanee Review* 101, no. 4 (fall 1993): 585–92.

The Old Army Game. Dallas: Southern Methodist University Press, 1994.

"One Kind of Anarchy." *College English* 25, no. 3 (December 1963): 163–69.

"The Other Side of the Coin." *Four Quarters* 6, no. 2 (January 1957): 20–28.

Poison Pen. Winston-Salem, N.C.: Stuart Wright, 1986.

"P.S. What Is Octagon Soap: A Tale from the Tumultuous Sixties." *Texas Arts Journal* 1 (January-February 1977): 39–49.

"Review of *In the Clearing,* by Robert Frost." *Houston Post.* "Houston Now" Section, March 25, 1962, p. 32.

"Review of *Promises: Poems, 1954–1956,* by Robert Penn Warren." *Georgia Review* 12, no. 2 (spring 1958): 106–8.

"Review of *The Assassination of Jesse James by the Coward Robert Ford,* by Ron Hansen." *Michigan Quarterly Review* 23 (fall 1984): 606–9.

"Review of *William Faulkner: New Orleans Sketches,* by William Faulkner." *Georgia Review* 14, no. 3 (summer 1960): 215–16.

Sir Slob and the Princess: A Play for Children. New York: Samuel French, 1962.

The Sorrows of Fat City. Columbia: University of South Carolina Press, 1992.

"The South." *American Libraries* 3, no. 1 (January 1972): 24–39.

Southern Excursions: Views on Southern Letters in My Time. Baton Rouge: Louisiana State University Press, 2003.

"A Story Goes with It." *Sewanee Review* 110, no. 4 (October-December 2002): 669–82.

The Succession. New York: Doubleday, 1983.

"The Survivor's Tragedy." *Washington Post Book World,* August 14, 1994, p. 5.

"Teaching Writing: A Letter to the Editor." In *Writers as Teachers/Teachers as Writers,* edited by Jonathan Baumbach, 59–75. New York: Holt, Rinehart and Winston, 1970.

"Technics and Pyrotechnics." *Sewanee Review* 88, no. 3 (summer 1980): 412–23.

That's What I Like (About the South): And Other New Southern Stories for the Nineties. Coedited with Paul Ruffin. Columbia: University of South Carolina Press, 1993.

"There Are Lions Everywhere." *Mill Mountain Review* 1, no. 3 (spring 1971): 217–19.

"To Guess the Riddle, to Stumble on a Secret Name." In *The Wedding Cake in the Middle of the Road: 23 Variations on a Theme,* edited by George Garrett and Susan Stamberg, 58–61. New York: Norton, 1992.

"To Whom Shall I Call Now in My Hour of Need?" In *The Girl in the Black Raincoat: Variations on a Theme,* 247–76. New York: Duell, Sloan and Pearce, 1966.

Understanding Mary Lee Settle. Columbia: University of South Carolina Press, 1988.

Which Ones Are the Enemy? Boston: Little, Brown, 1961.

Whistling in the Dark: True Stories and Other Fables. San Diego: Harcourt, Brace, Jovanovich, 1992.

A Wreath for Garibaldi and Other Stories. London: Rupert Hart-Davis, 1969.

"The Year in Fiction: A Biased View." In *Dictionary of Literary Biography Yearbook: 1983,* edited by Mary Bruccoli and Jean W. Ross. Detroit: Gale, 1984.

"Young Fenians in Love and History." *New York Times Book Review,* January 3, 1988, pp. 1, 26–27.

Secondary Sources

Bakhtin, Mikhail. *Rabelais and His World.* Translated by Helen Iswolsky. Cambridge, Mass.: Massachusetts Institute of Technology Press, 1965.

Bausch, Richard. "Many Voices." In *Bad Man Blues: A Portable George Garrett,* by George Garrett, ix–xi. Dallas: Southern Methodist University Press, 1998.

Bausch, Robert. "George Garrett's Military/Army Fiction." In *To Come Up Grinning: A Tribute to George Garrett,* edited by Paul Ruffin and Stuart Wright, 8–11. Huntsville, Tex.: Texas Review Press, 1989.

Bell, Madison Smartt. *Narrative Design: Working with Imagination, Craft, and Form.* New York: Norton, 1997.

———. Novel Panel. Southern Literature Festival: A Celebration of the Life and Work of George Garrett. University of Tennessee, October 2–4, 2003, Knoxville, Tenn.

Betts, Richard A. "'To Dream of Kings': George Garrett's *The Succession*." In *George Garrett: The Elizabethan Trilogy*, edited by Brooke Horvath and Irving Malin, 70–84. Huntsville, Tex.: Texas Review Press, 1998.

Birns, Nicholas. "Review of *Going to See the Elephant: Pieces of a Writing Life*." *Review of Contemporary Fiction* 22, no. 2 (summer 2002): 221–22.

Bowers, Neal. "What the Crow Knows." *Sewanee Review* 107, no. 2 (spring 1999): xliii–xlv.

Bryant, J. A., Jr. "Criticism in the Postmodern Age." *Sewanee Review* 101, no. 3 (summer 1993): 433–42.

Buckley, Jerome Hamilton. *Season of Youth: The Bildungsroman from Dickens to Golding*. Cambridge, Mass.: Harvard University Press, 1974.

Carr, John. "In Contention with Time: George Garrett's *Death of the Fox*." *Mill Mountain Review* 1, no. 3 (spring 1971): 19–26.

Chappell, Fred. "Fictional Characterization as Infinite Regressive Series: George Garrett's Strangers in the Mirror." In *Southern Literature and Literary Theory*, edited by Jefferson Humphries, 66–74. Athens: University of Georgia Press, 1990.

———. "Introduction." In *George Garrett: The Elizabethan Trilogy*, edited by Brooke Horvath and Irving Malin, ix–xxiii. Huntsville, Tex.: Texas Review Press, 1998.

———. "The Lion Tamer: George Garrett's Short Stories." *Mill Mountain Review* 1, no. 3 (spring 1971): 42–46.

Chaufour-Verheyen, Christine. *William Styron: Le 7e Jour*. Paris: du Rocher, 1991.

Cherry, Kelly. "Meaning and Music in George Garrett's Fiction." In *To Come Up Grinning: A Tribute to George Garrett*, edited by Paul Ruffin and Stuart Wright, 16–20. Huntsville, Tex.: Texas Review Press, 1989.

Clabough, Casey. "William Hoffman's Fictional Journey: An Interview." *Southern Quarterly* 41, no. 1 (fall 2002): 80–86.

Core, George. "Critical Essays Revealing, Nurturing Literary Pursuits." *Washington Times*, November 24, 2002, p. B8.

———. "Introduction." *The Old Army Game*, by George Garrett, ix–xiv. Dallas: Southern Methodist University Press, 1994.

Cross, Caroline. "George Garrett." *Broken Ink* 2, no. 1 (1971): 4–5.

Dillard, Annie. Untitled tribute to George Garrett. In *To Come Up Grinning: A Tribute to George Garrett*, edited by Paul Ruffin and Stuart Wright, 105. Huntsville, Tex.: Texas Review Press, 1989.

Dillard, R. H. W. "George Garrett." In *Dictionary of Literary Biography*, vol. 130: *American Short-Story Writers since World War II*, edited by Patrick Meanor, 163–77. Detroit: Gale, 1993.

———. "George Garrett." In *Dictionary of Literary Biography Yearbook: 1983*, edited by Mary Bruccoli and Jean W. Ross, 155–61. Detroit: Gale, 1983.

———. "George Garrett: An Appreciation." *Virginia Quarterly Review* 75, no. 3 (summer 1999): 459–72.

———. *Understanding George Garrett*. Columbia: University of South Carolina Press, 1988.

Durden, Douglas. "Writer Bridges Gaps between Worlds." *Richmond Times-Dispatch*, August 10, 1972, p. B8.

Easton, Richard. "An Interview with George Garrett." *New Orleans Review* 17, no. 4 (winter 1990): 33–40.

Fiedler, Leslie. "From Redemption to Initiation." *Newsleader*, May 26, 1958, pp. 20–23.

Fleming, Thomas. "Realms of Lead." In *To Come Up Grinning: A Tribute to George Garrett*, edited by Paul Ruffin and Stuart Wright, 21–30. Huntsville, Tex.: Texas Review Press, 1989.

Fussell, Paul. *The Great War and Modern Memory*. Oxford: Oxford University Press, 1975.

Grohskopf, Bernice. "An Author for All Seasons." *Virginia Quarterly Review* 79, no. 2 (spring 2003): 362–66.

Graham, John. "Fiction and Film: An Interview with George Garrett." *Film Journal* 1, no. 2 (summer 1971): 22–26.

Haar, Maria. *The Phenomenon of the Grotesque in Modern Southern Fiction*. Stockholm: Umea, 1983.

Harris, Mark. *Wake Up, Stupid*. New York: Knopf, 1959.

Hirsch, Edward. "Three Initiations." *American Poetry Review* 27, no. 5 (September 1998): 45–54.

Hoffman, Daniel. "From Daniel Hoffman." *Mill Mountain Review* 1, no. 3 (spring 1971): 195.

Howard, Jennifer. "Lives of the Fox." *Princeton Alumni Weekly*, December 7, 1994, pp. 17–21.

Howe, Susan. *Wilhelm Meister and His English Kinsmen*. New York: Columbia University Press, 1930.

Hutcheon, Linda. *The Politics of Postmodernism*. New York: Routledge, 1989.

Israel, Charles. "Interview: George Garrett." *South Carolina Review* 6, no. 1 (November 1973): 43–48.

Kellman, Steven G. "Who Killed Kit Marlowe? Who Wants to Know?" In *George Garrett: The Elizabethan Trilogy*, edited by Brooke Horvath and Irving Malin, 129–38. Huntsville, Tex.: Texas Review Press, 1998.

Lukács, Georg. *The Historical Novel*. Translated by Hannah Mitchell and Stanley Mitchell. London: Merlin, 1962.

Lytle, Andrew. "The Image as Guide to Meaning in the Historical Novel." *Sewanee Review* 61 (1953): 408–26.

Madden, David. "Continually Astonished by Everything: The Arm Stories of George Garrett." In *To Come Up Grinning: A Tribute to George Garrett*, edited by Paul Ruffin and Stuart Wright, 47–54. Huntsville, Tex.: Texas Review Press, 1989.

Malin, Irving. "Hermetic Fox-Hunting." In *George Garrett: The Elizabethan Trilogy*, edited by Brooke Horvath and Irving Malin, 9–21. Huntsville, Tex.: Texas Review Press, 1998.

———. "Review of *My Silk Purse and Yours: The Publishing Scene and American Literary Art*." *Review of Contemporary Fiction* 13, no. 1 (spring 1993): 278–79.

————. "Review of *Southern Excursions: Views on Southern Letters in My Time*." *Review of Contemporary Fiction* 23, no. 2 (summer 2003): 149.

Mazmanian, Adam. "Review of *The King of Babylon Shall Not Come against You*." *Library Journal* 121, no. 3 (February 15, 1996): 176.

McCullough, Frank. "George Garrett's Ralegh." *Mill Mountain Review* 1, no. 3 (spring 1971): 15–18.

McHale, Brian. *Postmodernist Fiction*. New York: Methuen, 1987.

McKee, Louis. "Review of *Days of Our Lives Lie in Fragments*." *Library Journal* 123, no. 11 (June 15, 1998): 82.

Meriwether, James B. "George Palmer Garrett, Jr." In *Seven Princeton Poets*, edited by Sherman Hawkins, 26–39. Princeton: Princeton University Library, 1963.

Middleton, David. "Review of *Southern Excursions: Views on Southern Letters in My Time*." *Southern Quarterly* 42, no. 1 (fall 2003): 133–36.

Moore, Richard. "The Poetry of George Garrett." *Mill Mountain Review* 1, no. 3 (spring 1971): 47–50.

Morris, Wright. *The Territory Ahead*. New York: Harcourt, Brace, 1957.

Nash, Charles. "Review of *My Silk Purse and Yours: The Publishing Scene and American Literary Art*." *Library Journal* 117, no. 16 (October 1, 1992): 86.

Omwake, John. "Garrett Assays Goldwyn Future in Film World." *Cavalier Daily*, February 26, 1964, p. 1, 4.

Peden, William. "The Short Fiction of George Garrett." *Ploughshares* 4, no. 3 (1978): 83–90.

Piller, John. "On Fire and in Love with the Taste of Words." *Virginia Quarterly Review* 75, no. 1 (winter 1999): 187–98.

Pouder, G. H. "An Extraordinary Novel." *Baltimore Sun*, August 29, 1965, p. D5.

"Ralegh Biographer Also Had His Hand in 'Frankenstein Meets Space Monster.'" *Greenwood (S.C.) Index Journal*, November 11, 1971, p. 3.

"Review of *The King of Babylon Shall Not Come against You*." *Publishers Weekly* 243, no. 4 (January 22, 1996): 58.

Robinson, William R. "The Fiction of George Garrett." *Red Clay Reader* 2 (1965): 15–16.

————. "George Garrett Discusses Writing and His Work." *Mill Mountain Review* 1, no. 3 (spring 1971): 79–102.

————. "Imagining the Individual: George Garrett's *Death of the Fox*." In *George Garrett: The Elizabethan Trilogy*, edited by Brooke Horvath and Irving Malin, 34–44. Huntsville, Tex.: Texas Review Press, 1998.

Rubin, Louis D., Jr. "From Combray to Ithaca; or the 'Southernness' of Southern Literature." In *The Mockingbird in the Gum Tree: A Literary Gallimaufry*, 21–36. Baton Rouge: Louisiana State University Press, 1991.

Ruffin, Paul. "Interview with George Garrett." *South Carolina Review* 16, no. 2 (spring 1984): 25–33.

Shear, Walter. *The Feeling of Being: Sensibility in Postwar American Fiction*. New York: Peter Lang, 2002.

Slavitt, David R. "The Huge Footprint: The Short Stories of George Garrett." In *To Come Up Grinning: A Tribute to George Garrett*, edited by Paul Ruffin and Stuart Wright, 55–60. Huntsville, Tex.: Texas Review Press, 1989.

Smith, Ron. "George Garrett." In *Beacham's Encyclopedia of Popular Fiction*, edited by Kirk H. Beetz, 2:712–19. Osprey, Fla.: Beacham Publications, 1996.

Spears, Monroe K. "George Garrett and the Historical Novel." In *George Garrett: The Elizabethan Trilogy*, edited by Brooke Horvath and Irving Malin, 45–57. Huntsville, Tex.: Texas Review Press, 1998.

———. "A Trilogy Complete, a Past Recaptured." In *George Garrett: The Elizabethan Trilogy*, edited by Brooke Horvath and Irving Malin, 124–28. Huntsville, Tex.: Texas Review Press, 1998.

Sullivan, Walter. *Death By Melancholy: Essays on Modern Southern Fiction*. Baton Rouge: Louisiana State University Press, 1972.

———. *A Requiem for the Renascence: The State of Fiction in the Modern South*. Athens: University of Georgia Press, 1976.

———. "Where We Have Been. Where We May be Going: Two Good Critics at Work." *Sewanee Review* 100, no. 4 (fall 1992): 662–68.

Sussman, Deborah. "Just for the Fun and Games of It: The Dramatic Writing of George Garrett." *Southern Quarterly* 33, nos. 2–3 (winter-spring 1995): 197–213.

Taylor, Henry. "The Brutal Rush of Grace: George Garrett's Poetry." In *To Come Up Grinning: A Tribute to George Garrett*, edited by Paul Ruffin and Stuart Wright, 73–89. Huntsville, Tex.: Texas Review Press, 1989.

Tew, Phillip. "B. S. Johnson." *Review of Contemporary Fiction* 22.1 (spring 2002): 65–69.

Tillinghast, David. "George Garrett." *South Carolina Review* 9, no. 1 (November 1976): 21–24.

Walsh, Jeffrey. *American War Literature: 1914 to Vietnam*. New York: St. Martin's, 1982.

Warren, Robert Penn. *All the King's Men*. New York: Harcourt, Brace, 1946.

West, Ray. *The Short Story in America, 1900–1950*. Chicago: Henry Regnery, 1951.

Whalen, Tom. "Eavesdropping in the Dark: The Opening(s) of George Garrett's *Entered from the Sun*." In *To Come Up Grinning: A Tribute to George Garrett*, edited by Paul Ruffin and Stuart Wright, 90–99. Huntsville, Tex.: Texas Review Press, 1989.

Wier, Allen. "Skin and Bones: George Garrett's Living Spirits." In *Bad Man Blues: A Portable George Garrett*, xiii–xxv. Dallas: Southern Methodist University Press, 1998.

Willingham, Calder. "What Is Rape?" In *The Gates of Hell*, 105–9. New York: Vanguard, 1951.

"Writer-in-Residence Garrett Takes Sabbatical for Next Two Semesters." *Cavalier Daily*, January 12, 1967, p. 1.

York, R. A. *The Extension of Life: Fiction and History in the American Novel*. Madison, N.J.: Fairleigh Dickinson University Press, 2003.

Index

Casey Clabough is associate professor of English and English Graduate Co-ordinator at Lynchburg College in Virginia. He also serves as literature editor for the Virginia Foundation for the Humanities' *Encyclopedia Virginia*. He is the author of scholarly studies of James Dickey and Fred Chappell, as well as the creative nonfiction book *The Warrior's Path: Reflections along an Ancient Route*.

The Art of the Magic Striptease

UNIVERSITY PRESS OF FLORIDA

Florida A&M University, Tallahassee
Florida Atlantic University, Boca Raton
Florida Gulf Coast University, Ft. Myers
Florida International University, Miami
Florida State University, Tallahassee
New College of Florida, Sarasota
University of Central Florida, Orlando
University of Florida, Gainesville
University of North Florida, Jacksonville
University of South Florida, Tampa
University of West Florida, Pensacola

The Art of th

University Press of Florida
Gainesville
Tallahassee
Tampa
Boca Raton
Pensacola
Orlando
Miami
Jacksonville
Ft. Myers
Sarasota